Crossing the Pacific

DREAMERS AND DOERS
PART 1

ARLENE GALISKY

SCRIPTOR HOUSE
THE EPITOME OF GREATNESS

Scriptor House LLC

2810 N Church St Wilmington, Delaware, 19802

www.scriptorhouse.com

Phone: +1302-205-2043

Paperback ISBN: 979-8-88692-006-2
eBook ISBN: 979-8-88692-007-9

Crossing the Pacific

DREAMERS AND DOERS
PART 1

ARLENE GALISKY

Dedicated to all the sailors
who've talked about going offshore,
the dreamers and the doers.

Contents

PROLOGUE

Dave and I lived pretty normal lives until the summer of 1994, which is when we decided to sail across the Pacific Ocean. He'd been talking about doing so for about a year, but I hadn't taken him seriously. Who would? We lived 500 miles from the ocean, and neither of us had set foot on a sailboat before.

In the twenty years that I'd known him, Dave had been committed to career, family, and community. He was a partner in a national accounting firm, a long-time member of the local hospital board, and had just helped organize the city's first air show. But he'd grown restless in the years since his two children left home and talked about retiring at age 55. When his finances wouldn't allow that, he reluctantly accepted that he'd have to work for a few more years. Then fate intervened. His firm offered early retirement packages to some partners, allowing them to retire at 55, and he qualified. It was enough to make the difference. He talked to his wife, they completed a separation agreement, and he began planning an adventure.

He first thought about buying a 4X4 pickup and driving from BC to the southern tip of South America, but lost interest after reading about the difficulties of traveling in Central America, particularly the Darien Gap. A friend of his was then sailing around the world, and it wasn't long before he made the leap from a truck to a boat, and from South America to the South Pacific. He began studying cruising magazines and researching sailboats.

Even so, I'm not sure what would have happened had not fate again intervened. Three times in that last year, he was brought face to face with his own mortality. His dad died in November, his house burned down around his ears in the middle of the night in May, and his mom passed away in July. His mother's death seemed to be the catalyst, as a few days later, he showed up at my house with his mind made up. "Lene," he announced, "I'm going to buy a boat and sail to Australia. Are you going to come?"

I first met Dave in November of 1974, when I moved back to Prince George, a small city in central BC with a boom-and-bust economy. I was an accounting student and had taken a job with the firm in which he was a partner. Not really happy in the hierarchy of public practice, I quit after a year and started my own accounting business.

Ultimately, I found a niche helping small businesses convert their offices from paper records to computers. Dave and I still worked together occasionally and over time found that we had much in common.

Ten years later, we participated in a whitewater canoeing course and found ourselves sitting at either end of the same canoe in a backwater of the Nechako River. He was over six feet tall and weighed 200 pounds, while I was eleven inches shorter and weighed 120, so we had a bit of a weight imbalance. We were leaning out on opposite sides, bracing with our paddles, while our instructor emphasized the importance of teamwork. I was then urged to sit up straight, which I knew would dump us both into the river. With other students egging me on, I turned and looked back at Dave, sitting confidently and a little smugly in the stern. I straightened, the canoe tipped over, and the rest as they say is history.

We started paddling rivers and lakes together and discovered that we shared an enthusiasm for outdoor adventure. In the early spring, we were part of a small group of enthusiasts paddling local rivers as soon as rising flood waters took out the ice. We also twice paddled a seventeen-foot canoe for 350 km around the lakes making up the headwaters of the Nechako River, and twice backpacked 316 km over the Grease Trail through BC's Chilcotin country.

I was now 48 years old and well entrenched in my own life, with a job, a house, family obligations, and community involvements. I'd never married and had no children, but basically had worked two jobs for the last four years. As well as my day job, I'd been at the forefront of a campaign to pressure the provincial government into holding a public review of a diversion project that threatened to destroy the Nechako River. Others had worked even longer and we were successful; the hearings had ended the previous week. But the long campaign had left me burnt out, exhausted both mentally and physically.

I knew that I would be making major changes in my life, but hadn't yet considered what they might be. Now, taking Dave seriously for the first time, I let the idea of sailing across the Pacific Ocean seep into my brain. The thought of being part of such an adventure breathed new life into my soul. I knew that I would be walking away from everything I'd achieved, everything familiar, but at some level knew I'd been dreaming of going to sea all my life.

CHAPTER 1

Windy Lady

Not entirely lacking in common sense, Dave and I drive to Vancouver a few days after he retires at the end of August and take a sailing course. With one other couple and an instructor, we spend five days in a 34-foot sailboat, cruising in the Strait of Georgia, the 150-mile-long arm of the ocean that lies between Vancouver Island and the BC mainland. We don't do much sailing as winds are light, but nothing happens to deter us and neither of us seems prone to seasickness, so our plans proceed.

By the end of September, Dave has found his boat. *Windy Lady* is a beamy, 40-foot-long, fiberglass sloop with a rear cockpit shielded only by a windscreen. She has large windows in the main cabin, high ceilings, and more living space than other boats we've inspected. Significantly, banging our heads in tight spaces isn't nearly the problem that it is on some boats. We take possession a week later and arrange to spend the preceding night onboard, as we want a full day to move the boat from Blaine, Washington, to Maple Bay on Vancouver Island.

Thick fog covers the marina come morning, and by the time it clears and the vendors, Ron and Diane, have picked up the last of their belongings, it's almost noon. We then see Ron standing on the edge of a pier, waving his arms, as we motor out of the marina. Above the throbbing of the diesel engine, I barely hear him yell, "*Engine Water!*" That means nothing to me, but sends Dave scurrying below to lift the sole (floor) over the engine compartment. In the excitement of the moment, he'd forgotten to open the thru-hull that allows seawater to flow into the engine cooling system.

The afternoon is gorgeous, with a warm, sunny sky and rippled sea, and we revel in every minute of the five-hour crossing of the Strait of Georgia. Dave steers toward a string of small islands some 25 miles away, and I'm momentarily alarmed when I realize that our chart doesn't show the pass through them. He isn't concerned, however, as he's noticed the spot where BC Ferries appear and disappear.

The sun is low on the horizon by the time we're through the pass, and as we're nowhere near our destination, we decide to stop at the harbor on nearby Saltspring Island. The light is fading from the sky when we tie up at the dock, and Dave immediately finds a phone and calls Canada Customs. When he'd asked about procedures for crossing the US-Canada border, Ron had replied, "I do it all the time. You just phone in as soon as you arrive."

That is not the message that Dave now hears. A very angry agent barks into the phone, "You bring that boat to the Customs Dock in Victoria *now!*" Well, we aren't capable of taking the boat anywhere after dark. After a good tongue-lashing, the agent relents, but issues a stern warning, declaring, "Everyone's entitled to one mistake, and you've just had yours!"

Next morning, we make our way to Maple Bay Marina, where Dave has arranged for a berth. We then return to Prince George where I finish my work obligations and find a house sitter for the winter. (I return for a week the following spring and sell my house, truck, and canoes.) We're slow to tell friends and family about our plans, perhaps because of our own uncertainties. Those we do tell have reactions similar to my mother, who is horrified and cries, "Why would you leave a perfectly good house to go live on a boat?"

We move onto *Windy Lady* at the end of October and then the work starts. We thoroughly inspect her from bow to stern, emptying and cleaning lockers as we go, and end up with three *to-do lists*. One is for jobs we need to do before going offshore, one for boat supplies, parts, and tools we'll need, and one for food and personal items, including vaccinations and dental visits.

In mid-November, Dave hires a diesel mechanic and together they work through the boat. Ian begins with the electrical panel, where a mishmash of different colored wires leads in all directions. The two men trace and label them, so that we know which piece of equipment is connected to which circuit breaker. He then moves on to the array of hoses that run between engine block and heat exchanger, as well as fore and aft on the boat. Some are part of the engine's salt-water cooling system; others belong to the fresh-water system that heats the hot-water tank and cabin radiators. I make sketches of everything.

Ian then works his way through the diesel engine and transmission, installing a secondary fuel filter and a propane alarm required by regulation. While he works, he explains everything he can think of about anything that might be useful, including the driveshaft packing-gland, and the three zinc anodes that protect expensive metal parts from galvanic corrosion. They will need to be replaced annually.

There are three batteries on the boat, one dedicated to the engine and two that make up the house bank. All need to be replaced. The house bank consists of two large 8Ds with a combined capacity of 450 amps; it provides an onboard source of power for instruments and lights. The boat is also wired for shore power, and I have my first lesson in energy management soon after we move aboard. I plug in the coffee maker and a small ceramic heater at the same time, blowing the 20-amp circuit breaker on the dock.

The winter months are cold and damp aboard *Windy Lady*, and she really isn't fit to live in, let alone take to sea. The main water tank leaks, as does the hot water tank, and water then accumulates in the bilge, along with oil from an engine leak. The cabin windows leak when it rains, as does the Plexiglas instrument panel in the cockpit, which funnels water onto the foot of the starboard berth. When nights grow colder, condensation forms on exposed fiberglass over the berths and water drips on our heads. The furnace, which should have dried the boat out as well as warmed it up, turns out to be an orphan and takes months to repair.

Our lone supporter is Dave's brother, Brian, who is also a dreamer, having crewed on two Atlantic passages. He visits regularly and his encouragement and enthusiasm help keep the dream alive when reality becomes a little too discouraging.

As the weeks pass, we adjust to living aboard and learn to recognize the sounds of water pump and refrigerator, as well as the movements caused by wind and ten-foot tides. We're in constant need of various bits and pieces, so Dave opens a charge account at a chandlery across from the dock. The owner, Jim, is a big help when it comes to dealing with unfamiliar products and equipment.

We order a new mainsail cover from a local sailmaker, then have him cover new foam mattresses for the stern berths. Eventually, he also makes us a canopy that shades most of the deck area. We find a carpenter to finish the two stern berths, put shelves over galley and chart tables, and installs grab rails throughout the cabin. By now, we've learned that *BOAT* actually stands for *Bring Out Another Thousand*.

Before we do any sailing, Dave has to service the four winches, all of which are seized up, and I spend hours with a scrub brush cleaning lines that are coated with green algae. When we do take the boat out, we don't do much sailing, as quirky winds in the islands frequently die, leaving us to return home under power.

But we do learn that maneuvering a fourteen-ton, forty-foot vessel at low speeds in the marina is no easy task. *Windy Lady* has six feet of hull below the waterline for much of her length and a fair amount of windage at the bow, so is affected by even light winds and currents. There is also something called prop-walk. When forward gear is engaged, the stern kicks sideways to port, and of course, the bow turns to starboard; the opposite happens in reverse gear.

By the beginning of May, we've completed many of the major jobs on our *to-do lists*. We've purchased new batteries, sails, lines, and anchor chain, and installed GPS, radar, VHF and HF radios. We now need to concentrate on learning how to handle the boat, so plan a six-week cruise up the BC coast. Dave then decides we'd make better use of the time if we circumnavigated Vancouver Island.

Vancouver Island is 285 miles long and 62 miles across at its widest point, so we're planning a voyage of over 800 miles. It's actually 700 nautical miles (nm), which is the measurement used at sea. As a rule of thumb, a nautical mile is about two kilometers. Wind and boat speeds are measured in nautical miles/hour or knots (kt).

CHAPTER 2

A Steep Learning Curve

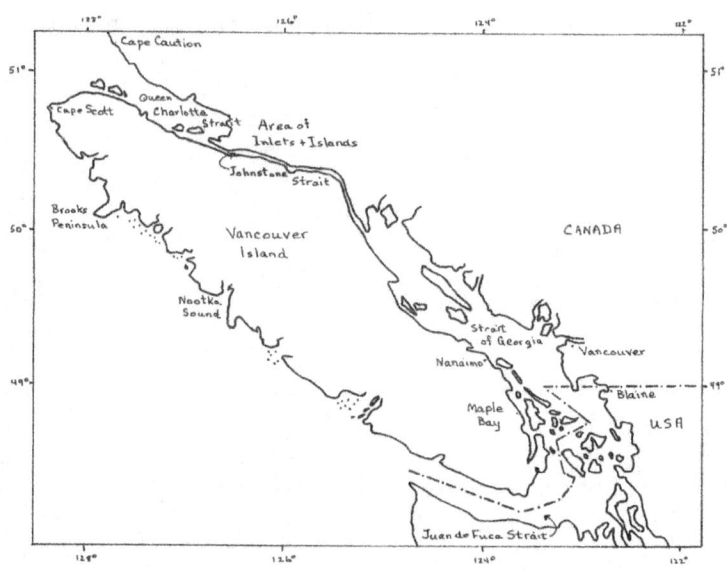

Map of Vancouver Island, Canada

This trip also has to serve as our shakedown cruise because there won't be time for a second. We set a departure date of May 13, which gives us ten days to complete as many jobs as possible, then frantically set to work. We also buy all the supplies we can think of and are still picking up items at the chandlery the morning we leave, so make a Hudson Bay start, untying about midday and not going far.

The wind dies thirty minutes after we leave the marina, so we motor-sail to our first overnight destination. Dave stands at the wheel in the cockpit and steers, while I sit on a bench across from him, relaxing for what seems like the first time in months. With his air of quiet confidence; he's unquestionably the captain of our vessel. He is able to turn his hand to almost anything.

Dave grew up in small towns in southern Saskatchewan, where his dad worked on the railroad. He'd been a big lad and a willing worker, and while still in school had summer jobs as a farmhand, a section hand on the railroad, and a roughneck on an oilrig. After graduating from high school, he'd joined the air force and qualified as a pilot. (He'd told me that, as a boy, he'd watched the troop trains bringing soldiers home from WW II, and I wondered whether that had influenced his decision.)

After leaving the service, he worked in an oil refinery for several years and then immigrated to Australia. Finding few choices there, he'd ended up working in a mine at Mount Isa. Six months in the heat and dust underground had convinced him that he didn't want to be a miner. Returning to Canada, he'd articled with a firm of Chartered Accountants.

My story is not nearly as interesting. My dad worked in the bush in central British Columbia, and I'd grown up in small nearby settlements. My first real job was working as a flunky in a cookhouse at a bush camp. After graduating from high school, I worked for five years as a secretary in a small office, then took time off to travel to Australia. When I returned, I also took up accounting. Other than being an able navigator, I have no particular skills that make me suitable for this endeavor, but I'm not afraid of hard work and am addicted to outdoor adventure.

However, I'm about to learn that I have a couple of traits that are problematic. First, I'm a worrier, something I inherited from my mother, which tends to make new experiences challenging. Second, I have comfort zones with well-established boundaries that I don't even know exist. It turns out, they keep me far too comfortable, and I really don't like being pushed beyond them.

So, as I begin to relax, I instinctively start fretting about anchoring, which we're about to do for the first time. We haven't discussed how we'll go about it, and the few articles I've read haven't been very helpful.

When we enter the long, narrow cove at Wallace Island, five sailboats are already at anchor. Their crews sit out on deck, enjoying the late afternoon sunshine, and watch with interest as we pass. They seem to take up a lot of space, and I notice that each boat has a stern line leading to a rocky outcropping on shore. Dave keeps an eye on the depth gauge and brings *Windy Lady* to a stop in a likely-looking spot with the stern facing the rock wall. Shoving the gearshift lever into reverse, he calls, "Lene, you want to come and take the helm?"

I've never driven the boat in tight quarters before because I have a problem with the gearshift lever. I can't put it in reverse and often struggle to get it into forward gear. When I now glance around the cove, it doesn't seem like a good place to start. In fact, it's suddenly unbelievably small, and *Windy Lady* has grown to the size of the *Queen Mary*. For the first time in my life, a wave of panic sweeps through me and my brain seems to freeze. *So, no, I don't want to take the helm.*

Instead, I walk numbly up to the bow, knowing that if I don't drive the boat, I have to drop the anchor. I stop and look down at the windlass, a foreign-looking piece of equipment bolted to the foredeck. I am also mechanically illiterate and have no idea how it works, or how to go about figuring it out. As I cast a desperate glance at the dark waters around the boat, another wave of panic overwhelms me. Dave tries to help, but I'm having a crisis of confidence and nothing he says makes sense. He finally just orders, "Put out 25 feet of chain," and walks away.

Left to my own devices, I eventually figure out how to release the anchor, and after several attempts am able to control the amount of chain that goes out. But each attempt is accompanied by an irritating clanging of chain and whining of windlass that just seems to emphasize how inept I am. I then can't read the measurement markings on the chain, and I painted them on myself! I'm now so demoralized that it doesn't help when I finally figure out that Dave attached the wrong end of our new 300-foot chain to the anchor.

When we finally have the anchor down in the right spot and the correct amount of chain out, we move onto the next step. Dave slowly backs up the boat, while I ease out another fifty feet. He then continues backing up, stretching out the chain and dragging the anchor. I stand beside the windlass with my foot resting on the chain, expecting to feel a change in vibration when it hooks, but nothing happens. I don't feel a thing.

After we've gone through this process three more times, a spectator in one of the boats, undoubtedly thinking we're going to go on all night, hollers, "Maybe you could try coming in from the side, then pull the stern around from shore!" Following this very logical piece of advice, we hook the anchor on the second try, as we're now using the length of the cove instead of the width, which gives us more room.

Feeling totally responsible for the fiasco, I try to redeem myself by volunteering to take the stern line ashore in my canoe. We'd brought it along, secured to the foredeck, and I now put it in the water. As I paddle away, I heave a sigh of relief, confident that this is something I can do. But I'm wrong, as pulling the stern of a fourteen-ton boat around ninety degrees is no easy task. The sweat pours off me in buckets as I struggle, but there's no way I will ask for help.

We don't have much to say to each other that evening, and I'm plagued with doubts all night. *Can I even do this? What is Dave thinking? Will he send me packing come morning?* I'm still depressed when I wake up.

We're out on deck early, and I stand at the helm while Dave brings up the anchor. As he works, I notice a soft, clear light bathing the quiet cove and my spirit starts to lift. Once the anchor is free, I steer the boat out into the channel, where the mirrored surface of the water reflects the surrounding rocks and trees. Awed by the picture-perfect images of this incredible new world, I am soon made whole again.

We now transit through a pass that takes us from sheltered waters out into the Strait of Georgia, where we stop to raise the sails. Following the routine that we've established, I take the helm and hold the bow into wind, and Dave hauls the mainsail up the mast. He then goes below and shuts down the engine, and I pull out the headsail. As *Windy Lady* moves forward, we adjust the sails.

We're soon sailing north up the strait, tacking back and forth into 18-kt winds from the NW. With no reefs in either sail, I find she's a bit of a handful, but Dave doesn't seem to mind. He steers her farther out, where winds are stronger, and she heels over as we race across the water. A 26-kt gust then hits the sails, spinning her around and knocking her down. She's left dead in the water and heeled over so far that the bottom of the headsail is only inches above the waves.

I'm sitting on a bench in the cockpit and am thrust back against the coaming. When I turn to look at Dave, he is fighting with the helm, trying to bring her upright, but she only responds when the wind releases its grip on the mainsail.

When I check below, the cabin is in chaos. Locker doors stand open, with cooking pots, cans, and books dumped out onto the sole, along with settee cushions and charts and pencils from the tables. Seawater has also come in through both galley and head sinks, and fresh water has sloshed out of the main water tank.

Dave immediately realizes that we left the galley thru-hull open, so we start *Windy Lady* sailing again and tack to port, causing her to heel over on the other side. When the sinks drain, I close the thru-hull, then wipe up most of the water and stuff things back in lockers.

At that point, I've had enough for the day, but Dave is the captain and wants more *experience*. We sail for another two hours, crashing into choppy, five-foot waves that soak the foot of the headsail and send spray flying over the foredeck. In the process, we learn there's nothing to hang onto forward of the mast, and when wet, the deck is dangerously slippery.

Dave starts the engine as we approach the narrow, rocky channel leading to the next anchorage, and we now furl the headsail but leave the main up. When we're part way through the channel, strong gusts hit the sail, heeling the boat over and turning the bow, threatening to put us on the rocks. Another gust then comes straight over the bow, jerking the boom quickly from side to side, causing the most gawd-awful racket.

The noise is like fingernails on a blackboard to my strained nerves, and stepping over to the end of the boom, I grab hold of the round head of the long-handled deck brush that Dave stowed there earlier. As I pull it free, another gust jerks the boom sideways, yanking it from my hands and slinging it astern. Astonished, I turn—and see Dave. He stands directly behind me with a dazed look in his eyes. Disbelievingly, I watch as a lump appears in the middle of his forehead where he's been hit. I am appalled and have felt guilty ever since. Stoically, he never says a word.

The anchorage that night is large and we hook the anchor on the first pass, but I'm too dejected to notice. We put the boat to bed, which includes lowering the mainsail, flaking it over the boom, putting on the sail cover, and coiling lines we've been using. Dave then prepares supper, while I restore order to the cabin and scrub down counter and floors stained by saltwater.

Winds are strong overnight, causing *Windy Lady* to dance at the end of her anchor chain, and occasionally a loud groan echoes underwater as it drags across the rocky bottom. Winds are still gusting at 20–30 kt next morning, so we stay put. There is no rest for Dave, however, as the head plugs up. In a foul temper, he spends hours removing hoses and cleaning out the buildup of calcium that blocks them.

When the sun comes out late that afternoon, we go up on deck and discuss the sails. Both are triangular in shape and have one side that slides into a track. The mainsail is pulled up a track on our 45-foot mast, and the foot of the sail is attached to the boom. The sail has three reefing points, which allow it to be lowered and tied to the boom in order to reduce sail. The track for the headsail runs up the forestay, which extends from bow to masthead. The sail is furled around the forestay when not in use, or to partially reduce sail.

The headsail we're using is a genoa, a huge sail meant for light winds. We decide to replace it with the working jib, a smaller, heavier sail better suited to current conditions. But large sails can be difficult to handle, and with winds still gusting up to 15 kt, I suggest waiting until they ease. Shaking his head, Dave responds, "Are we going to sit around at sea and wait for light winds before doing a sail change?"

No, of course we're not, I tell myself, watching him take a firm grip on the exposed corner of the sail (the clew) and start to pull it out.

He now orders me to release the furling line. The instant I do, the wind catches the sail and pulls it out half way, ballooning it out over the side of the boat and ripping the clew from his hands. He manages to hang onto the attached sheets (ropes) and is then dragged all over the foredeck as the wind whips the sail back and forth.

It looks to me like he's going to go overboard at any moment, and I don't know what to do but have to do something. Desperately, I jump to the furling line and with the help of a winch manage to re-furl the sail. We then start over again, but this time he ties the clew to the mast, which keeps the sail under control while we pull it out and down.

The working jib is a new sail, and even with a winch, we have difficulty pulling the heavy, stiff canvas up the track. As we raise it higher, the wind begins snapping the sail across the deck, causing the bow to slew about on the anchor chain. We don't pay much attention until we hear a sharp clanging noise, then turn to see the sail snapping wickedly at head level, with the metal ring sewn into the clew striking the mast.

Dave darts forward, grabbing the sail midway along the bottom, and gathers it into his arms. Unfortunately, he can't hold enough of the sail to subdue the clew, which continues to snap around his head. Certain that he's going to be brained at any moment, I manage to re-furl enough of the sail so that he's able to grab the clew and secure it. In my relief that he's safe, I'm suddenly furious. I'd suggested tying off the clew before we started and he ignored me.

Winds are lighter on Day 4 and the boat easier to handle, so we have a pleasant sail up to Nanaimo. Our new fiberglass dinghy is tied to the foredeck, and after anchoring, we winch it over the side. I then attempt to lower the 5-hp Johnson engine down to Dave, but find it heavy and awkward to handle, so he puts together a harness that makes it easier. When the engine won't start, he spends the remaining daylight hours tearing it apart and half the next day putting it back together.

We now dinghy ashore, find a chandlery, and purchase the lines we want before heading north. That evening, we sit out in the cockpit and make a snubbing line, meant to take the stress off the windlass when we're at anchor. Using a piece of three-strand rope, we figure out how to splice an eye in one end and back splice the other end.

We put two reefs in the mainsail before leaving Nanaimo harbor on the morning of Day 6 and sail comfortably in 18–20 kt winds and quite wild seas. Two hours later, the winds die. We motor farther out into the Strait of Georgia, which is 18 nm wide at this point, and start sailing again with winds steady at 12–15 kt.

I'm now standing at the helm, steering, and initially am just grateful for the quiet when Dave shuts down the engine. But *Windy Lady* is soon gliding smoothly over the waves at 5 kt, and I am enchanted. As my body sways gently with the slight roll of the boat, I'm lulled by the soft rustle of waves washing against the hull, feel sun and wind caressing my face, and look out on dark waters dotted with sparkling whitecaps that stretch to the horizon. It's magic!

That night, we easily anchor in a small bay on an island in the middle of the strait, and next day, with warm sunshine and winds of 15–20 kt, we experiment with the sails. We now learn all about *Windy Lady's* no-go zone. We want to steer 315 degrees, but the wind is coming from that direction, and a sailboat cannot sail into wind. The best we can steer is 275 degrees, so we steer that heading for a while, then tack (turn through the wind) and steer 355 degrees. In this way, we zigzag up the strait for six hours and sail 30 nm, but make only 15 nm towards our destination. The wind then dies, leaving us in the middle of the strait, and we motor for hours to reach the Copeland Islands on the north side.

The deep water and shelf-like rocky bottoms of the anchorages here present new challenges, and an eerie rumble reverberates through the water when the chain drags across rocks as the boat swings with the tide. With warm, sunny weather, we spend Days 8 and 9 here, exploring the marine environment.

At low tide, I paddle my canoe around the bay, noting the sea lettuce that covers the rocky intertidal zone. Every crack in the rocks has a resident purple starfish, and a long stream of water shooting through the air leads me to a clam bed, where water is squirting in all directions. I glimpse a small animal disappearing into the bush, a weasel I think, and see a seal resting easily in the water near the bow of the sailboat.

Dave goes fishing and takes the dinghy around to the far side of the island. He sees a powerboat pulled up on shore, but doesn't pay any attention until he hears whistling and turns to see a man waving his arms. When he motors over, the chap meets him at the water's edge with a relieved, "Am I glad to see you!"

With some prompting, the fellow explains, "You know where Lund is, on the mainland? Well, I left there about 1900 last night, going to a fish hatchery about forty-five minutes up the coast. But my engine quit, so I drifted around all night, then washed up on shore about 0500. I have no idea where I am."

Dave is happy to tell him, then gives him a hand hauling the boat down to the water. After watching the fellow yank on the starter cord, he asks, "Could you be out of fuel?" The castaway, who still smells strongly of liquor, switches over to a second tank; moments later, the engine catches and he's off in a cloud of spray.

CHAPTER 3

Desolation Sound to Queen Charlotte Strait

After leaving the Copeland Islands, we spend Days 10, 11, and 12 threading our way through the maze of channels between Vancouver Island and the mainland. The sunny weather continues and we sail when we can, but mostly motor. Growing more confident with every hour that passes, we transit through narrow passages, raise and lower sails, study GPS, radar, and engine instruments, charge batteries, monitor energy use, and conserve our limited supply of water.

The first day, we motor north into Desolation Sound, where high mountains with steep, rocky faces surround deep, dark waters. It feels closed in, more like a lake than an arm of the sea. We cautiously enter a marine park in late afternoon and anchor near a small stream rushing down over the rocks. As the wind eases, the air grows still and the water becomes a mirror, perfectly reflecting the surrounding mountains and forest. We set off to explore in the dinghy and learn that it is really too small, and the outboard motor is barely adequate.

Strong outflow winds funnel down through a notch in the mountains when we anchor in a small, isolated bay next day. Thinking that these conditions might serve as a final exam, we take extra care in setting the anchor. As we're still there next morning, I guess we pass.

The third day takes us to Yaculta Rapids, a mile-long passage with tidal currents of 5–7 kt. I nervously keep checking the tide tables, as we have to be at the south end of the passage before slack tide. A fishboat is waiting when we arrive and starts up the channel about fifteen minutes early, according to my reckoning. Conceding to local knowledge, we follow it up a back eddy on the eastern shore.

The current catches *Windy Lady* as soon as she pokes her nose out into the main channel, turning her almost broadside before she begins to come around. The bow then slews from side to side as she slowly pushes up through the lower rapid. At a sharp turn in the channel, we can't locate a marker buoy until we're almost on top of it. As our speed slows even more, I keep a wary eye on nearby whirlpools, my stomach in knots. We then cross a wide bay, proceed through the upper rapids, and are free and clear, another obstacle overcome.

Continuing under power, we relax and enjoy our surroundings, now seeing dozens of bald eagles. The big birds, both adults and juveniles, fly low over the water, perch on the rocks, and fight amongst themselves. We anchor that night in another isolated bay, where a pair of mergansers watch from the safety of the reeds, and a small hummingbird stops by to check out the cockpit.

Late that evening, with the sun low in the sky, we hear the throb of a diesel engine as a fishboat enters the bay. It circles around a small log boom tethered nearby, jumping and puffing as it works. Before long, the skipper has picked up the boom and the boat heads out. As silence returned to the bay, the songs of hermit thrush drift across the water, and as twilight deepens, the wild cry of a loon splits the air.

On Day 13, we wake to the sound of the chain dragging across the sea bottom. We're underway at 0530 and greet the sun as it peeps over the hills. With calm air, rippled seas, and an ebbing tide, we make good time and are soon turning west into the narrow, deep waters of Johnstone Strait, which forms the main route along this part of Vancouver Island.

Before long, we see whitewater ahead, as 20-knot outflow winds whip down an intersecting channel. *Windy Lady* is soon tossing about roughly in five-foot-high waves, and when Dave sees the dinghy bucking and twisting at the end of the towline, he decides to rescue the outboard motor. I'm appalled and try to talk him out of it, but he doesn't hear a word. Methodically, he sets about his task: reducing engine power, adjusting the autopilot, pulling the dinghy up close behind.

With the boat lurching about, he climbs over the transom at the rear of the cockpit, then steps down three feet onto the narrow bow of the dinghy. Stepping down again, he grabs the gunnels on either side and slides his way to the back. After loosening the clamps on the outboard, he lifts it up, which is when I expect him to go overboard as all the weight is at the back. He doesn't, just pulls it toward himself, then somehow manhandles it forward. Standing erect, he keeps his balance long enough to hand it up to me.

Dave takes his physical strength for granted, but I know my limitations well and cannot lift the engine up to the cockpit at the best of times. Knowing from the start that I would somehow be participating in this foolhardy venture, I seethe with rage. But I also know that if I drop the engine, I might as well follow it into the sea. Without pausing to consider, I lean out, draping my upper body over the transom, then grab hold and give a mighty heave— and swing it up into the cockpit.

We're through the worst of the waves in about fifteen minutes, then run into similar winds at the next two junctions, but seas are never as rough. The winds grow lighter as the afternoon progresses, and with a favorable tide, we keep going. After motoring 40 nm, we anchor late that afternoon on an island on the north side of Johnstone Strait.

I stay in a foul mood for hours, deeply resenting having been made to participate in this latest escapade. Writing in my journal that night, I bitterly complain that Dave is putting himself, *Windy Lady*, and me at risk. But, unbeknownst to me, those self-imposed boundaries of my comfort zone are expanding, and if I'm honest, that is what most prepares me for going to sea.

Next morning is clear and calm, and when we raise the anchor at 0615, the mirrored surface of the bay reflects a perfect image of the surrounding forest. Captivated by the view, I stay at the bow while Dave steers the boat out and around the point. The sun is already warm, and air and water so still that we seem to be gliding into a picture, with forested islands floating on tranquil waters and snow-topped mountain ridges beyond.

I then notice a small patch of fog nestled against the south shore of Johnstone Strait, and within a mile, it has spread across the entire channel. As sky and shoreline disappear, Dave orders me to the helm and goes below to the chart table. Falling back on skills honed in his flying days, he plots our GPS position on a chart and establishes waypoints that will keep us safely in mid-channel. He also has the radar on, which shows the contour of the shoreline and will reveal any traffic.

I stay on the compass heading that he was steering and watch as dense fog closes in around the boat. Soon I can see only ten, maybe fifteen feet into a dull, grey mist. As he monitors our progress, Dave calls for changes to our course, and I respond blindly, steering into nothingness. As time goes by, I have an eerie sense of being isolated in time and space, as if the boat is encased in a cocoon carrying us through a silent, ghostly world. My only links to reality are the dim light shining up through the companionway and the throb of the engine.

After some time, I hear a faint noise and turn to see a dozen dolphins swimming near the port quarter. I call down to Dave, and we watch them swim in close on the port side, dive, and surface to ride on the starboard bow wave. Seconds later, they drop back and disappear into the greyness, but their images remain in my mind. They had been solid objects in a formless world.

About midday, Dave calls up a warning; we're nearing a narrow channel between two islands. I search the greyness for shadows that might reveal their locations, but see nothing. I notice a log, mostly submerged, drifting slowly past and recall that we timed our departure to arrive here at slack tide. I look around for other debris but can't see in front of the bow, then hear thumps as we hit a few objects.

Unseeing and unseen, we motor west for six long hours, covering 30 nm as we pass down Johnstone Strait and out into Queen Charlotte Strait. By 1300, the fog isn't as thick, and we can see some fifty feet around the boat. I'm still on watch but no longer at the helm, as Dave has turned on the autopilot. When the fog shows no sign of lifting, we decide to head for Port Hardy on the north end of Vancouver Island. It's about 12 nm to the west and we figure will be the easiest harbor to enter.

Half an hour later, the sky starts to clear, and within minutes, the mountains on the island appear. As the fog dissipates, a light wind comes up and we optimistically revert to our original plan. Raising the sails, we head for an anchorage on the north side of the strait. Our enjoyment is short-lived, however, as we're soon heading into 20-kt headwinds and lumpy, three-foot seas that push the boat towards a small, rocky island in the middle of the strait.

I'm at the helm when we tack, but have no idea what now happens. Maybe my timing was off, maybe a wave or a gust of wind caught the bow. All I know for sure is that one moment *Windy Lady* is speeding across the strait; the next, she is sitting broadside to the waves, being tossed about like a toy. Both sails are backwinded, the deck is heaving and twisting beneath my feet, and the sheets thrash the water noisily as the wind whips the headsail. Dave jumps to a winch and furls it in, then we try to start sailing using the mainsail, but have to start the engine.

And so starts a three-hour-long ordeal, with *Windy Lady* plunging into high, steep waves pushed up by 30-kt winds. Waves break over the bow, sending spray flying across the foredeck, and water runs down the cabin roof and under the windscreen into the cockpit. Occasionally, a bigger series of waves sends the deck pitching ever steeper, and then Dave, who's at the helm, is on the receiving end of the spray. Inside the cabin, settee cushions are sent flying, locker doors pop open, and seawater runs into the cabin through the air vents.

As we draw closer to the north side, we peer anxiously at the misty shoreline, searching for small islands near the harbor entrance. When we finally spot them, Dave turns the bow toward them, as we need to find a lee shore where we can drop the mainsail. Almost immediately, the sounds of two shrieking alarms connected to the depth gauge begin bouncing off the cabin walls, and he jerks the helm back. He tries several times, with the same shrill results, before eventually finding a safe route. After we drop the sail, we locate the harbor entrance using GPS. Soon, we're safe and secure inside, relaxing for the first time in eleven hours.

Two large power yachts join us just before dark and creep out at 0500 in a cool, grey dawn. Dave hears the purr of engines as they go by, and bothered by their early departure, he tunes in the weather broadcast on HF radio. The forecast for the open coast to the north is good, calling for low swell, light wind, and visibility of less than a mile in fog. We had talked about going up the Inside Passage to Ocean Falls and decided against it, but now can't resist. It will add 250 nm to our route.

CHAPTER 4

North of Cape Caution

We lift the anchor at 0600 on Day 15, then motor out into the calm waters of Queen Charlotte Strait. As Dave turns the bow northward, I see a fogbank looming high in the sky to the southwest. *Windy Lady* is soon rolling in a slight swell pushing down from the open waters of Queen Charlotte Sound. As we proceed north, the swell grows higher and the roll more pronounced. At Miles Inlet, clouds sit low on the hills and the air is misty. After motoring for five hours, we round Cape Caution, staying a mile offshore, and the boat rolls heavily in water that is less than 100 feet deep.

An hour later, winds are gusting from 12–17 kt and seas have grown higher. Both subside as we turn into Smith Sound, where we find our way into a quiet cove. We stay over a day, and I use the time to study charts and guides covering the area to the north. Dave goes fishing, disappearing with the dinghy for hours, and returns with several rockfish. As soon as he's out of sight, I start thinking about how isolated we are and drive myself crazy with all sorts of imaginings. That night, swells push up into the cove and the boat rolls uncomfortably.

The early forecast on Day 17 calls for increasing winds and a low-moderate southwest swell. Dave is at the helm when we motor out through the entrance of the sound, and I can only stare in round-eyed wonder at the hills and valleys of moving water that sweep around us. We continue seaward until clear of a peninsula to the north, then turn and proceed up the coast.

We're soon crossing the wide entrance to Rivers Inlet, and swells now hit *Windy Lady* broadside. They sweep under the hull, rolling her onto her side, then drag at the stern, turning the bow, and leave her wallowing in troughs. It's a battle to keep her moving forward, and we share the duty for the next three hours.

As we proceed up Fitz Hugh Sound, the waters gradually calm in the lee of Calvert Island. This well-traveled portion of the Inside Passage is busy, and we see numerous powerboats, tugs, and barges, as well as three multi-storied cruise boats and a BC ferry. We also meet a huge pod of dolphins, with hundreds of animals leaping down the channel towards us. Half a dozen stop to check us out, and I feel a warm glow long after they disappear. With grinning mouths and boundless energy, they seem to embody the joy of living.

After a long day, we anchor in a quiet lagoon off Fisher Channel. It rains during the night, and come morning, the air is cool and clouds sit low on the surrounding hills. The six other boats in the anchorage are gone by 1000, leaving us to enjoy the solitude on our own. That evening, the sun streams through breaks in the clouds, the air grows still, and the water becomes a mirror, reflecting the surrounding old-growth cedar forest.

We climb into the dinghy, and Dave rows quietly while I string out a fishing line. We pass a great blue heron standing motionless on a nearby float, then the wild, pealing cry of a loon echoes over the treetops. Three seals soon appear, taking up positions around us, making it clear that if we catch a fish, we won't keep it. As I listen to bird songs floating through the air, something in the gloom on shore catches my eye. Nothing moves for so long that I decide I was mistaken—and then a small deer flicks its tail. The dinghy drifts to within seventy-five feet before the animal turns and walks away, then bolts into the forest.

As twilight deepens, we start back to *Windy Lady* and now a pair of Canada Geese fly overhead, followed by two smaller ducks. I notice dimples in the dark waters near the boat, and peering down see flashes of silver as a school of herring circles below. Next morning, an otter swims casually around the end of the float when we raise the anchor at 0630.

With heavy clouds and no wind, we motor westward through Lama Pass to Bella Bella. A light mist is falling when the small coastal village comes into view three hours later. A huge Holland-America cruise ship now appears in the channel in front of us, dwarfing the buildings and the island itself. We pull over to the side and let it pass.

Rain is falling steadily when we tie up at the marina dock. Going shore, we buy two charts and a dozen eggs at the store, then join some two dozen customers in the café, where we eat greasy hamburgers and breathe in a lot of second-hand cigarette smoke. The din in the room drowns out the TV news but we hear one story, as everyone stops talking long enough to listen to a report about a large sailing vessel that struck a reef and sank.

We wait for high tide before attempting to motor through the narrow, rocky channel known as Gunboat Passage. The buoys marking the channel are hard to spot in the rain, and I worry about our six-foot keel all the way. Once through, we stop at a nearby anchorage, where we stay for two nights. Despite low, grey clouds next day, I spend five hours paddling about in my canoe. I also check out a route past some large rocks at the entrance, which we didn't see on the way in due to the twelve-foot tide.

Clouds sit low on the mountains when we leave the following morning, and although mid-tide, the depth gauge never reads less than 24 feet. When we turn north into the calm waters of Fisher Channel, thousands of small ducks float in a long line down the center. With binoculars, I'm able to identify a few Buffleheads, but most are Common Golden Eye. Around the next point, some two dozen seals are draped across the rocks.

By midday of Day 21, we are in the isolated community of Ocean Falls, tying up at a dock in 100 feet of water. We talk to a few locals in a nearby small café and learn that the paper mill was shut down in 1982, after operating for some seventy years. The town's population dropped to a low of 25, but is now back up to 160. When the afternoon turns sunny and warm, we spend three hours wandering about the old town site and the dam. High on a hill, hidden in an overgrown street, we find a plaque that reads, *Owen, Jack and Bert lived here for 46 years, to 1989.* And then, *Home Again.*

All kinds of flowers bloom on the hillside, with domestic varieties like yellow day lilies and purple irises competing for space with native buttercups, daisies, and columbines. I also recognize thimbleberry, cow parsnip, and devil's club. But only when I see the little blue forget-me-nots do I think of the people who once lived here, their hopes and dreams now buried beneath the undergrowth and long forgotten.

As much as we enjoy visiting these remote areas, the long, narrow inlets provide little opportunity to sail, so we start south on Day 23. After motoring for four hours, we're approaching the site of the old cannery at Namu in Fitz Hugh Sound. Ahead of us, a flock of sea gulls circles above splashes of white in the water and then sunlight glints on dorsal fins. I assume that a large group of dolphins are feeding, then am delighted to see a few jumping and one tail-walks thirteen times.

Passing near the old buildings, we enter the anchorage just before high tide. Dave circles the boat around, checking for depth, then picks a spot and brings *Windy Lady* to a stop. I drop the anchor off the bow, realizing then that the process is no longer a mystery. I now know how much chain to let out, and with my foot, can interpret the vibrations, so have a good idea of what is happening below. Feeling good, I gaze around as we set the anchor. The sun is dropping in the west and shadows are lengthening, but that doesn't hide the sobering sight of an oil slick on the water and rusty barrels strewn about on shore.

Winds are light when we leave the anchorage next morning, but swells are pushing up the channel from the south. When we stop to raise the mainsail, a large swell rocks the boat just as Dave heaves on the halyard, and it instantly wraps around two of the upper mast steps. I turn and look at Dave, who looks back at me, as I've laid claim to the mast work. (I preferred having him on deck controlling my safety line, rather than the other way round. Besides, he did everything else!)

Wordlessly, I walk over to the base of the mast and start climbing up the steps, which are welded about three feet apart on either side. I'm almost twenty feet up, just below the spreader, when a second large swell rocks the boat. Feeling the strain on my arms as I swing out over the water, I close my eyes and hug the mast until the swaying eases. I then climb over the spreader, free the halyard, and scoot back down.

We alternate between sailing and motoring for the next few hours, and when halfway down Calvert Island, the breeze picks up to 20 kt. Soon, ten-foot swells are pushing their way up from Queen Charlotte Sound, and *Windy Lady* is bobbing around like a top. After fighting our way down to Rivers Inlet, we stop for the night.

Next morning, we sit in the cockpit with our coffee, enjoying clear skies and cool temperatures. When the noisy squawking of a stellar jay disrupts the silence, we trace the sound to flashes of blue diving at an eagle perched in a nearby tree. The jay then hops from branch to branch, scolding stridently, until the bigger bird finally moves down the bay. That doesn't satisfy the jay and it follows, bringing a couple of friends. After a little more haranguing, the eagle gives up and flies away.

We leave the anchorage at 1030 on Day 25, setting off under sail with a light SW breeze and calm seas. The wind dies soon after, then promptly picks up from the NW and grows stronger. By the time we reach the entrance to the inlet, winds are nearing 20 kt and *Windy Lady* is running on a beam reach, our fastest point of sail. She's becoming increasingly difficult to handle, and after a couple of strong gusts pull the bow around fifteen to twenty degrees, I nervously turn to Dave and ask, "Isn't it time to put a reef in the mainsail?"

Gesturing with his hand toward the heaving foredeck, he retorts, "If you think I'm going up there, you're crazy!"

Instead, he takes the helm and steers her straight out to sea. I grow increasingly anxious because seas are wild, with a strong westerly swell mixing in with the ebb current from Rivers Inlet and the northwest chop from Fitz Hugh Sound. Half an hour later, 25-kt winds have heeled her over so far that waves cover the lower half of the portholes. I think he just wants to see how fast she'll go because once the boat speed reaches 9 kt, he turns the bow southward.

As we follow the coastline around to Smith Sound, the sails are hit by a much stronger gust that violently spins *Windy Lady* around ninety degrees and lays her over on her side. With that, Dave races below to start the engine. I furl in the headsail, then step to the helm, steeling myself for the job ahead. It's time to put a reef in the mainsail.

Wind and sea are now at odds, so when I turn the bow into wind, *Windy Lady* is broadside to the swells, and the foredeck rolls and twists viciously, with spray flying everywhere. Dave hangs on with one hand and works with the other, so I watch closely. When he's working with reefing lines, I let the bow fall away; when he's working with the sail, I turn it back. Before he's finished, a huge swell rises up in front of the bow and I try to yell a warning, but my throat is so dry I can barely croak. Still, he hears and grabs on with both hands—and the boat just rides over top. It seems a long time before he's safely back in the cockpit.

Strong seas sweep under the keel as we motor south, and after fighting the helm for two hours, we turn east into Smith Sound. Swells now push against the stern, turning the boat sideways, first one way then the other. The seas only subside when we cross behind Brown Island, but 20-kt gusts follow us into the anchorage.

With clear skies and warm sunshine, we stay over a day, and Dave does more fishing while I paddle about in the canoe. The early weather forecast the following day reports that a low-pressure system is developing west of Vancouver Island. It's expected to send a series of storms onto the west coast, and we decide that it's probably time to get back around Cape Caution.

We leave Smith Sound on Day 27, motoring out on an ebb tide strengthened by melt water from the mountains. We meet a moderate westerly swell that rolls *Windy Lady* far over onto her sides when we make the turn southward. I grab onto the binnacle for support, and hear cursing from below, where Dave is trying to prepare breakfast. Swells hit us broadside all the way down to Cape Caution, and with light winds, the boat rolls heavily all the way.

Clouds sit low on the hills south of the cape, but the sky looks brighter toward Port Hardy, which proves to be an illusion as we run into fog near the Walker Islands. While I watch the island in front of us disappear into the mist, Dave takes his post at the chart table in the cabin. Piloting the boat through a grey, cotton-wool world isn't as unnerving the second time around, but that otherworldly feeling returns, especially when the mournful wail of a foghorn drifts across the silent waters.

We're in fog over three hours, and at one point, Dave hollers up, "Turn five degrees to starboard!" When I don't instantly respond, he urgently adds, "There's a boat dead ahead and three blips on the radar screen. I think it's a tug!" A short time later, I heard the throb of a diesel engine as the vessel passes 300 yards to port; a few minutes afterward, *Windy Lady* rocks gently in its wake.

About twenty minutes after making our last course correction, the winds pick up to 7–12 kt. The outlines of mountains on Vancouver Island appear, abruptly followed by the looming shape of a small island to starboard. Minutes later, we're in bright sunshine, with the sea sparkling deep blue and Hardy Bay only 2 nm away.

The marina at Port Hardy is no bargain at $42/night, particularly with dead fish floating in the water, rotting boards in the dock, and dog feces everywhere. We walk into town and treat ourselves to supper, but as soon as I begin to relax, I feel exhausted. Next morning, fog blankets the harbor; it lifts, returns, and lifts again, but a fog bank remains in the channel.

We phone Environment Canada for a weather briefing and are told that the current SE flow will be replaced by a NW flow in about two days' time. We won't be able to sail offshore, but there should be a brief weather window if we want to dayhop down the coast. We don't have the detailed charts we need for dayhopping and can't find what we want in the stores, but decide to go anyway.

We leave Port Hardy early that afternoon, heading for an all-weather anchorage at the north end of Vancouver Island. With headwinds of 20 kt, we motor most of the way. Wind and sea are calm when we approach the impressive cliffs guarding the entrance to Bull Harbor that evening. We take extra care in setting the anchor, then relax in the cockpit. The air is warm and still with dark clouds overhead, and a chorus of bird songs drifts across the water.

We spend three nights here, with overcast skies, frequent rain, and a day of gusty winds. When we go ashore, we stumble across several houses at the head of the bay that are boarded up and in need of paint. Dave finds a sign hidden in the bush identifying the site as an Indian reserve.

Crossing the narrow isthmus to Roller Bay, we stand and watch the surf pound against the steep, gravel beach, then look out on open water that extends all the way to Japan. I wonder how it came to be that two such different cultures developed on either side of that body of water. Then, feeling the pull of that far horizon, I know with absolute certainty that my future was meant to be out there.

CHAPTER 5

The West Coast of Vancouver Island

When we tune in the early forecast on Day 31, there is no weather window. A low-pressure system has stalled some 300 nm to the west, and a second low is strengthening off the Oregon coast. If we leave now, we'll face 20-30 kt headwinds and strong seas on the 30-nm run down to Winter Harbor. If we don't leave now, chances are we won't go at all.

I follow Dave up on deck and we stand at the lifelines, studying the grey, overcast sky. We need to cross a 4-nm-wide bar at slack tide, so if we're going, there's no time to waste. We were through the boat the night before, stowing and tying down everything we'd been using, and he now makes a quick decision, "Okay, let's get the anchor up." Trying to hide my apprehension, I sneak a long, last look around the snug harbor as I walk up to the bow.

Seas are calm as we round the end of Vancouver Island, and we cross the bar with no difficulty. The first swells appear several miles from Cape Scott on the northwest tip of the island, and they grow bigger as we near Scott Channel. After motoring for four and one-half hours, we stop on the verge of a stormy-looking sea and raise the mainsail, putting in two reefs. We then shut down the engine and pull out the headsail.

With SE winds of 20 kt coming up the coast, Dave steers *Windy Lady* out to sea, heading into a strong SW swell. Although the sea is pretty rough, we have a good run for 90 minutes and are then 7.5 nm from Cape Scott. After tacking back towards shore for 45 minutes, we're stunned to learn we're only 5 nm from the cape. We tack back out to sea again, and before long, winds are hitting 30 kt. I spend the afternoon sitting in the shelter of the windscreen, watching *Windy Lady* bob and twist as she crashes into waves, sending spray flying everywhere. My trust in her is growing.

At 1700, we've sailed 21 nm but made good only 7.5, so decide to head for a storm anchorage 2 nm away. Five minutes after we start the engine, a squall knocks *Windy Lady* over onto her side. Waves break over the bow, washing back over the cabin roof, and others break alongside, dousing the cockpit. She instantly bobs upright, shakes herself off, and struggles onward, but for the next hour, I sit huddled in the cockpit with my stomach in knots.

Frequent squalls now bring strong gusts and driving rain, and at times, we seem barely to inch forward. Waves crash over the bow, sending the sea streaming across the cabin roof and side decks, and spray flies everywhere. But only once does my heart leap into my throat, and that happens when a following sea tries to turn the boat sideways as we sweep through the narrow entrance into Sea Otter Cove.

Dave proceeds cautiously, squinting through wind-driven spray as he tries to locate the mooring buoys in the anchorage. When he turns the bow toward the closest one, *Windy Lady* promptly runs aground on a rocky shelf. He easily backs her off and then follows the circular deep-water route shown on our small-scale chart. I now walk up to the bow, dreading what comes next, because I have to secure her to a buoy.

Kneeling down beside the toe rail, some six feet above the water, I coil the mooring line in my hand, place the boat hook nearby, and wait. The foredeck blocks Dave's view of the buoy, so he steers blindly, but slowly we draw closer. When I lean out on the port side, preparing to throw my line, I see that the big metal storm buoy is mostly submerged. A squall then hits us, bringing a shower of cold rain and blowing the bow off to the side.

Undaunted, Dave repositions *Windy Lady* and brings her up to the buoy once more. I throw my line down under the heavy bar that runs across its top, reach down with the boat hook and pull the rope through, then bring the end back up on deck. As I secure it, I am ecstatic; I'm dripping wet, windblown, and cold, but finally I've done something right!

Gusty winds jerk the boat against its short mooring line for much of the night, and to our surprise, the other five boats in the anchorage are gone by 0600. When we leave thirty minutes later, the depth in the entrance is under ten feet and low tide still two hours away. With a light SE wind and smooth seas, we relax in the cockpit and enjoy the scenery as we motor down to Quatsino Sound. We ride the swells in through the entrance, passing near surf breaking on rocks below the lighthouse, and tie up at the dock in Winter Harbor about midday.

We now renew our acquaintance with a couple we met in Port Hardy, who are on a sailboat called *Starkindred*. They had a rough crossing to Sea Otter Cove and were towed into port when algae in the fuel killed their engine. We also meet the American couples on two Nordic tugs that shared our last two anchorages.

Lured out by warm sunshine, we stroll for an hour along the shady tree-lined boardwalk that follows the edge of the bay. We're back at the store when it opens at 1500, looking for charts, but see only the ones we already have. Gloria, off one of the Nordic tugs, comes to our rescue, lending me a coastal cruising guide, and I spend an hour furiously reading and making notes.

Next morning brings bright sunshine and strong winds that howl through the rigging of the boats. With the forecast calling for NW winds of 30–35 knots and moderate seas, we spend the day visiting and doing chores. I re-borrow Gloria's cruising guide and expand my notes, and she shows me another book she has. The title says it all, *Cape Horn: One Man's Dream, One Woman's Nightmare.*

When we untie early next morning, a few dark clouds sit low on the mountains and winds are light. Just outside the harbor entrance, I hear a sudden whoosh of air and turn to see a grey whale feeding near the shore; it disappears and resurfaces barely seventy-five feet off the stern. The whale appears to be about as long as our boat and its skin is rough, as though covered with barnacles. Mist rises from its blowhole when it again exhales, and it then disappears.

We run into moderate ocean swells at the entrance to the sound, and once again *Windy Lady* rolls far over onto her sides as we make the turn southward. I hang onto the binnacle to keep from falling across the cockpit, then have difficulty steering, so start bending my knees one at a time, trying to offset the roll. It actually works quite well. Thereafter, whenever the boat rolls heavily, I do deep knee bends in a sort of weird dance with the rhythm of the ocean.

Once we're clear of the entrance, we stop and raise the mainsail, then continue under power as we head south around Brooks Peninsula. Small mountains of water surge around the boat as we pass Solander Island, and we feel fortunate to have light winds and sunshine, as the weather station here had consistently reported 40-50 kt winds. That feeling deepens when we see two large Orcas (killer whales) passing some 300 feet away, their tall dorsal fins rising six feet above the water.

But my confidence deserts me when I see the rocky outcroppings and barrier islands littering the approach to Walter's Cove at Kyoquot Inlet. I check the coastal pilot and am further unnerved when I read that local knowledge is required to cross the bay because of many rocks and reefs, both above and below water. My faith in my handwritten notes and mud maps instantly disappears, so I direct Dave to a round-about, deep-water route.

That's okay until a sailboat with local knowledge crosses in front of us. My captain is then not very happy.

The entrance to a dredged channel into the cove is well marked, but it takes forever to find the second marker buoy. By the time we do, I can practically feel *Windy Lady's* bottom scraping on the rocks. My mud map then has some value, as it shows the relative positions of subsequent buoys, including two that mark ninety-degree turns. We go directly to the store after tying up, but still can't find any charts.

Dark clouds bring occasional heavy rain that afternoon, but during a lull in the storm, we walk across the island to a viewpoint overlooking the ocean. Strolling back around the harbor, we pass two clusters of buildings sitting across from one another. They look rather depressing on such a gloomy day. Farther down the road, we come to a small house and are greeted by a man walking across the yard. He is soon explaining that he is a teacher turned sawmill-operator and seems anxious to show Dave his bandsaw mill. I'm taken up to the house and pawned off on his wife.

When I enter the home, she is peacefully reading in a rocking chair and somewhat reluctantly marks her page, then puts her book down and politely offers me a cup of tea. As we chat, she talks about her seven children, who range in age from four to seventeen years, and her home, which is a converted one-room schoolhouse. Looking around, I note the bare wood floors and walls, the simple furnishings. Two ladders at either end lead up to a narrow loft running down one side of the room. It appears to contain large storage cupboards, and I suspect the two older boys sleep up there.

Initially, we're just two women, sitting and talking casually, but that soon changes. I begin to feel uneasy, then confused. I try to focus but can't; something is dreadfully wrong. It slowly dawns on me that I'd heard this conversation before, many times before. To my horror, I realize that I know what this woman is going to say before she says it. In fact, I know everything about her. The feeling of connection is so overwhelming that I ask myself, *is she living an alternate version of my life?*

As I struggle to make sense of what is happening, the image of a wood stove in a small kitchen flashes into my head. That completely rattles me, as I've never seen it before. The question then becomes, *is it my life or hers?* I hear my own wailing thoughts in protest, *but I'm going to sail across the ocean!*

I don't know how long the spell lasts, but it's only broken when the men return. I must have made a very strange visitor and drag Dave away quickly, needing to return to the familiar surroundings of the boat. But even there, my confusion continues while I try to understand what just took place.

I will never know what triggered my reaction that day, but the conditions certainly evoked memories of my mother, who raised her eight children in small, isolated communities in the BC interior. But it was myself that I saw in this woman, and I'm reminded that when I was born, there was no reason to believe that my life would be much different than my mom's. In fact, I was raised to be a wife and mother.

At one time, years before, I'd pondered over the fact that my life had followed a different path. But I was familiar with the struggles and sacrifices made by my parents and grandparents, so it was easy to conclude that my opportunities were a result of the efforts made by their generations to have a better life.

Having now met a woman who should have had those same opportunities, but still lived the old life, that explanation no longer satisfies me. *Was there more to it? Perhaps a type of genetic energy that flowed from one generation to the next? Did free will really exist, or was my life in some way a continuation of the lives of my parents and the path I followed preordained?*

We leave Walter's Cove at high tide next morning, motoring out through the dredged channel under a clear, sunny sky. High swells sweep into the bay while we're raising the mainsail, but winds are light. We then motor-sail down the coast, passing steep-sided, rugged mountains that rise up out of the sea. As *Windy Lady* rises and falls on twelve-foot swells, the motion magnifies the visual impact of scars left on the slopes by slides and zigzagging logging roads.

Shortly before midday, I see the shiny black backs and small fins of two Dahl dolphins swimming about fifty feet off the bow. Fish then start jumping and Dave hurries below for his fishing rod. Ten minutes later, he sits beaming from ear-to-ear, admiring the four-pound Coho salmon he's landed. At Esperanza Inlet, heavy surf pounds the rocks, causing a misty cloud to form above the shoreline, but I best remember Nootka Sound, as there the sound of the engine changes and it dies.

Dave rushes below, raises and ties back the sole, and starts checking the engine. I reset the sails, but winds are light and *Windy Lady* isn't moving fast enough to provide steerage. Realizing we're adrift, I uneasily study the hills and valleys of moving water around us, then fixate on the surf breaking on the shore and the high, isolated mountains beyond. Soon, my worried thoughts are going in circles. *Will we be washed up on the rocks? Are there any boats around to rescue us? Is there anyone in the inlet who could help us?* Unconsciously, I try to steer toward the inlet.

A few minutes later, I realize how absurd I am being. *We're a sailboat! We have to be able to maneuver without an engine.* Then the real irony strikes me. *Here we are, planning to sail thousands of miles across an ocean, and I obviously doubt our ability to deal with a minor emergency in light winds on a sunny afternoon.* With that thought, I call down to the captain, request permission to tack, and turn the boat back on course.

My actions are of little consequence that day, but it is an important milestone for me. For the first time in my life, I banished the worries swirling round in my head and started thinking sensibly. That I could do so would seem to indicate those fears were rooted more in my imagination than in reality.

Dave now appears in the cockpit carrying the Racor fuel filter wrapped in a cloth. Uncovering it, he explains, "The rolling of the boat dislodged a lot of gunk from the bottom of the fuel tanks. This filter and the glass bowl beneath it are filled with the stuff. We don't have a spare filter, so I'll have to clean it."

With that, he takes a deep breath, raises the filter to his lips, and blows long and hard into one end. A greyish-brown froth slowly oozes out all over, soaking the cloth and his beard with diesel. Choking and coughing, he blows again and again, until nothing more seeps out. He then replaces the filter, pumps fuel into the lines, and cranks the engine two or three times. It runs! We're underway within thirty minutes, but it takes much longer for Dave to rid himself of the smell and taste of the diesel.

That night, we tie up at the dock in Hot Springs Cove. Dave barbeques his salmon and we dine in the cockpit, enjoying the food, our surroundings, and the day's accomplishments. In the fading light of the long summer evening, we walk along a two-km-long boardwalk through lush, green rain forest, while listening to bird songs. Heavy cedar planks have replaced about half of the original split-cedar boards, and we note with interest the boat names and dates carved into the older boards.

We now see wisps of steam rising above the undergrowth and follow a stream of hot water down the hillside, seeing it grow bigger and plunge over an eight-foot wall. Below, in a rocky fissure, the stream widens into several bathtub-sized pools and quietly enters the ocean, marking the spot with a steam plume. I can't resist the temptation to ease my feet into a hot water bath, but my enjoyment is short-lived as darkness is almost on us and we have a long walk back.

Despite low cloud and fog, we're underway by 0600 on Day 37. The morning remains cold and grey, and with light winds and high swells, we motor. The sea flattens out about midday, and an hour later, the sun breaks through. Fish are jumping as we pass the Broken Islands in Barclay Sound, and Dave strings out a line and catches another Coho, a twin to the one he landed the day before.

While reaching down with a net to scoop up the fish, I catch the brim of my hat on a lifeline and it falls into the water. Unhappily, I watch it float away. It's a denim-covered cowboy hat that I rather like, and seeing my consternation, Dave tries to reassure me, saying cheerfully, "Don't worry; we'll get it back!"

So, as he takes care of his fish, I turn *Windy Lady* onto a reciprocal heading and start scanning the twelve-foot-high swells surging around us. I don't have much hope of finding the hat, but to my surprise, I spot the small, blue crown a few minutes later, barely visible as it floats down the back side of a large swell. I lose sight of it several times in the ensuing minutes, and it then hides behind the bow as we draw closer. Somehow, I bring the boat just close enough that Dave, stretching to his utmost limits, is able to snag it with the boat hook. It wobbles precariously on the end of the hook, but he brings it aboard. It's a very satisfying moment for both of us.

We anchor that night at the edge of Barclay Sound, and next day is again grey and cold, with fog, rain, and occasional high swells. We are well into the Strait of Juan de Fuca when I spot what appears to be a breaking wave ahead. Keeping a sharp lookout, I see a waterspout, a tall, black dorsal fin, and another waterspout. Soon, ten orcas are swimming abreast in a long line that stretches from our boat to the north side of the strait. Like in a dream, the tall fins break the water's surface, float through the air, then disappear. Another large whale surfaces three times as it swims by 100 feet away, providing a marvelous view of tall dorsal fin, shiny back, grey saddle, and black tail.

I continue scanning the waters ahead and soon spot another splash, then see numerous tall fins and waterspouts spread out across a large area. The whales are clearly visible as they swim by, arching in an out of the water, sometimes two together. Dave then shouts and points to the other side of the boat, where two orcas swim past 150 feet away. They are also side-by-side, with the smaller whale emerging from the water just as the larger one re-enters. I am utterly enchanted.

We're quickly past them, but ten minutes later, another large orca passes close by. It's traveling fast and all we see is a tall fin arcing in and out of the water. We think they're hunting Coho salmon.

We anchor that night at Sooke, on the southern tip of Vancouver Island. Next morning, we're underway before 0700; it is June 21 and the longest day of the year. Local fishermen also await the salmon, and dozens of small boats line the shoreline as we motor up the 5-nm stretch of strait to Race Rocks. Passing by the city of Victoria, we continue around the end of Vancouver Island and complete our circumnavigation at 1600 on Day 39, when we drop the hook at Saltspring Island.

That night, we visit with Brian and his wife and report on our adventures. Only then do we realize how much we'd accomplished. We'd simply been too busy living each day to put it all together. And as our competence and confidence grew, so did the attraction of that far horizon.

CHAPTER 6

Facing the Truth About Dreams

W e'd spent hours the previous winter devouring sailing magazines, cruising guides, pilot charts, and sailing directions. We learned that it would take two cruising seasons to complete our voyage. The first year would take us to New Zealand, and we needed to be there in November, before the start of cyclone season. The next year, we'd have time to visit several islands on our way to Australia.

We now need to choose a sailing route across the Pacific Ocean. The most popular route runs through Mexico and French Polynesia, but we decide against it after learning that many cruisers stay in Mexico. We really want to reach Australia. An alternate route runs through Hawaii and Samoa, but that means leaving no later than the end of August, which is when the offshore cruising season ends in the Pacific Northwest. We really should leave as soon as possible. As our *to-do lists* grew considerably during the shakedown cruise, we frantically set to work.

Five weeks later, on Thursday, July 26, we clear with Canada Customs in Victoria. We then motor for six hours to the American port of Friday Harbor in the San Juan Islands, where we pick up photocopies of 500 charts of the

Pacific Islands and the US west coast that Dave had ordered. We really hope to have the charts necessary to go ashore anywhere along our route.

When we untie at 0630 next morning, the day is overcast and cool. With light winds, we motor for thirteen hours through the Strait of Juan de Fuca, with the tide changing direction twice. We happily visit with several small pods of dolphins along the way. Then, as Dave sits peacefully reading in a rear cockpit seat, one animal surfaces about three feet from his elbow. Perhaps to get his attention, it exhales with a loud, explosive snort that is so unexpected, he almost drops the book.

The afternoon turns sunny and warm, and a nuclear submarine now steams up behind us. I study the sealed black exterior cutting through the blue waters of the strait and cannot see a single sailor. My own head swims with the immensity of the adventure ahead, and it seems extraordinary that they would go to sea and never see the ocean.

The sun is dropping low in the sky as we near the entrance to Neah Bay on the American side of the strait, where we plan to spend the night. Spotting a waterspout, we peer intently at the shadowy shoreline and see the long, dark mottled shapes of two large, grey whales. We're then inside the harbor and dropping the anchor. With winds on the nose next day, we stay over and finish a few more jobs.

On Sunday, July 30, the sky is again overcast and winds are light. We're away before 0800, and I take a long, lingering look around the quiet harbor as we leave. Hilo, Hawaii, is 2,500 nm across the ocean, and I'm feeling both exhilarated and intimidated at the thought of spending three weeks at sea. Minutes later, we run into high standing waves near the entrance to the strait. They keep growing higher until *Windy Lady* is pitching almost straight up and down in a way that I really don't like. Thankfully, we're through the worst of them fairly quickly. We then round Cape Flattery, and with the ocean heaving around us, I turn the boat into wind and Dave raises the mainsail.

We're in trouble right from the start, as a strong westerly swell rolls *Windy Lady* over onto her side, turning the bow and knocking the light SW wind from the sails. As she rolls and twists in the waves, the boom lurches back and forth across the cabin roof. Dave now brings up the preventer, which is just a long rope with pulleys and two hooks that attaches a pad eye on the bottom of the boom to the toe rail. It's meant to keep the boom from swinging.

He's careful to keep a good grip on the handrail as he starts down the heaving side deck, but when the boom lurches overhead, he can't resist trying to snag the pad eye. Stretching upwards with the hook in one hand, he releases his grip on the boat with the other and flails around with it, trying to keep his balance. It doesn't take much imagination on my part to picture him going overboard. Only then, looking at the waters around us, do I think about how difficult it would be to rescue him.

Eventually, to my relief, he continues on to the mast, where he's better able to hang on. He then steps up onto the cabin roof, crouches beneath the boom, and stretches his free arm out toward the pad eye. Just as he's about to clip on, the end of the boom shoots up eight feet into the air and swings out over the water on the port side. While we gape in disbelief, the wind plays with the sail and the boom dances beyond our grasp.

I'm still gawking when Dave returns to the cockpit and furls the headsail. He has me turn the bow into the swell, bringing the boom back over the deck, then eases the mainsail halyard. As the sail sags, the end of the boom drops, and he secures it to the top of the windscreen. I now see that the traveler, which controls the side-to-side movement of the mainsail, is lying on the cabin roof. The pad eye it was attached to has sheared off.

I'm sure we could have jury-rigged something, if necessary, but at this stage it only makes sense to turn back. I'm unbelievably disappointed. Dave starts the engine and we return to the entrance to the strait, where the standing waves have been replaced by flat water; it's like a large lake. We've been out six hours and the tide is now high, so I assume the steep waves earlier resulted from ocean swells sweeping in the entrance at low tide.

We motor all night, in and out of fog, and clear with Customs in Victoria the following morning. After anchoring in the harbor, we remove the boom and take it ashore in the dinghy. The days then drag by, and we wait nearly two weeks for repairs.

We spend another night at Neah Bay before rounding Cape Flattery on Tuesday, August 15. Winds are from the south at 15 kt when we raise the sails, and with the preventer in place and our plans back on track, we now relax. (But I'm still hoping for good weather for the first 24 hours while we settle in.)

By 1500, the wind is down to 5 kt and *Windy Lady* is rolling heavily in a westerly swell. Dave now tries the autopilot for the first time under sail. It groans long and loud with each adjustment, makes them constantly, and sucks up a lot of power. He soon decides to use it only when the engine is running.

We've already agreed to share the watch equally and plan to trade off every three to six hours, depending on conditions, and he now asks, "Which shift do you want tonight?"

Absurdly, that's when I first think about sailing in the dark, and the idea is not particularly appealing. Quickly realizing that it's a bit late for that, I respond, "The sunset watch," thinking that transitioning from daylight to darkness would be easiest.

So, at 1800, Dave goes below to rest and I start my first watch, now responsible for keeping the boat safe and on course. We're 20 nm off the coast of Washington State, and the mountains on the horizon are starting to fade. As they grow smaller and hazier, I find myself glancing in their direction more often.

The time comes when I look and see nothing. Uneasily, I stand and turn slowly in a full circle, scanning the waters around the boat. That is when I first realize what it means to go to sea. My entire world has just been reduced to the deck of a forty-foot sailing vessel surrounded by an ocean of moving water.

High swells and light winds keep me busy steering the boat, and I actually don't notice as light fades from the overcast sky. There's then enough ambient light after nightfall to see. I know because a sudden, loud snort behind me sends my heart leaping into my throat. Quickly turning around, I see the tail of a dolphin disappearing into the waves. Dolphins swim with the boat for two hours during the following watch.

We're passing through a fishing fleet at change of watch at 0200, and isolated lights bob here and there in the darkness. With a half-moon and a few stars peeking through the clouds, it's really very pleasant. An hour later, the wind drops and the swells push the boat sideways. I turn the wheel from lock to lock, trying to stay on course, and soon my shoulders ache.

The wind fills the sails again just before daylight, and *Windy Lady* makes 5 kt for the next six hours. About mid-morning, I'm puzzled by an area of white water off to the southwest. Peering closer, I see dolphins leaping in the distance, and minutes later, hundreds of animals surround us. Most show only a dorsal fin, but others arch through the air or perform back flips. A few jump straight up, twist, and land with a heavy smack on their sides. We watch them for over half an hour and I try to count the ones I can see at any given moment, but there are just too many. We estimate there are over a thousand.

A thunderstorm brings gusty winds early that afternoon, then takes the wind when it moves on. By 1800, high swells are pushing the boat sideways, and Dave goes below to start the engine. While going through his pre-start checklist, he stretches out on the sole with his head hanging over the engine compartment. A few minutes later, he's standing on deck with his head hanging over the lifelines. It's the only time either of us are seasick, and he blames it on diesel fumes and the rolling of the boat.

We start sailing again just before midnight, and when I come on watch at 0200, the light of a half-moon reflects off the waves and stars fill the sky. It's another beautiful night. But by the end of my watch at 0500, the boat again rolls heavily. I cradle my body with pillows after climbing into my berth but can't sleep.

Soon after I come on watch at 0800 on Day 3, a thunderstorm with cold, driving rain and gusty winds soaks me through as I stand at the helm. We then have steady winds and good sailing for the rest of the day. The color of the ocean now changes from the blue-black of northern waters to a warmer, deeper shade of blue. The breeze dies at sunset, leaving *Windy Lady* rolling in a westerly swell, so I reduce sail and let the boat drift, hoping Dave will be able to sleep. He resets the sails during the next watch.

When I return to the cockpit at 0200, the wind has strengthened and the sky has darkened ominously. Before Dave goes below, we turn on the spreader lights and put a second reef in the main. Thirty minutes later, winds are up to 20-kt and *Windy Lady* charges into swells, sending spray flying high over the foredeck. The night is now pitch-black and a dense black wall looms close in front of the bow. I find it a bit unnerving at first and keep telling myself that there's nothing in front of us but open water.

I steer using only the compass, which is surprisingly difficult. I hadn't realized how much I depended on visual cues, like swell direction and cloud formation, when steering a course. As the wind vane hides in the darkness at the top of the mast, I try to determine wind direction by feeling it on my face. A wave then washes over the starboard rail, and I worry that winds are getting stronger and wonder if we have too much sail up. The last hour seems to go on forever, but I log 24 nm during that watch, which is pretty good.

Winds are steady at 18 kt for much of Day 4, and we have another good day. That afternoon, I join Dave in the cockpit for an hour, the first time we've spent together in three days. I've not been getting much sleep and he obviously hasn't either as he looks tired. He's also obsessed by the fact that we're hand steering so much and grumbles, "It's crazy! We don't have time to do anything else! And it's exhausting, we sure couldn't do it in heavy weather." He then declares, "I'm going to install wind-vane self-steering as soon as we get in port."

The wind drops that evening, and almost becalmed, we drift for hours through light rain showers. Dave then wakes me just after midnight, calling me out to the cockpit. I turn on the dim light over my berth before crawling from my blankets and must be half asleep when I get there because the bright lights behind him don't register. Waving a hand in their direction, he has to ask, "What do you make of that?"

I wake up instantly as I focus on the mass of lights about one-quarter mile away. Alarmed at how close they are, I scream, "Why did you come so close?"

He yells back, "It wasn't me; they came and looked at us!"

Even as he speaks, we hear the hum of powerful engines and the lights start to move away. As visibility is limited to about a half-mile in rain showers and mist, we go below and turn on the radar. The unit takes two minutes to warm up and then a very large image appears on the screen. It's nearly 2 nm off and moving away rapidly. Dave calls repeatedly on Channel 16 on VHF radio, which all ships monitor, but there is no response.

When the vessel is 6 nm away, we turn off the radar and return to the cockpit, staring out into the darkness where the ship disappeared. Dave explains that he first saw lights on the horizon about midnight. When he looked a second time, they were much closer, and in spite of his best efforts, the vessel continued to close. He is exhausted, wet, and very wired—and convinced that it was a UFO. As I'm about to take the watch, I try to find a rational explanation.

We review what we know, which isn't much. *Windy Lady* had been drifting with the waves for hours, and our running lights would have been hard to see in the poor visibility. On the other hand, our visitor had many lights and definitely did not have a diesel engine. The vessel appeared to change course after I turned on the cabin light, then sped away into the darkness. As we try to make sense of what we've seen, I make a note of the time and place: Saturday, August 19, 1995 at 0100; latitude 43°51.4' N; longitude 126°59.2' W.

Was it a US naval ship? Did one pick us up on radar and come over to make a visual sighting? If so, why didn't it respond to our VHF call? Perhaps it was the nuclear submarine we saw two weeks earlier in the Strait of Juan de Fuca. If it was running on the surface, maybe it didn't want to be identified; but would it have had all those lights?

The more we talk, the less likely my theories become, and when Dave goes below, I stand at the helm feeling as if I have a bull's eye painted between my shoulder blades. When the mist starts to clear, I peer around looking for lights and hear again the hum of the ship's engines in my head.

Winds remain light overnight, and the swells rolling relentlessly out of the west grow higher. The sails flog, *Windy Lady* rolls heavily, and we each in turn struggle to keep her moving forward. Neither of us get any sleep.

I'm feeling exhausted when I drag myself back to the cockpit at 0900, but tell myself; *you only have to make it through the next four hours.* I then see Dave and my heart sinks; he looks even worse than I feel. Knowing that we depend on each other, I give my first order, "You need to get some sleep. I don't want to see you back on deck until you've had three hours. I don't care how long it takes!" He returns two hours later, protesting that he'd just been lying awake in the berth.

At noon, as we go into Day 5, steep ten-foot swells make it almost impossible to keep *Windy Lady* moving forward. We turn to a heading ninety degrees to the east, but turn back two hours later, as all we did was add a following sea to our other problems. Now desperately fighting fatigue, we're pretty much at the mercy of the ocean and reduce our watches to three hours, then two.

Conditions reach a new low during my 2000 watch, when 15-kt gusts start snapping the flogging sails. Turnbuckles on the stays supporting the mast then bang against the chain plates, sending a shudder throughout the entire boat. This situation continues into the next watch, then abruptly changes an hour before midnight.

I'm in my berth, semi-conscious I think, when I feel the boat rolling slowly and abnormally far over onto her sides and hear unfamiliar sounds. Disturbed, I get up and look out the companionway, but Dave isn't in the cockpit. Suddenly terrified, I call his name. A dull, detached voice mumbles out of the darkness behind me, "The boat's hove-to and I'm monitoring her drift." Dave is sprawled on the settee, and with both sails backwinded, *Windy Lady* is doing what she was designed to do.

Returning to my berth, I listen to the gurgling of fuel/water running over the baffles in the tanks as the boat continues to roll extremely. About 0200, the rolling eases, and soon I hear Dave moving about. When he sees that I'm awake, he asks, "Can you take the helm?" He adds, "The wind has died down, and I want to charge the batteries."

Fifteen minutes later, I'm dressed and standing at the wheel. It's difficult to maintain a heading in the pitch-black night, almost harder with the engine running than it was under sail. Sometime after 0500, I start to nod off on my feet, so wave my arms and tap my toes, but am conscious only of a desperate need for sleep. An hour later, I feel the autopilot take control of the helm, then Dave pokes his head out into the cockpit and announces, "The autopilot seems to be working and I've had a few hours' sleep. You can come in and go to bed."

I sleep fitfully until 0900 and wake to find Dave standing at the chart table. He comes over and sits on the berth beside me, and I see that he's had a bath and changed his clothes. He now states, "We can't go on like this. We have to get self-steering equipment. I figure we're halfway between Victoria and San Francisco, so we can have the work done in either place."

Dismayed at the thought of returning to Victoria, I protest, "If we go back, chances are we'll never leave!"

"Well, that's a risk I'm prepared to take. We know the suppliers and marinas in Victoria, so it makes the most sense to go there. If you want, we can do it in San Francisco, or even hire someone to take the boat to Hawaii."

When I remain silent, he adds, "I've already turned the boat around."

I'm stunned, but know there's nothing more to be said. While digging out the charts that we need to return north, I attempt to adjust my mindset. But in my heart, I know that the dream is dead. It died at 0900 on Sunday, August 20, after we'd sailed only 370 nm down the west coast.

The trip north takes four days, and perversely, we relax in warm sunshine for the first two, with hardly any wind and calm seas. We motor, using the autopilot, and I learn that its control unit is located under my berth, and the burring noise it makes is like a drill in my ears. I move to the settee amidships, discover that the boat movement is actually smoother there, and sleep soundly for three hours.

As we now need to check engine instruments, we spend time inside the cabin while on watch, but still try to scan the surrounding horizon every fifteen minutes. We can see only 8 nm, and a ship making 24 kt would cover that distance in twenty minutes, so that gives us a bit of time to take evasive action, if necessary.

By noon on Tuesday, an icy wind is on the nose at 10 kt. A US Coast Guard plane now finds us, swooping down to read the name on our bow, then calls on VHF radio. They want to know our destination, and when Dave explains our situation, they ask if we need assistance. We don't, but it is comforting to know they are there.

By nightfall, the wind has strengthened to 15 kt, and it's up to 20 kt at 0200. Wind waves from the northwest are then over three feet high, making for a very lumpy ride. Early Wednesday morning, we pass a number of ships standing off river mouths, probably waiting for high tide. We sail for a few hours that day, but mostly motor, and pass the buoy off Cape Flattery in total darkness.

The trip back up the Strait of Juan de Fuca is long and slow, as we push against two ebb tides and one nebulous flood. Our speed over the ground hovers near 3.5 kt but occasionally drops down to 2.5. Just before noon on Thursday, August 24, we tie up at the Customs dock in Victoria. No one shows any particular interest in our early return to port, and a few hours later, we anchor in West Bay. We try to wait the usual time for the boat to settle but are soon fast asleep.

CHAPTER 7

A New Reality

When I wake next morning, *Windy Lady* sways gently on her anchor chain and water laps softly against the hull. Getting up, I make myself a cup of coffee, then stand in the cockpit, looking morosely around the quiet harbor. The contrast to past days is neither welcomed nor wanted. I feel disoriented, partly because the last nine days were all consuming, and partly because our focus for months has been on preparing to leave. In many respects, we've already cut ourselves off from life in Canada. I don't know what the future holds, but am bitterly certain that we will never go to sea again.

Dave finds a berth for the boat at a marina in Victoria's outer harbor, and two weeks later, we pack up some camping gear and head for Saskatchewan. We meet up with his two brothers in Chamberlain, and honoring their mother's last request, the men spread her ashes on her father's grave. I'm intrigued by her request, as she'd lived in Victoria for 22 years, her husband's ashes were spread in nearby Esquimalt harbor, and her sons all lived in BC. For her, however, home must have been the area where she grew up and raised her children.

When we return, we sail frequently, trying to build on what we've already learned. The marina couldn't have been more convenient, as ten minutes after untying, we're raising the sails out in the Strait of Juan de Fuca. That winter,

Dave qualifies as a ham operator, and studies everything he can find on reefing systems, boom vangs, and wind-powered self-steering systems. I take correspondence courses in celestial navigation and coastal cruising. To our surprise, we wake one morning to find a couple of inches of snow on the deck and pancake ice in the waters around the boat.

Dave's older brother, Gordon, lives in Victoria and they use the time to renew their ties; they'd been very close as boys. He also flies to Ottawa and spends a week with his son and family, then visits with his daughter in Vancouver when she has surgery on her shoulder. After Christmas, we make a trip north to see my parents. My mom is not well, although she says nothing. A month later, we learn that she has terminal cancer.

I'm now haunted by our conversation of a year earlier, when she found out that we were going to sail to Australia. She'd shaken her head in disbelief and asked, "What do we do if there's an emergency?" I had responded, "You'll just have to have it without me." I will see her in April and speak to her from overseas in July and September. She passes in October. It's a very difficult year for those who love her.

Somewhere along the way, we start making lists again, and Dave eventually orders a Hydrovane self-steering system. In mid-April, we leave on a ten-day cruise up the Strait of Georgia, during which he decides on the rigging changes he wants to make. We stay out in the middle of the strait to get the strongest winds and the sailing is good, but temperatures are cool and we turn back after 100 nm.

Dave now meets with a sailmaker and a rigger in Victoria. They review the work he wants done, assure him that there is plenty of time to complete it before the end of May, and he agrees to their price. On May 3, we motor to a boatyard about four hours away, where a crane waits to remove the mast. The boat is then propped up on the hard stand, and we camp onboard for the next eleven days.

Living on the hard is not an enjoyable experience, as *Windy Lady* quickly turns into a disaster area, both inside and out. We clean and antifoul the bottom, wash and wax the hull, sand and varnish hatches, and a hundred other tasks. Our last job before she goes back in the water is installing the self-steering unit.

We now learn that the mast isn't ready, although the crane is booked for early the following morning. When Dave learns that the crane is available later in the day, he badgers the rigger and gets the mast delivered and installed then. Meanwhile, we sit around for hours, twiddling our thumbs.

We work frantically for three days on the work dock, preparing *Windy Lady* for the move back to the marina. I'm at the helm when we leave, and when we're about ten minutes away from the dock, Dave hollers up, "We've got a problem! Water is pouring onto the galley floor out of the head. I think it's coming from the sink drain."

I want to return to the dock immediately, or at least get back into shallow water before we sink, but a closer look reveals the water is coming from a sink tap. One of us opened it when we were on the hard, and a few minutes earlier, Dave had accidently switched on the water pump while working on the GPS.

The next two weeks are a nightmare as we try to complete the countless and diverse tasks on our lists. Dave spends half his time chasing after the rigger, trying to get him to complete his work, but finally gives up and installs the new deck hardware himself. When the new sails arrive, they don't fit, and the self-leveling radar mast is lost while being shipped. When it finally arrives and is installed, it interferes with one of the running backstays needed for the new inner forestay. (*Windy Lady* is now cutter-rigged, so we can raise a third sail.)

By the end of May, *Windy Lady's* lockers are bulging. We have power and hand tools, miscellaneous engine parts, boat fittings, fuel and oil filters, repair kits for sails and fiberglass, and anything else Dave can think of needed to maintain the boat, the sails, and the engine. These are stored in large lockers under the settee in the main cabin. (I keep inventory lists, so that I can find things when needed.)

The big lockers in the galley are filled with large plastic buckets with snap lids that protect the contents from humidity and water leaks. Inside are bags of rice, macaroni, flour, powdered milk, sugar, and everything else needed to run a kitchen. I keep about a month's worth of supplies in smaller containers, handy for the cook. We won't use the refrigerator at sea because of the power it consumes, so home-can three dozen jars of meat and vegetables. We also obtain a couple of cases of tinned salmon and canned tomatoes, and I prepare meals in advance for the first four days.

The extra sails fill a large locker at the bow. Spare halyards, sheets, and anchor rode are stuffed beneath the companionway steps. After inventorying the charts, I roll them up and store them in sections of PVC pipe, which are stowed beneath the chart table. We have a wet locker for coats and boots, while items like engine oil and filters are stored in small lockers in the sole. There is some storage room in the head and the two stern cabins for clothing and personal items. Then there are equipment manuals, pocket books, my portable sewing machine, material for tarps, first-aid supplies, and so on, all of which need to find a home.

Remembering how our last attempt ended, Dave asks Brian to join us on the crossing to Hawaii. He feels confident that, with a third crew member, we'll be able to handle any problems arising at sea. As the voyage will take over three weeks, Brian arranges to take the month of June off work.

The pressure then builds at the days of June start ticking by. On June 4, Dave signs off on everything but one headsail. The next day, the two brothers move the boat to the public dock in front of the Empress Hotel in Victoria's inner harbor. The last sail is delivered there on the evening of June 6. On Saturday, June 8, we check the marine weather forecast at 0600 and heave sighs of relief. The day promises to be fair with favorable winds.

In a final flurry of activity, we set about readying the boat. Gordon and his wife arrive at 0830, and an hour later, I hear the sounds of excited voices and laughter, as Brian appears with his wife and daughter. At 1030, Dave and Brian load the dinghy onto the foredeck, then we climb down onto the dock for some last-minute pictures. Someone asks me if I'm excited, but after so many weeks of intense pressure, I'm just numb and glumly answer, "I've been so busy that we'll probably be halfway to Hawaii before I notice that we've untied."

Gordon, who spent thirty years in the navy, asks us to gather round, saying he'd like to bless the boat. He reads a passage from the bible, followed by the Twenty-Third Psalm, and the blessing. Presenting the bible to Dave, he explains that their parents gave it to Granny Ball for Christmas in 1937. I am touched by the brief ceremony, and it remains one of the few things that I remember from those tumultuous weeks.

CHAPTER 8

Passage to Hawaii

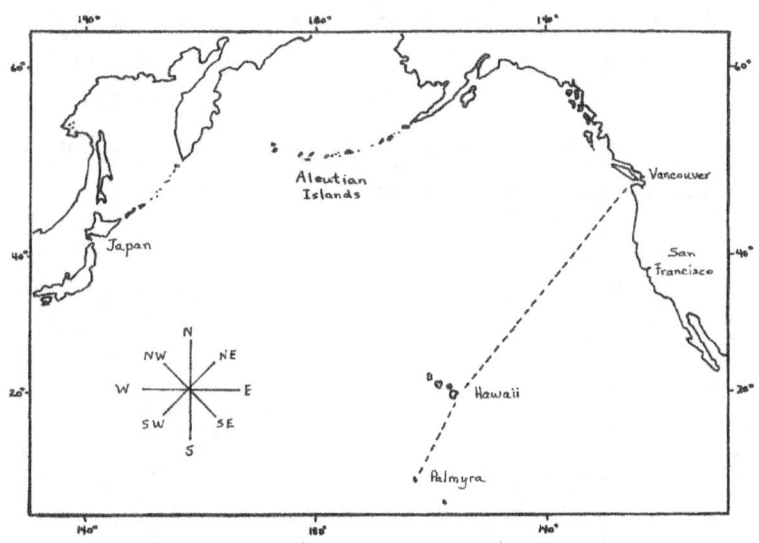

Rhumb Line Route – North Pacific

The sky is grey and overcast as Dave steers *Windy Lady* away from the dock, and Brian and I stand on the foredeck, waving goodbye. We then cross the harbor to the fuel dock, top up the diesel tanks, and untie for the last time at 1115.

There is no time to relax during the 60-nm run down the Strait of Juan de Fuca, and the two brothers, both big men, take over the cockpit for the first two watches as they check out our new equipment. I spend the time sorting through lockers with my inventory lists in hand. For days, I've desperately been stowing stuff wherever it would fit and now feel like I don't know where anything is. As I move and repack items, I try to ensure that heavier objects won't shift and start banging in the first rough seas.

When I come on watch at 2000, both wind and sea are calm and we're motoring. The sun is low in the sky, and I confess to looking rather wistfully at the entrance to Neah Bay as we pass. It seems odd to be heading out to sea at the end of the day. Brian relieves me at midnight, and I keep him company until we round the marker buoy off Cape Flattery at 0115. With smooth seas and a gentle swell rolling beneath *Windy Lady*, we then head out into the blackness that is the Pacific Ocean.

This year, we intend to sail farther off the coast, so steer southwest from Cape Flattery. When we're out 100 nm, we'll head south to Mendocino Ridge off Eureka, California. At that point, we'll again turn southwest towards Hawaii. We're hoping this route will keep us out of the center of the North Pacific high-pressure area, where winds will be light.

I don't sleep much that night, as the engine is noisy, but am in the cockpit ten minutes before the start of my 0800 watch. Looking east toward shore, I first notice that the coastal mountains have disappeared from view. I then turn slowly in a full circle, in what becomes my pre-watch ritual, scanning the horizon for ships and searching sea and sky for clues as to what the next four hours might bring.

With southerly winds now steady at 7 kt, Dave and I set the sails before he goes below. He shuts down the engine on the way to his berth, and I tweak the sails a few times, then happily settle into a rear seat and study sails, clouds, and waves. Swaying with the gentle roll of the boat, and listening to the soft swish of water against the hull, I begin to relax. Two hours later, winds increase to 12 kt and *Windy Lady* flies over the water. Feeling the magic, my spirit soars for the first time in months and the dream is reborn.

When Brian relieves me at noon, I fill in the ship's log. We record GPS position (latitude and longitude), course, distance logged, barometric pressure, and wind and sea conditions at the end of every watch. In the event of an emergency, our last recorded information will be no more than four hours old. As navigator, I also plot our noon position on a chart, which stays beside the HF radio. After twenty-five hours, we log 108 nm for Day 1.

When I take the watch again at 2000, dark clouds hang low overhead, southerly winds are steady at 16 kt, and *Windy Lady* tosses about roughly in lumpy, grey seas. The forecast calls for cold, stormy conditions overnight, and I wear a safety harness over my bulky cruising suit and clip onto a jack line as soon as I step into the cockpit.

Uncertain of what the coming hours will bring, I settle into a rear seat and watch the sky grow darker as winds increase to 20 kt. The night now turns pitch black and a solid wall seems to loom in front of the bow. With wind and sea roaring in my ears, I concentrate on my job, keeping wind in the sails and the bow on course, and gradually my apprehension eases.

During the night, winds back to SSE and ease for a while, but during my morning watch, they veer to the south and again strengthen. *Windy Lady* now charges into waves and spray flies everywhere. We wait too long before putting a reef in the mainsail, and winds hit 29 kt while Dave is working at the base of the mast. He grimly hangs on with one hand and works with the other, while being doused with buckets of salt water. At noon, we log 94 nm for Day 2.

For the next sixteen hours, winds gust from 20–30 kt, and with only one reef in the mainsail, *Windy Lady* crashes through the hills and valleys created by the swells. Like an airplane, she moves in three dimensions; the bow can go up or down, or turn right or left, while the deck rolls from side to side. In rough seas, she does all three at the same time. As she rolls and twists, waves crash over the bow, sending spray flying across the deck, and water is soon leaking in through the head hatch, the galley hatch, and the front and side cabin windows.

The rough, erratic, and sometimes violent movements make it impossible to sleep and difficult to do chores. I soon have a collection of bruises on my legs and hips. Dave and Brian end up putting a second reef in the mainsail at change of watch at 0400, working under the spreader lights with the boat hove to, the wind howling through the rigging, and waves crashing all around.

By 0800, winds have started to ease, and as seas calm during my morning watch, I notice that the color of the water has changed to the warmer, deeper blue I remember from the prior year. A pod of some fifty dolphins then appears, racing back and forth alongside the boat for an hour. At noon, winds are down to 10 kt, and we're 100 nm off the Oregon coast, just south of the mouth of the Columbia River. We log 106 nm for Day 3.

When Brian relieves me, he's acquired his sea legs. He'd been seasick ever since we left and hadn't eaten a thing, but never missed a watch. We've all now pretty much adjusted to the watch schedule, as well as our other duties. Dave looks after the engine and batteries, keeps in touch with a HAM network, and prepares meals. (He will run the engine for four to five hours every fourth day to charge batteries.) I monitor weather broadcasts, plot our noon positions, clean up after meals, and keep the cabin tidy. We all conserve our limited supply of fresh water.

The two men spend the afternoon in the cockpit, brainstorming about sails, seas, and boat performance. When winds back to the north, they rig the boat for downwind sailing, dropping the mainsail and easing the headsail out in front of the starboard bow. With winds steady at 10 kt on the stern, *Windy Lady* makes 4 kt, but rocks uncomfortably as the westerly swell sweeps beneath the keel.

The temperature cools quickly as the sun drops toward the horizon, and I'm glad for the warmth of my insulated cruising suit when I come on watch at 2000. I sit in my usual seat in the rear of the cockpit, and as the light fades and the waters grow darker, I notice a small, solitary bird flitting between the waves and realize again how much I enjoy this last hour of the day.

By morning, the wind has backed to the west, heavy clouds darken the sky, and it's rainy and cold. The early forecast includes a gale warning for the southern Oregon coast, so I worry. A later forecast extends the warning to northern and offshore waters, and I worry even more. Fully expecting 40-kt winds within twelve hours, I go through the galley and tie everything down.

The winds aren't as bad as forecast, but they are steady at 25-30 kt for the next three days. They move constantly, slowly veering or backing through ninety degrees between west and north. Sea conditions are extremely rough and *Windy Lady* races through the waves with her hull heaving and twisting, so sleep is almost impossible.

We end up putting in or taking out reefs at every change of watch, but don't reduce sail lightly, as that slows the boat and we have a schedule to keep. The two men again work under the spreader lights at 0400, this time using the engine to keep the boat under control as they put three reefs in the main and partially furl the headsail. We log 107, 140, and 135 nm for Days 4, 5, and 6.

After six full days at sea, we've sailed 686 nm and are approaching the western extremity of Mendocino Ridge. The winds have taken us farther offshore than expected, and we're now concerned that we could be close to the center of the high-pressure area. We don't know its position because I'm no longer picking up weather broadcasts. Keeping our fingers crossed, we turn and head southwest towards Hawaii.

The blustery conditions begin to ease next morning and by noon the NW breeze is steady at 15 kt. When it drops to 10 kt that afternoon, we put away our cruising suits and safety harnesses. Conditions remain much the same for the next twenty-four hours, and barometric pressure goes up and down a point. We log 109 and 107 nm for Days 7 and 8.

Our luck then runs out; the barometer climbs five points overnight and the wind dies. As *Windy Lady* rolls in the swells during my morning watch, the sails flog, the rigging bangs, and a few heavy items in the lockers hammer back and forth monotonously. It's all I can do to stay at the helm until noon before tracking them down. We log 92 nm for Day 9.

Concerned about getting Brian to Hawaii, Dave spends an hour on the HAM radio and confirms that we are in the center of the high. He starts the engine, and as the sea calms, I take advantage of the quiet, sunny afternoon and tour the foredeck. I find a few fittings that need tightening, then see that the mainsail halyard has chafed halfway through. Checking these items now becomes part of my regular duties.

As I stand at the bow that afternoon, admiring the sparkling blue waters around us, I have no idea that we are 700 nm away from the closest land and the ocean floor is almost 3 nm (5,225 meters) below the hull. After nine days at sea, however, I'm beginning to realize what an insignificant speck we are on the surface of this ocean.

That evening, I spot a plastic bottle bobbing on the rolling surface of the water and then see more bottles, fenders, and the upturned bottom of a bucket. Without wind waves, they are easy to spot. There's supposed to be a huge pool of rubbish out here somewhere, and I wonder how far we are from it.

We motor for forty-two hours, and with the autopilot doing the steering, our watches are easier, but the engine throbs loudly and the boat rocks uncomfortably from side to side. We raise the sails again at 0800 on Day 11, with westerly winds at 5–10 kt. We log 120 nm and 122 nm for Days 10 and 11.

Someone now asks, "Shouldn't we be getting close to the trade winds?" Instantly, we all share a vision of a steady 15-kt breeze filling the sails. We watch the wind vane closely and perk up when the arrow drifts to the northwest. We grow excited when it moves to the north a few hours later, and actually cheer when it settles in the east. But winds remain light and variable for two more days, and under sail, we record 95 and 88 nm for Days 12 and 13.

We've now sailed a total of 1,327 nm and are halfway to Hawaii. As Brian has only ten days left in his holidays, Dave starts the engine again. An hour later, the trade winds find us, and by 1400, we're under sail with a steady 10-knot breeze from the NNE. As winds are on the stern, the men drop the mainsail and ease the headsail out over the starboard bow. Later, they attach the whisker pole to the sail for the first time, stretching it out like a big vertical kite. It works well in a steady wind, but I'm not really comfortable with the configuration during my watch that night, thinking it too inflexible. We log 110 nm for Day 14.

The trades prove unreliable and now veer seventy degrees to the east. With the wind coming over the port quarter, the brothers stow the whisker pole and reset the sails. When I come on watch at 2000, Dave reports that he had to hand-steer for most of his watch. Even so, with winds at 10 kt, I figure I can handle it and decide not to reduce sail, as that would slow the boat. But I don't consider the effects of a following sea, and by the time I do, both men are in their berths. I tell myself that I can cope until midnight, but then the winds strengthen and my watch turns into a nightmare.

With too much mainsail up, I'm fighting the helm constantly. Winds then increase to 15 kt, pushing up higher seas that turn the bow a few more degrees. The mainsail now blankets the headsail, and when the headsail loses the wind, the boat spins around like a top on the crest of the waves. On one occasion, *Windy Lady* pivots over 100 degrees, backwinding both sails. I furl the headsail and start sailing again using the main, but feel like we're going in circles.

After that, I'm much more vigilant when checking conditions at the start of my watch, especially at night. I no long ask myself; *do I want a reef?* Instead, the question becomes; *can we forget about putting in a reef?*

Next morning, winds are down to 10 kt and sea conditions have eased. We bask in bright sunshine and warm temperatures for the rest of the voyage.

With more settled weather, we log 107 nm for Day 15, and similar distances for the following two days, then average 120 nm a day for Days 18 through 24.

Dave and Brian spend an afternoon experimenting with the sails, figuring out all the things that we should have known before leaving home. With lighter winds, they also come up with an explanation as to why the Hydrovane self-steering system doesn't work. We'd all spent countless hours playing with it, but it would only hold the boat on course for a few minutes at a time. They conclude that there had to be slippage in the hydraulic steering system, allowing movement in the main rudder.

Another afternoon, they string out a fishing line and catch a twenty-pound tuna but can't lift it into the cockpit. They then hook a four-pound mahi-mahi that makes a welcome change to our dinner menu. A few hours later, just before sunset, I glimpse a school of flying fish, their gossamer wings looking like a net thrown out over the waves. During the next few days, the fish appear frequently, emerging from the waves and gliding through the air, almost appearing to fly. In the mornings, I find the remains of a few that came aboard during the night.

A few squalls one night bring gusty winds and rain showers, and next morning, the world has been scrubbed clean. The day absolutely sparkles, with bright sunshine dancing on whitecaps dotting deep-blue waters, and rows of small, fluffy, white clouds arranged across the sky by a brisk wind. Again, as I scan the horizon, I'm overwhelmed by the sheer size of this ocean.

We cross the Tropic of Cancer when three days out, and the following morning, I pick up a weather report for the first time in two weeks. Two large freighters pass two nm behind us early the next day, and by midmorning, we are searching the sky for signs of Mauna Kea, the 13,800-foot volcano that towers over the island of Hawaii.

At 1410, when we are 30 nm off, we finally make out the mountain's dim shape through the surrounding cloud cover. As we won't make harbor before dark, we spend half of our twenty-fifth day at sea hove-to about twenty miles off. As I stand my watch that evening, I am relieved that the passage is over. We'd been at sea a long time and the days had long since blurred into one another.

As *Windy Lady* drifts slowly in a light breeze, I watch the muted shades of sunset spread across the sky and think about the voyage. Much of the time, we'd gazed out over waters that were usually blue and skies that were often grey. The view was always the same yet constantly changed, and I was never bored. I saw a bird or two most days, and occasionally, one had spent up to twenty minutes trying to land on the masthead. The VHF antenna on top of the swaying mast had thwarted all efforts. We'd also been visited by several small pods of dolphins.

During the last hour of the day, I'd watched the light fade from the sky, while night's shadows crept silently across the water. Often, as the sun sank into the sea, it created a golden pathway to the horizon, while the rising full moon created a silvery pathway of its own. On quiet nights, the stars had cast their reflections on the water, and one stormy midnight, I'd been astonished to see what can only be described as the shadow of a rainbow.

It occurred to me that such scenes would have been familiar to the mariners who first sailed these waters, and I'd been awed when I thought of their courage. They'd relied on their skills as seamen, as well as their faith in God, to keep them safe. Our passage was made easier with detailed charts and electronic devices. But we shared the same vulnerability to the whims of wind and sea; if bad weather developed, there was no place to hide. And I had worried that we would run into a bad storm.

I'd also brought personal baggage with me, and in the lonely vigils of my evening watch was obsessed with thoughts of home and family. I grieved, knowing that I would never see my mom again, regretting that I'd been unable to spend time with her in those frantic weeks before leaving. I felt like I'd deserted my dad and siblings when they needed me most, but actually, I was needing them. I took what solace I could from the natural world around me, but for days a dark cloud hung over my head. I came to resent the presence of a third person on the boat, and although I knew it was totally unreasonable, I couldn't change, so kept to myself.

Late one afternoon, well into the second week, I came up on deck and stood, staring out at sea and sky. I don't know what happened, or why, but suddenly the view in front of me was extraordinary. It was like I was seeing it for the first time. As I marveled at my good fortune, actually being able to sail across the ocean, I realized that in my despair, I had already missed a big chunk of this voyage.

The thought of losing a single moment of this once-in-a-lifetime adventure was more than I could bear. So, I started another journey, one in which I focused on each day as it came. Accepting that I could not change the past, I tried to put it behind me. As for the future, well, I knew that we were as prepared as we could be for whatever was going to happen, and it was time to stop worrying.

I wish I could say that I came to terms with Brian's presence, but that only happened when I acknowledged how much easier the passage was with his help. (I later explained and apologized, and with his usual sunny good-humor, he shrugged it off, saying he hadn't noticed.)

That night, while hove-to, we drift 8 nm west and 2 nm north. An enormous black cloud hangs over Hilo harbor when we set the sails at 0700, and two hours later, Dave starts the engine. He wants the batteries fully charged when we arrive in port. At 1130 on July 3, having spent 26 days at sea and sailed 2,756 nm, we drop the anchor in Radio Bay.

CHAPTER 9

Hilo and the Big Island

We make landfall in Hilo because it is the closest port of entry to our route. After we've anchored, the men lower the dinghy into the water and Dave rows ashore, taking boat papers and passports. He returns two hours later, having dealt with Immigration, Customs, Agriculture, and Port Authority. Next morning, Brian catches a flight back to Canada, and that night Dave and I have ringside seats for the fireworks celebrating the American Independence holiday.

The small anchorage known as Radio Bay is tucked into a corner of Hilo's busy harbor, with a cement plant on one side and a container dock on the other. Trucks and equipment work nonstop, and an occasional aircraft takes off from the nearby airport, so it's very noisy. We discuss moving to Maui or Kona, but don't, mostly because we have to check out of Hilo when we leave.

Living on a boat in Hilo in summer is nothing like a winter vacation in a nice hotel in Waikiki. The temperature in the cabin is over ninety degrees Fahrenheit, and without shore power, we cannot use the fan. We can't open the deck hatches either because of frequent, heavy rain that has us bailing out the dinghy three or four times a day.

The oppressive heat and humidity leave me feeling bone-weary and unable to sleep, and I spend four miserable days before a vacancy opens up on the retaining wall, where there's room for maybe twelve boats to stern-tie. We waste little time in dropping the anchor at the edge of the channel and backing into the berth, then tie stern lines to the wall. It's far enough away that we have to ferry across in the dinghy, but we're now able to rig tarps over the two forward hatches and leave them open, which lowers the temperature inside the cabin by ten degrees.

For a moorage fee of $8 US/day, plus a $50 deposit for the key, we have access to a small ablution block containing toilets and showers. Within a few days, we also locate a coin-operated laundry. We eat our main meals ashore, as dumping almost anything in the harbor can bring fines. We leave fresh fruit in the cockpit, but fruit flies/black flies are still a problem in the galley, where even a few crumbs on the floor can start an infestation. I occasionally clean house with a fly swatter.

After so many days confined to the boat, we want exercise, and within a week are walking five miles a day, sometimes farther. The frequent downpours aren't a problem, as they cool the air and our clothes are dry half an hour later. Streets are busy, with vehicles constantly whizzing by, but the areas we walk through aren't very prosperous. There are few people in the malls and stores are mostly empty, so clerks tend to pounce on customers. I search for some sign of the sights, sounds, and smells remembered from earlier visits to Hawaii, but don't find them.

We learn that the local sugarcane industry was shut down because it couldn't compete on world markets. A local teacher tells us that the majority of her students come from homes that receive welfare and have problems with alcohol use and wife and child abuse. Discussions with native Hawaiians over land claims have stalled, and they've taken over much of the beach area around Hilo. A ramshackle settlement has grown up near Radio Bay, and on weekends, we hear loud voices as people party.

When we return to the marina one afternoon, we find that a squall with 30-kt winds has caused havoc. *Compass Rose* dragged its anchor and drifted into *Swak*, which then ran into *Irish Lady*. *Compass Rose* attempted to motor away but ran afoul of *Swak's* mooring line, which then wrapped around its prop. Crews were still trying to sort them out. Our neighbor tells us that *Windy Lady* barely moved, which is good news.

In the late afternoons, boat crews gather at a picnic table set up in a grassy area near the retaining wall. The crews are mostly couples going back to the Pacific Northwest from Tahiti, and we now hear first-hand information about the countries and harbors that we hope to visit. At the same time, I begin a running battle with sand fleas or some other such pest that hides in the grass, and small, red bites soon cover my legs and itch for days.

Dave rents a car during our second week, and we drive up to Kilauea Volcano, which has been erupting for twelve years. Rain falls steadily as we peer into Halemaumau Crater and hides the steam coming from vents along the Circle Rim Road. Driving down the Chain of Craters Road, we emerge high on a range of hills overlooking a broad, flat plane beside the ocean. The view is spectacular.

Recent lava flows follow the contour of the hills, dropping down maybe 200 feet or so before crossing flat countryside. Several streams from one flow send up steam plumes as they fall into the sea. The plumes combine into one huge column that can be seen for miles. We park the car, then walk over new lava to the ocean's edge, marveling at this display of nature's power. I admit that I also recall the spooky tales of Madam Pele, the volcano goddess, that I'd heard from Hawaiian friends in times past.

The current lava flow originates from a cone on the mountainside and reportedly runs through a lava tube for six miles. We visit a section of older tube, and standing out in the rain, I study story boards that explain how the outer layer of lava cools and forms a pipe through which the inner core drains. We then climb down to the entrance and walk through about 200 feet of tunnel. Lamps placed along one wall provide the only lighting but it appears to be about fifteen feet high and twelve feet wide. The light glints off small pools of water on the floor, and with roots hanging down from above and shadows all around, it's more than a little spooky.

Our last stop that day is at a park in a small community on Hilo Bay, where a tall clock stands with its hands frozen at the time a tsunami hit in 1960. At a nearby café, lines on a wall mark the height of the water that day, as well as the height of a previous tsunami. Impressed as I am by these reminders of past disasters, it never occurs to me that one day we would be on the periphery of just such an event.

The following weekend, I find traces of the old Hawaii when we wander past a downtown park as the International Festival of the Pacific is getting underway. Drawn by the lyrical sounds of Hawaiian music, we watch for an hour as hula dancers perform on the beach. The first group is from Japan and the dancers are professional. Members of several local clubs follow and they're not quite so polished; the littlest ones have more enthusiasm than grace but prove to be just as entertaining.

Toward the end of our stay, a small fish boat ties up beside us. The crew takes the boat out every evening, works all night under lights, and returns in the morning with their catch. They are after yellow-fin tuna and never bring in more than four fish, but they are impressive. When the fish are weighed, two are over two hundred pounds.

Our maintenance work is well underway at this point. Working between rain showers, we replaced the sealant around the cabin windows, which was a big job. Dave also found a leak in the hydraulic pump at the inside steering station. He disconnected it, as we don't use it, and is now hopeful that the Hydrovane will work. But the furling drum on the forestay is frozen and pouring buckets of freshwater through it doesn't help. Having nothing else available, he sprays it with WD40 and metal filings wash out. Not a good sign!

I climb the mast a couple of times, attaching a halyard to my climbing belt so that Dave can tie me off. I first replace the cups on the wind gauge, as one broke off after a week at sea. I then re-attach the radar reflector to the top of the backstay, as it slid down during the crossing.

As well as replacing supplies, we buy material to make flags. When arriving in a country, we're supposed to fly their flag, the Canadian flag, and a yellow quarantine flag (Q-flag). Before I start on that project, however, I discover that a dozen jars of home-canned meat are covered in mold. It seems that the humidity attacked a film of grease left on the jars when I removed them from the canner. As the jars are sealed, I wash them down with hot water and bleach and they're fine.

After two weeks in Hilo, we start to think about the next leg of our journey, which will take us 1,000 nm south to the privately owned coral atoll of Palmyra. We trek downtown to a realtor's office and apply for a visitor's permit, giving July 23 as our departure date. We return a few days later to pick it up.

On Monday, July 22, high swells from a storm off Tahiti are pounding Hawaiian beaches, and all south-facing shores are under high surf warning. While mulling over whether or not to leave next day as planned, we go up on deck and find the dinghy missing. We see no sign of it anywhere. About the time we're wondering if we'll need to replace it, a sailboat anchored behind us swings with the tide, revealing two dinghies tied alongside. Keeping our fingers crossed, we wait. Bob, a single-hander on *Adios*, brings it back at 0900, cheerfully saying, "I found your boat drifting out to sea last night."

Deciding not to leave with headwinds, we delay our departure. Dave installs two small 12-volt fans that we purchased, one in each berth. He also makes a couple of half-hour round trips to a nearby gas station, jerry-jugging diesel fuel. This is an anxiety-filled chore as fuel spills, even small ones, are subject to $10,000 fines.

With time on my hands, I start thinking about the upcoming voyage and can't stop the doubts that surface in my mind. *We're going to be sailing into a very remote area of this huge ocean and will have to rely on each other. But I'm not Brian, I don't have his strength and experience. Will I be able to give Dave the help he needs?* I then distract myself by finding more chores to do.

On Wednesday, the 24th, we obtain an exit clearance from Customs, then take down canopies and fill the water tank. That night, the temperature inside the boat falls below eighty degrees for the first time. Next morning, the early forecast calls for easterly winds of 10 kt, so we race through the boat, checking that everything is secure inside and out. We return the washroom key to the Harbor Master's office, recover our $50 deposit, then untie the mooring lines.

CHAPTER 10

The Doldrums

When we leave Hilo on Thursday, July 25, we are starting the 2,400-nm passage to American Samoa. We will break our journey at Palmyra, 1,000 nm to the south, and expect to be at sea ten days on this leg. The coral atoll has a resident caretaker, and our visitor's permit provides GPS coordinates for the entrance channel, which was dredged out by the US Navy during WW II. It's also supposed to be marked by a buoy.

We will now be passing through *the Intertropical Convergence Zone (ITCZ),* the buffer zone between northeast and southeast trade winds that lies north of the equator. Once known as *the Doldrums,* the area is notorious for fast-moving tropical storms and dead calms. We're about to learn that the worst storms hit in the dead of night, while the calms set in during the heat of the day.

We clear the breakwater outside the harbor just before midday, then continue motoring as the batteries need charging. I wear a shady hat to keep the sun off, but the humid, 90-degree-plus temperature is only bearable because the rear cockpit seats catch a light breeze. Bright sunlight glints off the dark waters and green slopes around us, but cloud hides the tops of both Mauna Kea and Mauna Loa. Steam venting from Kilauea's volcanic cone adds an exotic touch, drifting downslope and eventually mixing with plumes rising from the lava building new land to the south.

As we follow the shoreline around to Hawaii's East Point, Dave frets over the batteries. They're taking a long time to charge and become overly hot. The energy monitor (EMON) controlling the high-output alternator was set by a technician in Canada, and he worries that the charging rate is too high for the tropics. If so, our expensive gel cells could be damaged.

We shut down the engine at 1600, and with ENE winds of 10 kt, *Windy Lady* glides smoothly through a low, two-foot swell. Dave brings up the sail for the Hydrovane self-steering unit, and soon Otto (as we name it) is steering for the first time. Minutes later, as we draw away from the island, remarkable vistas of open sea and sky stretch out before us.

We've decided to stay with a four-hour watch schedule, as neither of us slept more than three hours at a time during the passage to Hawaii. In practical terms that means going to bed and getting up three times a day, and it will take three or four days before we start getting enough sleep. So now, as the light starts to fade, Dave goes below to rest.

I find myself looking back, studying the island as night's shadows creep across it. When the features of the landscape start to disappear, I strain my eyes, trying to keep them in focus. All too soon, only a few pinpoints of light are visible in the blackness and I can't tear my eyes away. When the last light suddenly goes out, a wave of absolute terror sweeps through me, and all the doubts that I've been suppressing surge upwards.

But with nothing to hold my eyes, the spell is broken. Turning my head away, I take in the quiet beauty of the dark waters and night sky around me, and my soul calms. My doubts are replaced by the knowledge that, whatever happens, I will deal with it. In fact, I wouldn't trade places with anyone on earth.

When I return to the cockpit at midnight, the sky is bright, with the light of a three-quarter moon shimmering on the water. Winds are still from the ENE at 10 kt, and *Windy Lady* glides smoothly through a ruffled sea. Two hours later, the moon drops below the horizon and the sky fills with stars, with the glow of the Milky Way spreading across the heavens from northeast to southwest. The brightest stars are reflected on the ocean's surface, and tiny flashes of light sparkle in the wake of the boat, a form of bioluminescent organism disturbed by our passing. It's unbelievably beautiful!

The winds veer to the east near the end of my watch at 0400, and for the next eight hours, a line of squalls brings 25-kt gusts and rain showers. Otto can't handle the stronger gusts, and during my morning watch, I learn to ease out the main and partially furl the jib before the wind hits. That takes most of the pressure off the helm, and it's then a simple matter to reset the sails afterwards.

Just before the end of that watch, the wind suddenly shifts to the SE (on the nose) and settles at 15 kt. I'm not paying attention and both sails are backwinded. To my chagrin, I have to circle the boat around using the mainsail to start sailing again. At noon, after 25 hours at sea, we log 119 nm for Day 1.

For the next 48 hours, winds fluctuate from 10–20 kt, while shifting between east and SE, often moving thirty degrees during a watch. Squalls also bring 25-kt gusts, periods of rain, and six-foot seas. The daylight hours are hot, humid, and very unpleasant, but the nights are pure magic, with cooler temperatures, a waxing moon that lights up the water, and bioluminescence that sparkles in the shadows. We log 114 and 128 nm for Days 2 and 3.

Winds now back to the NE and soon fast-moving squalls are bringing 30-kt gusts. By sunset, winds have veered to the east and heavy, grey clouds fill the sky. At midnight, winds are steady at 20–30 kt, and we've put three reefs in the mainsail. *Windy Lady* now races through the water on a beam reach, twisting and tossing as she crashes into swells, and before long, the cabin windows are leaking. Water seems to seep in more easily than ever, and the wild movements of the boat disperse it everywhere.

When night reluctantly gives way to dawn, there is no horizon, just a leaden sky that merges into a dull, grey sea. Twelve-foot-high swells break on the portside, rocking the boat, and spray flies everywhere. A grimy layer of salt soon covers the deck and cockpit and tracks down into the cabin. By noon, winds have dropped to 15–25 kt, still on the beam, but seas remain unchanged. Only the occasional burst of white spray breaks the monotony around us for the next 24 hours.

Heat and humidity in the cabin are almost unbearable, and sweat pours off us at the slightest exertion. Other than standing watch, Dave limits his duties to preparing meals and checking in with a HAM network. I keep the galley clean and plot our noon positions. As boat movements are unpredictable and sometimes vicious, I soon have a new collection of bruises.

We spend maybe an hour together each day, during breakfast and supper; and one night, I scrape my dinner off the cockpit sole after a moment's inattention. I try to soften the movements of my berth by making a nest using two fenders and several cushions. But the fact that I get any sleep at all is thanks to the small 12-volt fan blowing air on my head. We log 133 nm and 131 nm for Days 4 and 5.

The winds now ease a bit, dropping to 15–20 kt that afternoon, but seas stay high and grow rougher. By midnight, winds have backed to ENE and are down to 10–15 kt but seas remain erratic. As Otto can't cope, we hand steer through our watches. Eight hours later, Dave records his frustration in the journey log, "The vane, the vane, it's driving me insane!" At noon, we log 118 nm for Day 6.

A couple of hours later, the wind dies, and *Windy Lady* rolls in rough seas for half an hour. It then rises in the SSW, again on the nose, and settles at 8–10 kt. Unable to make our course, we start drifting westward. About midnight, a storm brings 20-kt winds and two hours of steady rain. When it clears, the wind dies.

We fight to keep the boat moving forward for another eight hours, then Dave starts the engine. Fifteen minutes later, the autopilot quits working and we're back to hand steering. (We later learn that water from the leaking windows seeped into the unit.) We log 80 nm for Day 7.

By 1800, winds are steady at 10 kt from the NE and we're sailing again. Two hours later, lightning flashes on the horizon, and by midnight, the sky has turned pitch black and rain pours down. Winds now gust from 15–25 kt, with frequent squalls bringing 30-kt gusts and heavier downpours. During Dave's 0400 watch, winds veer to the east and grow stronger, gusting up to 39 kt before dawn. Thankfully, Otto mostly handles the conditions. By 0800, winds are easing, but two hours later are again on the nose, pushing us westward. We log 92 nm for Day 8.

We tack to the east for a while that afternoon, but end up farther off course, so return to our original heading. Knowing that we'll have to make up any easting we lose, we now hold the bow as close to the wind as possible, willingly trading speed for direction. Meanwhile, we keep a close eye on two of our instruments. The Signet log measures the distance the boat travels through the water, while the GPS gives us the distance to our destination.

Dave sails 12 nm through the water during his afternoon watch, but makes good only 5 nm toward our destination. I sail 10 nm during the following watch and also make good 5. At midnight, he sails 8 nm, but ends up a mile farther away from our destination. I'm downright spooked when I take this in and stare at Dave in shocked disbelief. My mind races. *It's like we're being sucked backwards into a big, black hole! How is that possible? Is something affecting our instruments?*

Dave starts the engine, and with a throttle setting that should have given us 4.5 kt, *Windy Lady* creeps forward at 2.0 kt. We then see that the course shown on the GPS differs by thirty degrees from the compass. They should be the same! Standing in that dimly lit cabin, in the middle of the night, in the middle of the ocean, I'm suddenly conscious of feeling very alone.

Five minutes later, the boat speed increases by a knot, and compass and GPS come into sync. We then suddenly understand that we're in the grip of a strong current. Much the same, it turns out, as if we'd been crossing a 100-mile-wide, west-flowing river. With the mystery solved, I take the helm and Dave goes to his berth.

The current continues to impede our progress, and the night grows blacker as we head south. At 0600, the wind dies away completely and the heavens open up, inundating us in a torrential downpour for eight hours. Dave stands out in it for the first two hours, and then I'm out in it for four. My foul-weather jacket is quickly soaked through as rain streams down over my head, shoulders, and bare legs. Water pools around my feet, then is thrust out the scuppers by the rolling of the boat.

The passage has become a grueling test of stamina, and we endure only because there is no choice. We are tired, frustrated, and not being particularly nice to one another. But at the end of my watch, seeing me huddled at the helm, miserable and wet, Dave shakes his head contritely and mumbles, "I'm sorry I got you into this." We log 67 nm for Day 9.

Dave puts in another two hours before the rain finally stops. The sky then remains overcast, with rolling seas and no wind. At change of watch at 1600, he voices the doubts that nag at us both and asks, "Did we make a mistake in deciding to head for the South Pacific?"

We continue motoring until 0400, when winds pick up from the SSE at 10–15 kt. We motor-sail for another eight hours and are within 10 nm of Palmyra when we first see the tops of palm trees on the horizon. Sailing down its south side for 7 nm, we come to the spot on the chart that shows a passage through the reef. With the boat sitting precisely on the GPS coordinates, Dave turns the bow toward the lagoon. Visibility is poor as we study the choppy waters in front of us, and there is no sign of a buoy. I do see two small islands, complete with palm trees, that aren't on the chart.

Confused, we motor westward along the reef, gradually drawing closer as we search for a channel. Suddenly, with the depth gauge reading thirteen feet, the keel is grinding on coral. Dave backs *Windy Lady* off and sends me up to the bow with orders to find a safe route. Of course, we know better, we should have hightailed it back out to deeper water, recalculated our approach, and tried again—but we don't.

It's midday and a maze of dark, circular shadows are visible in the clear, blue water that stretches between us and the lagoon. I quickly realized that the light blue water is very shallow, and that the black shadows in deeper water are coral heads. They look to be about five feet in diameter, but it's impossible to tell how close to the surface they come; in fact, that's what we've just hit.

There is no way through them, so I direct Dave back to the east, but even that route isn't clear and *Windy Lady* isn't very maneuverable. After several bumps and another grounding, I desperately yell, "Let's get the hell out of here!" Dave steers out into deeper water and we continue to motor eastward.

I stay at the bow, anxiously scanning the dark waters for some sign of the channel, and several minutes later spot a dark, misshapen buoy bobbing low in the water. Approaching cautiously, Dave again turns the bow toward the lagoon, and soon I see the far edge of the channel beneath the water. We then pass the two small islands that caused our earlier confusion. Later, I realize that on our chart, which was made during WW II, they appear as reefs that covered at high tide.

CHAPTER 11

Palmyra

As we enter the lagoon, the masts of three sailboats are visible against the palm trees on the far side. We then see a small boat speeding toward us, and soon make out the figure of a man standing in the stern of a hard-bottomed dinghy. This is Roger, the resident caretaker, and he's all decked out, with torn shirt whipping about his upper torso and diving knife strapped to the calf of one muscular brown leg. Yelling and gesturing for us to follow, he meanders back and forth in front of *Windy Lady* as he leads us to an anchoring spot.

He obviously wants to speak to us, so we rush through our anchoring, then make arrangements to meet him ashore in an hour's time. We now start putting the boat to bed, but are interrupted by the arrival of a second dinghy. I'm soon standing at the lifelines, chatting with our visitor as though she was a long-lost friend. We'd met Maree and her husband Dave in Hilo and had dinner with them one night, but I'd been suffering from the heat and pretty poor company. Dave now has to interrupt us after 45 minutes, so that we can put the dinghy in the water.

When we go ashore, Roger tours us through the camp facilities, emphasizing that the area is off limits, except by appointment. The grounds are neat and tidy, as is a small, frame-construction house with thatched roof. The rain catchment system has huge storage tanks and there's a tub (urinal) for washing clothes, and a big bathtub sits in an open glade. He informs us that we can have all the drinking water we need, but are limited to one bath each and can wash clothes only once.

He then shows us through the house, pointing out several yellowed newspaper clippings pinned to a wall. The articles contain the gory details of two murders that took place on the island twenty years earlier. Two couples on two yachts shared the lagoon at the time, and one of the men was eventually convicted of killing the other couple and chopping up their bodies. We're told that the incident happened in the small bay where *Windy Lady* sits at anchor.

We're almost dropping from exhaustion when we return to the boat. As Maree has invited us to dinner, we try to nap, but are wide-awake as soon as we lie down. We settle for leisurely baths in the cockpit, then relax until it's time to row across to *Byjingo*. Significantly, we don't mention the passage, not even to note that we were at sea eleven days and sailed 1,081 nm.

Dave and Maree are Australians and a good twenty years younger than we are. They built their boat themselves and left from Sidney the previous year, sailing north to Japan, then across to Alaska and down the BC coast. After wintering near the US-Canada border, they followed the same route as we did to Hawaii and left Hilo a week before us.

With sympathetic ears listening, Dave and I are soon feeding off each other, and all our doubts and frustrations come pouring out. Our hosts patiently listen to our tale of woe, then respond with some sorely needed encouragement. They tell us about similar experiences they'd had the previous year, providing exactly the therapy we need. *Byjingo* Dave (BD) ends by saying, "In my opinion, most cruisers don't even like passage making."

When we climb down into the dinghy to leave, Maree hands me a bottle of betadine that she says is great for coral cuts, and BD advises us to check beneath the boat before going in the water. He explains that a large barracuda had been resting in the shade beneath their boat, but now appears to be residing under ours.

With our spirits considerably lifted and some confidence restored, we now return to *Windy Lady*. In future, we will find similar levels of companionship and generosity in other members of the cruising community. Whether it is sharing charts, boat parts, or just common frustrations, most happily provide all the support they can.

The next morning, we awake to the light patter of a rain shower on the cockpit floor above us. Taking our coffee outside, we start our first day in paradise by watching a small manta ray cruise beneath the rippled surface of the lagoon. Water laps softly against the hull, and in the background, the roar of surf on the outer reef is constant, but varies in volume depending on the wind.

We plan to spend the day resting but the temperature rises quickly, so we rig a tarp over the cockpit for shelter. We then lower our new 4-hp Suzuki outboard engine onto the back of the dinghy and take a quick spin around the lagoon. I'm astonished by the number of birds nesting in thick vegetation along the water's edge. That night we return *Byjingo's* hospitality, as the other couple indicated they could be leaving at any time. Over a simple dinner, we share the bottle of wine that the marina manager in Victoria gave us before we left.

It starts to rain that evening and is still raining when we wake at 0600, so we doze awhile longer. Just after daybreak, we hear loud, sharp knocking on the hull and a man's voice urgently calls for Dave. He scrambles from the berth, pulls on a pair of shorts, and runs up to the cockpit. I'm a minute behind and emerge to find the lagoon hidden behind a grey wall of rain.

BD and Maree are standing in their dinghy alongside, wearing swimsuits, and rain streams down over their heads and shoulders. They're looking down at a triangular shape poking up through the surface of the water. I only recognize the bow of our hard dinghy when I see the painter attaching it to the toe rail. The rest of the boat, including the engine, is straight below.

The rain filled it up overnight, and with a bit of wave action, the weight of the engine caused it to sink stern first.

Dave is already passing a halyard to BD, who attaches it to the bow. He then winches the dinghy out of the water, and after most of the salt water has drained, the two men swing it up on deck, remove the motor, then return it to the surface of the lagoon. With our thanks ringing in their ears, the other couple hurry back to the relative dryness of their own boat, leaving us staring at a waterlogged motor hanging in the cockpit. Dave quickly scans the owner's manual, then takes the engine ashore, sets it in a barrel of fresh water near the landing, and works on it in the pouring rain.

Two hours later, he has it running and stops by *Byjingo* and again thanks them. When he returns, he tells me that the other couple think the two boats are getting a little close. I've already had the same thought and remembered that Roger interrupted us when we were anchoring. We re-anchor a few hours later, when the rain takes a breather, but make three attempts before we're satisfied. The problem is that the cove is small but the water deep, and we need to put out 225 feet of chain.

The rain continues overnight, and we catch buckets of water off the small tarp sheltering the cockpit. We also catch a foot of water in the inflatable dinghy, which we'd set up on the cabin roof. We now have plenty of water for washing clothes, so won't have to impose on Roger's hospitality.

Dave wants to check the keel to see if it was damaged by our encounter with the reef, but the barracuda mentioned by BD is spending a lot of time under our boat. It's six feet long and trails some thirty feet of fishing line. He goes ashore and asks Roger about the fish, and the caretaker just shrugs his shoulders and replies, "Aw, that fish isn't a problem; there's plenty of food in the lagoon."

A minute later, he changes his mind, "You know, they have attacked fishermen over on Fanning Island." At that point, Dave decides to wait until the fish is gone before diving under the hull. When he does, he finds no damage.

We make numerous trips around the lagoon in the dinghy and see thousands of birds nesting near the shore. Many of them are blue-billed boobies, and the babies are nearly the size of the parents and still unable to fly. At first glance, they look like large balls of white fluff caught in the branches. Most of the coral in the lagoon appears to be dead, but we see a few reef fish along one end. Several small manta rays regularly hunt in the waters and two black-tipped sharks, about four feet long, swim by the boat one evening.

As the weather becomes a little more settled, we start to explore the atoll. We walk for hours along the beaches, finding many empty bottles, then stumble across cement bunkers hidden in the undergrowth. The cement foundation of a WW II gun installation dominates the white, sandy beach on the northwest corner, a grim reminder of the harsh reality under which so much of the world then lived. Palmyra, it turns out, had been a naval air station, and some 2,400 military personnel were stationed here.

A more recently wrecked airplane is piled up near one end of the old airstrip, where thousands of sooty terns are nesting. At dusk, the birds fill the air with raucous calls. One evening, when the wind dies, we are inundated with bugs and I have to wonder whether any of the seabirds on the island actually feed on them. We see hundreds of hermit crabs on the trails and a few fiddler crabs on the beach. Roger then shows us four huge coconut crabs that are penned in a small shed in the shade of the trees; they're about twelve inches across and have enormous claws.

Dave can't leave his first island paradise without husking a coconut, so one morning we set off in search of a coconut palm. The first challenge is knocking one down from high in a tree, and he then spends considerable time removing the husk. The small nut that is left doesn't have much liquid. Later, we manage to twist a green coconut off a tree. It is full of water, as the nut hasn't yet formed, and provides a mild, refreshing drink.

On August 8, Dave's 57th birthday, *Byjingo* departs for Apia, Western Samoa. We've enjoyed their company, and I watch soberly as they raise the anchor and motor out through the reef. After rocking in the swells outside, they disappear to the south. That afternoon I do a large wash, and even the sheets and towels are dry two hours later. We spend the next day preparing the boat for sea.

CHAPTER 12

Passage to Pago Pago

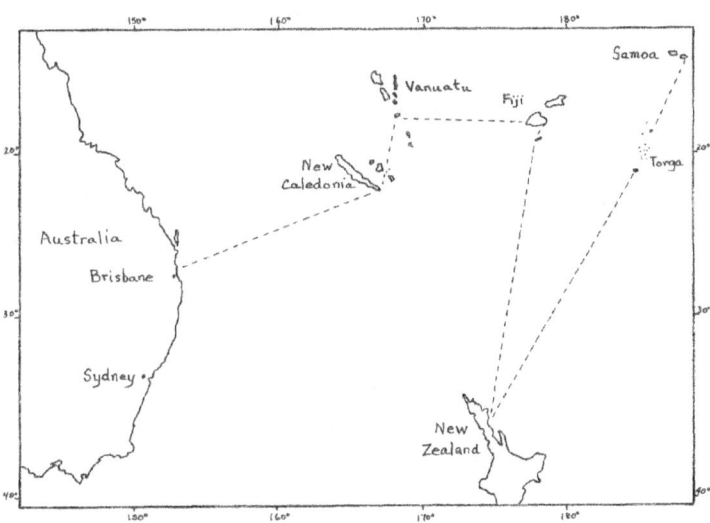

Rhumb Line Routes – South Pacific

We leave for American Samoa on Saturday, August 10, having spent six days on the atoll. Our spirits are much revived, and we talk optimistically about doing the entire 1,300-nm passage under sail. We'll now be crossing the equator into the

Southern Hemisphere and want to stay east of a rhumb-line course, as that will put us in the best position to approach the harbor city of Pago Pago on the island of Tutuila. If we drift to the west, we'll have a difficult beat into SE trade winds at the end of the voyage. (A rhumb line is the shortest distance between two points at sea.)

We time our departure for noon, as reefs are most visible with the sun high in the sky. Our planning is for naught, however, as the day is overcast and squalls bring gusty winds and rain showers sweeping across the lagoon. The anchor is then caught on something and we can't break it loose, no matter in which direction we pull. We end up tightening the chain, which pulls the bow lower and lower in the water, until the weight of the boat breaks it free.

I now steer *Windy Lady* out into the lagoon and hold the bow into wind while Dave raises the mainsail. He gives a mighty heave on the halyard, pulling the sail halfway up the mast, then smoothly wraps the end of the line around the port winch. Attaching the winch handle, he gives it a turn—and the winch flies apart. Pieces hit the deck in all directions, some of them rolling towards the toe rail and threatening to go overboard.

He quickly chases them down, while loudly cursing the incompetence of the workmen in Victoria, who installed the new winches. Fifteen minutes later, with the help of some Loctite, he has the unit re-assembled and secured to the mast. All I can do is watch and muse, *better here and now, than later, out there!*

With the mainsail up, we motor across the lagoon to a buoy that lines up with the range marker, which is a notch cut into the trees on shore. Keeping the buoy centered on the stern and in line with the notch takes us safely out through the reef. At Sand Island, about halfway, the notch is barely visible in haze, but the flat bottom of the channel is now visible about twenty feet down.

In the crystal-clear water, we see the shadowy outlines of several schools of fish, all about three feet long, and I see a sea turtle swimming into the lagoon, its head poking out of the water. It dives down about three feet, giving me a good view as it swims by, and I figure the shell's at least two feet long.

Once clear of the channel, we turn to a heading of 190 degrees and continue motoring until the batteries are charged. Although winds are light and seas calm, we pass through a strong west-flowing current about two miles off the island. *Windy Lady* is then tossed about rather unpleasantly for fifteen minutes by high standing waves.

After motoring for two hours, we shut down the engine and drift along under sail, making 2 kt in light SSE winds. By 1600, Palmyra has disappeared from view, and when I start my watch, the ocean is unusually quiet, the silence remarkable. We continue to drift until midnight, when a squall brings 25-kt gusts and rain showers.

When the storm moves on, winds settle at 5–10 kt, still from the SSE, and sheet lightning flashes brightly on the horizon for hours. The winds increase to 10–15 kt with the dawn, bringing more squalls. At noon, after 24 hours at sea, we log 71 nm and are then 10 nm east of our rhumb-line course.

Winds now increase to 20 kt, pushing up lumpy, three-foot seas, and Dave spends the afternoon hand steering, as Otto can't cope. When *Windy Lady* rides up on a wave, he sees a freighter, one of only a few that we see mid-ocean. It's just in radar range at 8 nm. We put a second reef in the mainsail when I take the watch at 1600, which slows the boat some, but Otto now returns to work.

By midnight, the breeze has eased, seas are calmer, and the sky is covered with brilliant stars. There's a definite chill in the air before daybreak, and with the rising of the sun, the wind veers southward. At 1000, it's on the nose at 8–10 kt, pushing us westward. At noon, we log 102 nm for Day 2 and are 25 nm west of our course line. I check and recheck my work then have to tell the captain that we lost 35 nm of easting in the previous 24 hours.

Wanting to regain some easting, Dave starts the engine at 1300. The wind now drops to 5 kt and the sea calms, until only a trace of swell is visible.

With the sun beating down from a cloudless sky, the temperature soars. The rear cockpit seats still catch a bit of a breeze, but it's ninety-five degrees inside the cabin, and Dave unbolts the galley hatch and leaves it wide open for over thirty hours. The berths are now as stable as a bed ashore, but we're only able to sleep because of the small 12-volt fans blowing air on our heads.

While we suffer through the daytime heat, the night watches are extraordinary. I first look for a green flash when the sun disappears, which Dave's brother, Gordon, told us about, but we're too low in the water to see it. I then search for the first pinpricks of light as the stars come out. There is no haze or cloud on the horizon, which is rare, and the night sky soon extends down to the sea in every direction. More stars are visible than I've ever before seen, with the brightest reflected on the quiet waters. For the first time, I see Betelgeuse climbing over the eastern horizon.

But most remarkable, for two nights we watch the Perseid Meteor Showers. With the moon dark, hundreds of meteors streak amongst the stars for hours. The first night, a fireball lights up the sky behind Dave as I climb up the companionway at midnight. It flares to half the size of a full moon before vanishing; he thinks it's lightning.

After motoring for 39 hours, we start sailing again at 0400, with winds at 8–12 kt from the SSE. Although we're now within 50 nm of the equator, Dave is looking for a sweater before dawn. The morning that follows is spectacular, with clear, cloudless sky, warm sunshine, and cool breeze. Within a few hours, SE winds of 10—20 kt have pushed up three-foot seas, and the views around me are extraordinary.

In every direction, inky-blue ocean waves roll ceaselessly toward the west. White caps sparkle here and there, and occasionally, a shower of white spray rolls off *Windy Lady's* bow. Overhead, not a single blemish mars the huge blue dome of the sky, with the deep, dark center at the zenith blending smoothly into a whitish-blue hue around the horizon. Other than a few flying fish and a couple of birds, we could have been alone on the planet.

Shortly after midday, the winds increase to 15—20 kt while backing to ESE, and *Windy Lady* then flies across the waves on a beam reach. Unwilling to give up a moment of such a perfect day, I forego my rest and spend the afternoon in the cockpit. While crossing the equator, we stand in front of the GPS and watch as it changes to 0 degrees of latitude at 1625. As the sun drops into the sea and the stars come out, the waves grow a little higher, and our magic carpet ride continues for nearly twelve hours.

Gusty 25-kt winds start to overpower Otto during my midnight watch, so I hand steer. Meanwhile, I continue to tweak sails and vane settings, and although nothing seems to change, Otto surges back to life three hours later. At noon, winds are from the SE at 15–20 kt, and seas are six-feet high and lumpy. We log 97, 106, and 120 nm on Days 3, 4, and 5, and more than recover the easting we'd lost.

Before long, winds have dropped below 10 kt and backed to ESE, and that night, our instruments again reveal strong currents. With the compass steady on 180 degrees, the course on the GPS fluctuates between 148 and 227 degrees, while the boat speed varies between 3.7 and 5.0 kt.

Clouds are building on the horizon at sunrise, and fast-moving squalls sweep down on *Windy Lady* all day, bringing gusts of 25 kt in the morning and 30 kt in the afternoon. In between the squalls, there's barely enough wind to fill the sails. The squalls disappear at sunset and winds are light for a second night.

By morning, the breeze hardly registers and *Windy Lady* rocks uncomfortably in three-foot swells. The temperature soars, and we roast in the cockpit and swelter in the cabin. When on watch, we cover up with long-sleeved cotton shirts and wide-brimmed straw hats. We average 100 nm/day on Days 6 and 7.

Late that afternoon, ENE winds settle at 10–15 kt, and soon six-foot waves rock the boat mercilessly. We struggle with gusty, 25-kt winds overnight, and when they ease at daybreak, seas grow even rougher. We log 136 nm for

Day 8 and make another 10 nm of easting. We're now over halfway to Pago Pago.

Winds then settle at 10–20 kt from the east, with six-foot waves breaking along the port rail. Occasionally, a wall of spray flies over *Windy Lady*, and seats and deck are soon feeling grimy. But we spend an hour sitting on the starboard bench late that afternoon, captivated by the sight of fifty dolphins playing in the oncoming waves. They mostly surf, staying just below the breaking tops and riding the waves in towards us. I'm reminded of a fish I saw the previous day, swimming off the stern in a following sea. It was white, very large, and instantly disappeared. I assumed it was a shark.

Sea conditions are very rough overnight and grow rougher with the dawn, when winds increase to 15–25 kt and veer to ESE. At noon, we log 125 nm for Day 9. Wind speeds then alternate between 10–15 and 15–20 kt over the next six watches. During one watch, the GPS records a boat speed of 11.1 kt and logs a half mile more than the Signet, so currents are still with us. We log 123 nm for Day 10.

The winds now take a breather, but it turns out to be the lull before the storm. And the storm is the one I've been dreading ever since leaving home. When I come on watch at 1600, winds are hitting 25 kt, still from the ESE, and seas are rough. By the end of my watch, winds are up to 30 kt and seas have grown much rougher.

I happily turn the duty over to Dave when he appears, then am bounced and jolted about in my berth, so don't get much rest. As I tiredly climb out at midnight, the boat lurches sharply and I whack my head painfully against a bulkhead. Hanging tightly onto grab rails, I make my way forward six feet to the settee amidships. I've left my clothes and rain gear there, where it's easier and safer to get dressed in heavy weather.

In the dim light of the 12-volt system, I see Dave standing at the chart table, hanging on with one hand while trying to fill in the journey log with the other. He tells me winds are steady at 35 kt, and seas are ten feet high and lumpy. As I dress, I listen to the storm raging outside and my heart sinks.

I notice water dripping off his foul weather gear and watch, hypnotized, as it pools on the teak floor boards, then runs back and forth with the movements of the boat. Next thing I know, I'm dressed and groping my way up the companionway. I have no idea how I got there.

Now almost paralyzed with fear, I step out into the pitch-black night, then inch my way around the helm. I feel the wind tugging at my jacket, rain stinging my face, and cold water sloshing over my bare feet. Sinking down onto a rear cockpit seat, I manage to respond to Dave as he adjusts the sails. He furls in the headsail a bit, then eases out the main so that the end of the boom stretches well out over the waves.

Before going below, he pauses to watch me brace my feet against the end of the forward bench, then shouts, "Are you going to be all right?"

Looking up, I see him framed against the weak light shining up from the cabin, bobbing about as the boat rolls and pitches. Nodding my head, I manage to squeak, "Yes, of course," but the words are lost in the roar of the storm. He starts below, then stops and boards up the entrance to the companionway. We've never done that before.

The cabin light now goes out and I am alone in the dark. I glance at the wind gauge and read 35 kt; I don't look again. Seeing that the storm has overpowered Otto, I grab the wheel and turn to a heading of 180 degrees. Braced in my seat, with my neck craned out to see the compass and a death grip on the wheel, I ride out the twists and turns of the boat with rain streaming down my face and jacket. My eyes are glued to the face of the compass like it was a lifeline to reality and time ceases to exist.

At some point, I become conscious of feeling cold, but only much later, when I feel the helm respond to Otto, do I realize that I'm shivering and soaked through to the skin. When Otto starts holding the boat on course for minutes at a time, my confidence begins to return. I dash below for a sweater—and see that two hours have gone by. When I return to the cockpit, I notice some definition in the sky behind and hope surges through me that maybe the worst is over.

I take a seat on the port side and make a grab loop by knotting a short piece of rope that hangs on the push pit railing. Holding onto it for security, I look over the cabin roof and see low, dark clouds scudding across a black sky. I then dare to look farther, and as *Windy Lady* rolls, turns, and pitches, the flashing strobe light on the masthead reveals angry-looking waves all around. The wind gauge reads 30–35 kt.

The winds now veer twenty degrees and ease a bit, but seas grow higher and the cockpit wetter. Breaking waves dump the equivalent of a bucket of water over me at least six times, and I can't count the number of times I take a glassful in the face. As the last hour of my watch drags on, I feel the occasional gust of warm air on my cheeks and wonder where it came from. We make 23 nm during that watch.

When I go below at 0400, settee cushions are lying on the sole, as are charts and pencils off the chart table and a basket from the galley table. Water has come in the forward hatch and sloshes about on the sole of the head, but the cabin windows are dry, as Dave re-sealed them in Palmyra. I wipe up the water we tracked below and find myself wondering why we didn't put a third reef in the mainsail.

The dinghy oars, which we'd stowed beside the port berth, are now lying in the middle of the mattress. When I re-position them, they simply return with the next roll of the boat. As I struggle to secure them, my hand touches a soggy corner of the mattress and I realize, with a sinking feeling, that water is seeping in from the nearby porthole. Grabbing my pillows, I head for the starboard berth, where I sleep fitfully.

At 0800, winds are coming from the SSE at 20–30 kt and seas are higher and rougher. Dave made 22 nm during his watch and writes in the journey log, "Oh, what a night! Wild and wet!"

I start my shift by standing at the starboard rail, studying the oncoming waves, and soon am experiencing the oddest mixture of terror and delight. The waves build until they form small mountains, steep-sided, close together, and twelve to fifteen feet high. After cresting overhead, they come crashing down somewhere along the length of the boat, dousing the deck and cockpit with salt water. Now and again, a large wave breaks amidships, washing the keel to starboard, but *Windy Lady* quickly bobs upright. Of more concern are those occasions when she pitches almost straight up the face of a wave, then drops down the backside, burying the bow in the bottom of the next one. At noon, we log 127 nm for Day 11.

Seas ease during the afternoon and are down to ten feet when I come on watch at 1600. An hour later, I sense a change in the wind, just momentarily at first, then gradually the lulls become longer and more frequent. At 2000, winds are 15–30 kt; at midnight, they're 15–25 kt; and at 0400, they're 15–20 kt. During that time, seas go from ten feet to three.

I awake next morning to a beautiful, clear, sunny sky, with winds of 18 kt and friendly seas. Shortly after 0800, we catch our first glimpse of the misty outline of the island of Tutuila. Relaxing in warm sunshine, we watch the surging sea break on rocks and reefs, while the ridges and ravines of the island's rugged eastern slopes reveal themselves. With quieter seas, we made good time and log 130 nm on Day 12.

We're required to contact the Harbor Master in Pago Pago before we arrive, and Dave starts calling on the VHF radio when we're four hours out. He tries every fifteen to twenty minutes, but no one ever responds. We stop outside the harbor, drop our sails, and raise the yellow quarantine flag, then motor in through a passage in a broad reef, with surf tumbling tumultuously on either side.

As we make our way to the customs dock, we pass near an anchored sailboat, and some joker standing on the foredeck points in front of us and bellows, "Reef! Reef!" We almost have heart attacks and quickly check the chart, but there is no imminent danger. On our thirteenth day at sea, Thursday, August 22, we tie up at 1430 local time, having sailed 1,376 nm.

CHAPTER 13

American Samoa

Because we haven't yet cleared into the country, Dave is careful to step off the boat only as needed to secure mooring lines to the dock. But that doesn't prevent us from coming to the attention of a rather irritated off-duty policeman, who slouches over to the side of the boat while I'm coiling lines at the bow. Beckoning me over with his finger, he snaps, "Go get your old man!"

In response to his questions, Dave explains that he'd been unable to raise the Harbor Master. The officer insists that he try again and he does, with the same result; he's told to keep trying. The man then disappears for a while but returns wearing his uniform and stays until dark. Meanwhile, another boat rafts up beside us, and a parade of people begin walking across our deck.

The Harbor Master doesn't answer his radio until the following morning; turns out, he'd taken the afternoon off to go fishing. Officials arrive soon after and clear us in, then I hose salt off deck and hull while Dave arranges for a fuel delivery. When we're finished, we anchor in the inlet, putting out extra chain as 20-kt winds are frequent and the holding poor.

Eager to go ashore and stretch our legs, we put the dinghy in the water and head for a small jetty near the head of the inlet. Wind waves now strike the side of the dinghy, spraying me with salt water and somewhat dampening my enthusiasm. I lose my remaining interest as we walk down a lane leading around the bay. Garbage is strewn everywhere. Styrofoam food containers and drink cans are particularly plentiful around several *No Littering* signs. A few scrawny chickens and mangy-looking dogs poke through the mess near some dilapidated old buildings, and the one man we see is occupied throwing rocks at a dog.

Plastic shopping bags also dot the water in the inlet, and they can be hard to see. We soon manage to wrap one around the prop of our dinghy motor. They sometimes end up on the bottom and reportedly can make anchoring difficult. The water is dirty, too, and *Windy Lady* soon has an oily scum on her waterline. Two tuna canneries and a power plant occupy the narrow beach-front on the north side of the inlet, and the canneries are smelly when the wind blows, the power plant noisy when it isn't.

When trade winds ease, wind waves are no longer a problem. We still get wet in rain showers, but our clothes dry quickly and don't have that damp, sticky feeling. There really isn't a gathering spot for crews on boats anchored in the inlet, but we meet a few cruisers while ashore. We also find a wet market within easy walking distance and buy fresh bananas, coconuts, and papayas.

We now discover the dozens of small, wildly painted buses that make up the city's transportation system. The vehicles are highly personalized, with rugs, plastic flowers, and ornaments around the driver's seat. They also have elaborate sound systems, and one has two music video screens. We never wait more than five minutes for a ride and observe the curious habit of a few young riders, who carry a 25-cent coin tucked in their ear. The fare is 25¢ or 50¢, depending on how far you are going, and the vans hold about twenty passengers. We also notice many small pickup trucks on the roads, all of them with two-to-eight passengers sitting in the back.

The Samoan people we meet are soft-spoken and friendly, but very large. At some point it seems, normal sized children suddenly explode into immense adults. We're told that diabetes is a problem, apparently made worse now that traditional diets have been replaced with modern food, particularly fast foods and coke.

Trade winds then return and tear through the anchorage at 30 kt, keeping us onboard for two days. I don't see any boats dragging their anchors, but do notice a lot of folks getting sprayed in their dinghies. I start wearing my poncho when we go ashore, which more or less keeps me dry.

We now find newer homes and larger shopping areas around the point, south of the inlet, and begin to wonder how people earn a living. Other than the fish canneries and power plant, there doesn't seem to be much work available, but everyone has money for fast foods and laundromats. After visiting the local hospital, where Dave pays a $2 fee to have a rash treated on his foot, we conclude that the American taxpayer probably foots the bills one way or another.

We stop at a government building in search of information on swimming and snorkeling areas, but it turns out to be a fisheries office. Even so, the young woman at the counter is very helpful, saying that she likes to snorkel, too. She first warns, "The harbor is polluted, as is the coast near the tank farm. There are strong currents in some areas, and not enough water over the reef to swim in others, so you have to be careful."

She then goes on, "There is one spot that was dynamited when the airport was built. Access is across the end of the runway and then you just follow the trail of garbage." We decide to give it a pass.

We stay in American Samoa just long enough to rest up, about the same length of time that it took to get there from Palmyra. I have no qualms about going back to sea, which strikes me as odd when I later think about it. *After that storm, why hadn't I been apprehensive?*

My journal reveals another side to the story. I'd recorded a rather surprising conversation with a fellow cruiser soon after we arrived in port. When asked about the crossing, I'd responded, "It was just about perfect." I then explained, "We had mostly good weather and smooth sailing, a couple of exciting days towards the end, and then an easy entry into harbor."

I start to wonder whether the euphoria of making landfall could have caused temporary amnesia, then realize that I never again experience the paralyzing fear of that night. We go through worse storms and I am afraid, but I can still function. *Having surviving my worst nightmare, it seemed that my fear no longer had the ability to take control of my mind.*

CHAPTER 14

Neiafu, Tonga

We leave Pago Pago just before noon on Tuesday, September 3, motoring out through the reef under a grey, overcast sky. When we raise the sails, winds are from the east at 10–15 kt, and with winds on the beam, we're expecting a fast passage to the Vava'u Islands in the Kingdom of Tonga, 325 nm to the southwest.

We spend the afternoon together in the cockpit, enjoying these first hours at sea, then start our watch schedule at 1600, when Dave goes below to rest. The island has now disappeared from view and winds are gusting at 15–25 kt from the ESE. Although seas are lumpy, Otto is working well. At the end of my watch, winds are up to 30 kt. By midnight, winds are steady at 15–20 kt, but they move around overnight, and at 0800 are coming from the SE.

Sailing conditions are close to perfect during my watch that morning, with a few fluffy, white clouds floating in a bright sky, and deep-blue swells about three feet high rolling silently past the side of the boat. Lulled by the soft rustle of water curling off the bow, I contentedly soak up the sunshine, while enjoying a coolness in the breeze. I'm enjoying it so much that, instead of resting, I spend the afternoon in the cockpit with Dave. The sun gets a bit warm for a while, but the rays lose their heat quickly as it drops toward the horizon, and I'm digging out a sweater before sunset.

The sky is studded with brilliant stars when I start my watch at midnight. An hour later, a half-moon rises up out of the sea, creating a pathway across the quiet waters behind us. As it climbs higher, shadows appear in the cockpit and it's just a very pretty night. By 0400, the breeze has dropped to 6 kt, and *Windy Lady* is making under 3 kt.

Six hours later, winds are back up to 10–15 kt and conditions are similar to the day before, with a few scattered clouds, quiet rolling seas, and comfortable temperatures. We log 129 and 107 nm for Days 1 and 2.

Winds now drop below 10 kt for about ten hours, not strengthening again until after midnight. By 0400, they're gusting from 10–20 kt and seas are choppy. At first light, the islands of Vava'u are visible in the distance. We start the engine when we run into currents near an outer island, then motor past a couple of smaller islands before turning north into a channel leading to the village of Neiafu.

The channel narrows and curves around the base of a distinctive-looking hill, and buoys now mark the deep-water route, with a range marker on the hillside. We then enter a large, sheltered lagoon that is probably one of the safest harbors in the South Pacific. The village of Neiafu sits along one side, and Customs is located at a large commercial wharf near the entrance.

Concerned about currents and gusty winds, Dave keeps the boat speed up as we approach the high, solidly-built, wooden wharf. I'm standing at the bow, thirty feet closer, and am immediately intimidated. We've only tied up at floating docks before, and the deck on the wharf appears to be about the same height as our stanchions and lifelines. We seem to be coming in very fast. A group of young men obviously think the same. They are hidden behind containers piled on the dock, so appear out of nowhere and throw themselves against the toe rail, straining to hold *Windy Lady* off while her fenders are squashed flat. I suspect the ten men had been drinking or smoking, or whatever similar activity these young men did.

After thanking them for their help, Dave asks about Customs and is told that it's closed for the weekend. Turns out, we've crossed the International Dateline and it's Saturday, not Friday. We assumed that the line followed 180 degrees of longitude, but it actually jogs around a number of Pacific islands, including them in the eastern hemisphere. Maybe that is why Tonga calls itself *the Place Where Time Begins.*

With our yellow Q-flag up, we motor away from the dock and pick up a mooring buoy. Contacting the owner on VHF radio, we arrange to use it for two nights. Loud music drifts across the water for a couple of hours that evening, coming from a tourist bar, we assume. Sunday morning, we awake to the pealing of church bells. The day that follows is sunny, warm, and peaceful, and we spend most of it sitting out in the cockpit. The sounds of *sweet song* occasionally drift to our ears, the singing coming from different locations, as if church choirs are in competition.

According to our cruising guide, most Tongans in Vava'u are religious and live traditional lifestyles. It's against the law to swim on Sundays, although that apparently doesn't apply to tourists, as long as they don't do it close to villages. In fact, we seldom see local people swimming, and when we do, they go in fully clothed.

We expect to be in the islands for two months, so start planning our activities. There are thirty anchorages within a few hours' sail of Neiafu. Some sites have good swimming beaches, others are close to snorkeling destinations, and a few provide a weekly feast featuring local foods and entertainment. Boats move freely between them but it's necessary to follow channels and go through passes, as coral grows everywhere, even in what appears to be open water.

I'm not very happy at the thought of taking *Windy Lady* back to the wharf on Monday morning, and the grey, showery day pretty much reflects my mood. When I then see two Tongan Navy patrol vessels tied up alongside the high wall of the wharf, hope surges through me that maybe it won't be necessary. But my hopes are dashed a few minutes later, when both boats anchor out in the lagoon.

We then watch, disbelievingly, as the bow of a huge American warship enters the lagoon, completely blocking our view of the hill marking the entrance. The *USS Frederick* (LST 1184) moves slowly, dwarfing the lagoon and surrounding hills, then carefully turns around and approaches the wharf. The crew throw lines down to a small powerboat that delivers them to men on shore. Once the mooring lines are secured, the massive vessel pulls itself in. The warship is some 550 feet long and the wharf only 250 feet, so the stern sticks out a bit on one end, the bow far out on the other.

During this process, Dave dinghies ashore twice to find out what we are supposed to do. A Customs officer first tells him to bring *Windy Lady* alongside the end of the wharf once the Americans are finished docking. When that isn't possible, an officer tells him that they will come out to the boat.

I'm still watching this activity when our dinghy appears from behind the stern of the ship. I can't believe my eyes. Talk about three men in a tub! The two Tongans are big men, bigger than Dave, and the dinghy sits low in the water, with barely an inch of freeboard all around. It mushes forward, looking as if a ripple might swamp it. Fortunately, there are no other boats moving around.

Only slightly damp, the two officers, Customs and Agriculture, are on board for half an hour, looking around, asking questions, filling in forms. When Dave takes them ashore, he returns with the Immigration Officer, who barely steps aboard before demanding a soft drink. With no refrigeration, we can only offer him warm tang, which he unhappily accepts. It's almost noon when Dave takes him ashore, and we then lower our Q-flag and anchor out in the lagoon.

During the week that we're here, daytime temperatures are very comfortable and rain frequent. We spend hours walking through the village, studying small wooden houses nestled under trees on large, residential lots. Yards and streets are reasonably clean and vehicle traffic almost non-existent. (We see maybe one pickup truck a day.) Pigs of all sizes and varieties roam freely, as do chickens and dogs. The dogs are much healthier-looking than the ones we saw in Pago Pago.

The shopping district stretches for three blocks along a narrow, dirt road running beside the lagoon. Small, dark shops occupy wooden buildings along part of it, and the stores have limited supplies of canned goods and staples such as potatoes, onions, rice, and flour. A few also have some frozen meat, mostly lamb. Farther down, there are a couple of eating places, a bar, a bank, and two supermarkets. Spam and tinned corned beef appear to be popular but prices are high, and a can of spam costs $5.50.

The bank doesn't have an ATM and can't provide a cash advance on a credit card because telephone lines are down to Nukualofa, the country's capital city. We're told to return in two hours, by which time service has been restored and we're able to obtain funds. In the meantime, we locate the wet market and several businesses catering to the cruising community.

A bar overlooking the lagoon turns out to be a favorite with some yachtees, as five minutes after dropping the anchor out front, they can be sipping on cold beers while keeping an eye on their vessels. Another business offers boat repair services, rents mooring buoys at $5/night, and sponsors a weekly potluck barbeque for cruisers.

We make plans to attend the next one, as it will give us an opportunity to meet members of this year's cruising fleet. I make a pot of homemade baked beans to take along, and Dave tracks down a local entrepreneur by the name of Hans and buys a couple of very expensive steaks. (Hans has a freezer on board his sailboat and brings up frozen meat from the capital city.)

Over forty people attend the barbeque, and we learn that boating is the main tourist attraction in the islands, but business is slow. Upwards of fifty sailboat operators work out of Neiafu during the cruising season, and two bareboat charter operators cater to sailors who fly in for a week or two. There are also overseas cruisers like ourselves, who come from different countries. Many this year are Americans, some coming from the east coast, others sailing from the west coast after spending the winter in Mexico.

The conversation, however, mostly swirls around the drama being acted out by a threesome on a sailboat. While Dave and I hear different details, the general theme is the same. A British couple, not married, have been together on a boat for nineteen years. The boat is registered in his name, but they both worked at various times to maintain the boat and their lifestyle. A temporary female crewmember was recently taken aboard, and the man has announced that he intends to marry her. All of them still live on the boat and, in fact, are present.

Friends of the first woman are incensed, as laws in Tonga do not provide her with any protection. An effort is made to pressure local business people and lobbying goes on all night, then continues on the cruisers' net on VHF radio in the days that follow. We only learn how the situation ends when we return to the islands three years later. The first wife has the boat and still sails in the islands; the new couple married, bought another sailboat, and moved on.

This incident causes some soul-searching amongst yachtees, and not necessarily because of concerns about romantic third-party involvements. It's simply a reminder that the laws offshore do not provide the same protection as those at home. We check to ensure that I could legally take *Windy Lady* out of the country, if anything were to happen to Dave. A few months later in New Zealand, however, rumors circulate about marriages taking place on two of the boats that were here.

The cruisers' net is a VHF channel used by yachtees to get in touch with one another; they then switch to a different channel to talk. It's also used by a local couple with a beach restaurant, who provide a brief newscast each morning with information on weather, tides and local activities. One morning, they report that the sailors and marines on the *USS Frederick* are in Tonga for exercises with their local counterparts, and that the ship will be open for tours later in the week.

Taking advantage of the opportunity, we make our way over to the ship at the appointed time. A young sailor shows us around the main deck and explains that an LST is a tank landing ship. Taking us up to the bow, he points to large doors below and describes how the ship is driven up on a beach, the doors opened, and equipment driven off. While I'm getting my head around this, he mentions that on their way down from Pearl Harbor, they stopped at a small island and picked up an injured sailor off a yacht.

Dave immediately asks, "Was the island Palmyra?"

The sailor shrugs and responds, "I don't know, but we steamed back a couple of hundred miles." He then explains, "We sent in a boat with a doctor, but only had him onboard because of the contingent of marines we carried. So, the man was very lucky. We took him over to Christmas Island and put him on a US Coastguard Hercules that flew down from Honolulu." He then recollects something else and adds, "The man was in pretty bad shape; he'd been swimming and was attacked by a barracuda."

Of course, we just know that the island was Palmyra, and the fish the one that rested under our boat. The details are soon confirmed by yachtees on HAM networks. A Kiwi boat stopped at Palmyra when returning home from the Trans-Pac yacht race. A crewmember jumped into the water and was struck by a barracuda, severing an artery in his thigh. We figure that the fish was resting in the shade under the boat and lashed out when the water erupted beside it. Remembering how close he'd been to going into the water with it, Dave winces and mutters that his own thigh is aching.

A few days later, the marines and a few sailors parade through town in the pouring rain. We hear music wafting on the breeze and get quite wet standing in the cockpit, but are rewarded by a rather misty glimpse of 100 men marching along the cliff road. I think of the Kiwi sailor in Palmyra, who undoubtedly owed them his life, and realize I've gained a new perspective on the US military.

CHAPTER 15

Life on the Hook

As we settle into life in the islands, the dinghy becomes more important because we can't step off the boat without it. Dave takes it ashore every three weeks to scrub barnacles off the bottom and seems to work on the engine constantly. We spend hours each week bailing out rain water, which gives us out initial supply of wash water. After that, we collect enough from the tarp over the cockpit to meet our needs. We reserve the water in our tanks for cooking and drinking, and the house battery bank provides a bit of power for lights.

We pretty much live in the cockpit, even showering there after dark, as it's less humid than in the head. Normally, we're early to bed and early to rise, with not even a barking dog breaking the silence. We become adept at washing clothes with bucket and plunger, then hang sheets and towels on a line strung across the foredeck and peg other items to the lifelines. Usually, even heavy shorts and towels dry quickly. I use the rinse water to scrub the cockpit and am always puzzled by the amount of dirt that tracks aboard, given that we're sitting in the middle of a lagoon.

We return to Neiafu regularly during our stay in the islands, as the wet market provides an irresistible supply of fresh tomatoes, cucumbers, green peppers, papayas, bananas and coconuts. Large papayas cost 50¢ each and a three-pound bag of sweet, juicy tomatoes is $1.00. We buy a few potatoes and onions in a store occasionally, and when we're ashore, we're able to dispose of the little garbage we accumulate.

We usually anchor near a landing used by the villagers, and early on Friday mornings, which is market day, a few small, overloaded boats come chugging up to the dock. Passengers are crammed into every available space, including on top the cabin roof. Later, produce is piled high in the stalls at the wet market, and the plaza outside is stacked with large roots, leaves, and melons, as well as smaller amounts of watermelon, cabbage, spinach, lettuce, and even potatoes.

We do wonder about fish stocks in the lagoon, but decide that villagers probably need whatever there is. Early one morning, in one of the outer anchorages, I watch as four men in a small boat pull in a long net. They catch many fish, but most are small and only two or three look big enough to fill a frying pan.

We now learn about ciguatera, a debilitating illness that comes from eating fish that feed on coral. Villagers seem to have developed an immunity, but we meet two cruisers who tell us they were seriously ill. The bigger the fish, the more toxins it accumulates, and the effects are cumulative, so a second attack can be life threatening.

I find the dark-haired, brown-skinned Tongans a handsome people and very much enjoy visiting the village. The men wear shirts and long pants, and some have a soft, short, woven-grass mat wrapped around the hips and tied at the waist. The women, both young and old, wear long dark skirts, usually with tunic tops. On market days, a few younger women stand out like butterflies in bright, colorful muumuus. Schoolchildren are most noticeable, as girls and boys alike wear uniforms with white tunic tops and blue wrap-around skirts.

I try not to be intrusive, never taking pictures without permission, but as time goes by, I start to feel uncomfortable. I seem to be under constant scrutiny. Assuming that the villagers don't approve of my clothes, I start wearing my baggiest shorts and loosest tee shirts when going ashore. When that doesn't make a difference, I try to ignore my discomfort but it never goes away. In fact, one morning, when the town is especially busy and many men are sitting on benches in front of the stores, I feel like I'm walking a gauntlet.

It never occurs to me that perhaps my coloring is responsible for the attention; that my blondish-white hair and blue eyes are just unusual to them. But years later, in Asian countries, total strangers come up and ask me to pose in their pictures. The first time it happens, I think I'm being asked to take a group photo, but no, the woman wants me in the group. I then realize that I probably look at people with very black skin in much the same way. They've always fascinated me because they seem to have a glow that comes from within.

With the memory of our encounter with the reef in Palmyra still fresh, I spend hours studying our charts before we start traveling through the islands. Choosing a quiet, sunny morning for our first trip, we don't go far, just around the corner to Port Morelle, anchorage #7. As we approach the small bay, we see the masts of three sailboats etched against the palm trees. While Dave circles *Windy Lady* around, checking for depth, I stand at the bow and study the waves softly washing up on the white-sand beach. As coral grows out to a depth of thirty feet and damaging it is frowned upon, we drop the hook in sixty feet of water.

We try three times before our CQR anchor digs in, so put on snorkeling gear and check it out. Pulling ourselves down the chain, we see the anchor buried in the sand. We then swim ashore, passing near the other boats, and see their anchors and line/chain dumped in a pile beneath them. This turns out to be standard operating procedure for many captains, which makes me nervous whenever I see a boat anchoring near us.

We now use the inflatable as a swimming platform, but I find the water cool and can stay in only thirty minutes at a time. Trying to get comfortable with my snorkeling gear, I swim along a narrow strip of coral growing around the outer edges of the bay. The reef is home to many schools of small fish, including some that are very tiny and electric blue, while a few larger white fish poke their beaks into the sand nearby.

It is here that we catch up with Dave and Maree off *Byjingo* and invite them aboard for dinner. But our plans go awry when the grill plates for the gas barbeque disappear into sixty feet of water. Fortunately, we're still able to cook on the propane stove in the galley. The evening is warm and pleasant, and we sit outside talking long after the stars appear. Maree happily points out the constellation known as the Southern Cross.

Losing items overboard happens all too often when you live on a boat, and we've lost tools, spare parts, and keys. What makes it most frustrating is that the item seems to float through the air in slow motion, so you clearly understand what is happening but are powerless to stop it. Dave had clamped the barbeque onto the starboard rail, then placed the grill plates inside. He heard a grating sound as he turned away, then turned back to see it rotating slowly backwards and the plates flying through the air.

CHAPTER 16

Hunga Island

With a fresh supply of fruits and vegetables aboard, we next make our way to Hunga Island, on the leeward side of the archipelago. With the sun peeking through the clouds, *Windy Lady* races across smooth, sparkling blue waters in a steady 20-kt breeze for over an hour. She rolls in a low swell when we turn down the outside of the island, then the wind dies and we finish the trip under power.

The narrow passage into the lagoon is a surprise, as it cuts through a low ridge that I thought was part of the island, but actually is the outer perimeter of the lagoon. A rock outcropping bisects the channel part way through, then a number of buoys mark a safe route through shallows on the far side. The large lagoon is almost rectangular in shape, with a village in one corner on the far side, and a small restaurant, Club Hunga, on a white, sandy beach on the other.

We anchor near three sailboats south of the village and spend the afternoon quietly, with our small Canadian flag fluttering off the stern. We notice a number of small powerboats and outrigger canoes coming and going from the village, and then, when we're below preparing dinner, we hear soft tapping on the hull. Going up to the cockpit, I see a dignified, older Tongan man sitting in a dugout canoe. After greeting each other, he admires our boat and I admire his canoe, noting that fishing line has been used to attach the curved sticks of the outrigger pole.

Speaking softly, he explains, "My name is Vaha and I live in the village. I've come to invite you to my church on Sunday and then to my home afterwards for a Tongan dinner."

I promptly call down to Dave, and when he appears his first question is, "Real Tongan food?"

Upon being reassured, he enthusiastically accepts. He then asks if it's possible to buy a few bananas or coconuts. When that too is confirmed, the men agreed to meet at the village jetty at 1000 the following morning. Intrigued, we stand and watch the Tongan paddle away, not then aware of the unique experience awaiting us.

Promptly at 1000 next morning, we arrive at the jetty, which turns out to be a pile of rocks and dirt dumped into the water. There's nowhere to tie up, so I scramble out onto the bank and Dave anchors the dinghy, then wades ashore through the mud. Vaha appears ten minutes later, carrying a large basket made of loosely woven leaves. In it are plantains, coconuts, a sweet potato, and a stock of green bananas.

After some discussion about payment, he states quietly, "I am a friend and this is my gift to you." Somewhat taken aback, as this is not what we expected, we accept the basket as graciously as we can. He then surprises us again by asking, "Do you want to see my plantation?"

Of course we do, so he leads us up the hill and through the village. As we climb, I notice two low fences, made of sticks, running out into the lagoon on either side of the jetty. In response to my question, he explains, "The fence surrounds the village and keeps the pigs inside and away from the crops."

He now adds, "There are seventy families here, about 380 people. We have five churches, three Tongan (Wesleyan), one Mormon, and one

Methodist." When asked, "Why three Tongan?" He responds, "Some people want to be on their own."

We cross a large, closely-cropped grassy meadow that forms a common area between the houses. A few chickens, goats, and horses roam about freely, and several pigs root beneath the trees. The area is remarkably clean, even to the point that the ground beneath the larger trees has been swept.

The small homes are mostly of frame construction, with low fences of barbwire, sticks, and corrugated steel around them. The sheds and outbuildings have thatched roofs and walls of corrugated steel. Each house is equipped with a small solar panel that provides power for a few lights, and a large, cement cistern holds the rainwater that comes off the metal roof. Curiously, Dave asks, "Have you ever had a drought?"

Vaha smiles and responds, "No, we always have lots of water." He then continues, "But we have no power tools, all the work in the village is done by hand. We use horses to carry supplies up from the beach and to move crops down from the plantations." However, I do hear a generator near the jetty and see someone using a power tool on the bottom of an upturned boat.

We see only a few people as we walk through the village, and Vaha politely greets each one. A woman peels bark off a sapling, making tapa cloth we're told, and clothes hang on lines, drying in warm sunshine. We're then spotted by a group of slim, dark-haired, dark-skinned, brown-eyed little ragamuffins. The girls are maybe five years old, with bare feet and dirty, torn dresses that hang below the knees. They eagerly ask me my name and want to know where we're from. They then volunteer their own names. When I hurry to catch up with the men, two of the girls grab my hands, trying to hold me back, but as we get closer, they let go and quickly disappear.

At the back fence, Vaha opens a rough gate made of sticks and corru-gated steel, then leads us down a narrow path that winds through the trees. After a short walk, we come to an opening in the forest that is his plantation. He points to various plants as we pass; banana, coconut, papaya, sweet potato, yam, breadfruit, cassava (from which comes tapioca), dalo (the local name for taro), and mulberry (for tapa cloth). He then shows us a few vanilla bean plants that are part of an eight-acre patch and explains that they had to pollinate them by hand.

Pointing to a large plant with long, narrow leaves, he tells us that villagers dry the leaves and use them to weave their mats. He then finds a small mulberry sapling, strips off its bark and skins it, revealing the fiber used to make tapa cloth. He explains that it is dried, then soaked overnight and beaten, and the process can stretch an inch-wide strip out to a foot, maybe wider.

On our way back to the trail, he picks up a conveniently placed long pole and knocks down a green coconut. With his machete, he slashes off one end, then wipes the point of the blade on a piece of husk before poking a hole in the nut. As he wants none, Dave and I share the cool, sweet liquid inside. Dave now points to notches cut into the trunks of the coconut palms and queries, "For climbing?" Vaha nod and smiles as he responds, "But only for young men!"

We return through the village and are back at the jetty by 1230. Retrieving our fruit basket, which he'd placed in a locked shed, Vaha now asks if he can come and see our boat. Not wanting to risk swamping the dinghy, Dave makes two trips out to *Windy Lady*. After showing him through the cabin, we sit outside, as the Tongan smokes continuously. Wanting to offer him some refreshment but not really having anything, I make tea and spread peanut butter on homemade bread.

Disliking the idea of showing up empty-handed for dinner, Dave asks if we can bring coffee. Vaha shakes his head, saying, "The fruit and the meal are gifts from a friend, no charge, but if you truly want to help, you can make a donation to my church." He then explains, "Some members are going to a meeting in Neiafu on Wednesday, and we could use the cash, but only if you want to help. It's really not necessary."

Dave nods his understanding and soon politely suggests that it's time for the visit to end. Vaha thanks me for the food and drink, saying that he will go and start preparing for tomorrow. That leaves us in a quandary, wondering just how much of a donation would be appropriate.

But I have another problem. I cannot wear shorts to a Tongan church and have nothing else to wear. I rummage through the cabin lockers, looking for anything that I can cut up to make a skirt, then settle on an old mauve-and-white checked cotton sheet. I dig out my portable sewing machine and eventually, by trial and error, produce a garment that is roomy enough to wear over a pair of shorts, and covers my legs to the knees. I tell myself that it doesn't even look like it was once a sheet.

Earlier in the day, Dave made dinner reservations at Club Hunga over the VHF radio. He now keeps an eye on the mooring buoys out front, and when he sees that one is free, we motor across the lagoon and pick it up. We don't want to be searching for *Windy Lady* in the dark. We go ashore at 1800 and find fourteen other cruisers seated at a long table; we've met most of them before. Soon, we're sipping on cokes at the happy hour price of $1 each.

The restaurant is operated by Pete and Happi; he's a fortyish Kiwi, and she is some years younger and Tongan. They offer only one meal, priced at $12. Part of the meal is cooked in an umu, an underground oven, and we traipse outside to watch Pete start a bonfire. He lets it burn down to the coals, heating several large rocks in the process. The rocks are arranged in a shallow hole in the sand, small packets of food wrapped in leaves are dropped inside, then it's covered over. The meal consists of fish, chicken, and potatoes, all of which are a little bland for our tastes, but the contents of the packets from the umu are a mystery.

Happi is an attractive woman and seems to do everything at the club, cooks, sews, cleans, and gives the daily report on the cruisers' net. She sits with us for a while after dinner and explains that she left the village with her mother at age seven and returned two years before. She tells us that adjusting to village life has been difficult and is particularly critical of the medical services, saying they are inadequate, and the churches, claiming they have too much control over people's lives.

Next morning, we leave *Windy Lady* on the mooring buoy and dinghy across the lagoon to the village. About fifty meters off the beach, we hit a rock and break the shear pin on the prop. Scrambling out in knee-deep water, we wade ashore through the mud, then half-carry, half-drag the dinghy up onto a narrow strip of sand. After climbing over a low spot in the fence, we hurry up the hill.

We thought we'd still be on time for the 1000 service, but hear singing as we approach the building that Vaha pointed out the day before. We clean the sand from our shoes as best we can, then remove them before stepping over the doorsill. One of the men standing at the back edges over to let us squeeze in beside him.

The singing continues for a few more minutes and then women and children sit down cross-legged on grass mats that cover the floor. The men at the back remain standing. We use the time to move forward to a vacant mat in the center of the congregation, while everyone in the room watches.

The minister now reads from the bible, and at the end of every verse, a deep rumbling sound comes from the throats of the men. I'm not sure whether it signifies agreement or dismay. Meanwhile a couple of little girls, maybe four years old, wander back and sit in front of me, then stare at me for at least half-an-hour. The reading of scriptures is followed by more songs, with the men singing one part and the women another. Although they have no musical instrument to guide them, they sing beautifully and enthusiastically.

Now comes the sermon. The minister is an older, grey-haired man and speaks quietly at first, but soon his voice grows louder and more emphatic and his arms wave about excitedly. I don't understand a word but start to feel uneasy, so look about the room. Doors on both sides and the end are propped open with sticks, as are the rough shutters than cover the windows. Grass mats cover the floor wall to wall, and I can feel the uneven surface of poles beneath my ankles. A long, white cloth is draped over a desk up front; similar cloths cover two shelves located high on the wall behind it. On each is set a kerosene lamp. The building is maybe twenty feet by forty, and I noticed corrugated steel sheets covering the outside.

People grow restless as the sermon drags on, and now and then someone slips outside. A woman takes a child out first, then a man leaves and I see him standing near the door smoking a cigarette. One woman has a woven grass fan and occasionally bats the heads or shoulders of two ten-year old boys with it; they obviously aren't paying attention. Small children walk back and forth among the seated adults, stopping briefly beside a familiar figure and then moving on. Several of the little girls wear shoes and socks, and all wear colorful, lacy party dresses (most are pink.)

There are maybe twelve men in the room, about the same number of women, and double that for children. The men wear black jackets over lava-lavas (wrap-around skirts) and most have on shirts and ties. Many of the women wear colorful shirts and long skirts, along with flat-brimmed, woven-grass hats held in place by long pins stuck through their hair buns. One woman stands out, as she wears an off-the-shoulder taffeta dress with long, dangling earrings and makeup. She is accompanied by two lighter-skinned, blondish boys.

We all rise for another song, and then a second man goes forward and sits at the desk. Opening a ledger, he calls out names, and as he announces each one, a young child goes forward and throws money on the table. He counts it, calls out the amount, and enters it into a ledger. The room is now very quiet, and I think of Happi's criticism that the church had too much control over people's lives. Certainly, such a public accounting would place a lot of pressure on them.

Singing from other churches now drifts into the room, and I have the distinct impression that the rivalry amongst them includes which choir can sing the loudest. The hour-long service then ends with a final song. I slip out with the first group but Dave lingers inside, where all the men come over, shake his hand, and thank him for coming.

The little girls attach themselves to me as soon as I leave the building, then everyone quickly disperses. As we walk away with Vaha, one of the little girls dances around us. When I ask about her, he explains that he and his wife adopted her when she was a month old. He quietly adds that his wife passed away two months earlier, and now his mother looks after her.

Removing our shoes outside the front door of the house, we enter a large, plainly furnished sitting room and sit down on a settee positioned along one side. Vaha sits in an easy chair at the far end and introduces his married daughter and 16-year-old son, who sit on a settee across from us. After politely greeting us, they ask a few questions and then leave. Meanwhile, our host has changed his clothes as has the little girl, who appears only briefly.

The room is neat and tidy, and there are many small framed pictures sitting on a TV set in the corner and on a nearby small table. Fluorescent lights are powered by the 12-volt solar panel, but the TV doesn't work. Through the open back door, I see an older woman hobbling back and forth and assume she is Vaha's mother, but we don't meet her. Another woman walks by the door carrying a plate of food, and soon after the son enters the room and lays a colorful floral cloth in the center of the large grass mat that fills the space between the settees. Dishes of food are set on it, along with three plates, two forks and a spoon. Vaha then invites us to eat.

Dave gets down on his knees and fills a plate, asking about the food as he does so. The dishes include tuna, corned beef with coconut cream (wrapped in a leaf), breadfruit and tapioca root, and papaya with more coconut cream (hot). Dave hands me the plate he's prepared and fills a second for himself. Vaha waits until we are eating before filling his own plate. I find the food tasty but very rich.

Our conversation ranges from fishing and farming to family life in Tonga, where Sunday is "for church and cooking only, to be spent with the family!" Vaha explains that his 16-year-old son has four years of schooling and likes to spend time in Neiafu, with his girlfriend. I am asked if I'd like to take his picture and do so happily. With three studs decorating one ear, he looks like he'd fit right in at home.

We attempt to explain that modern life in North America is not without its problems, while emphasizing what we see as valuable in their traditional lifestyle. I think the message is lost, however. They know the hardships of their own lives and see only that we travel the world in a big boat with everything in it you could possibly want.

About 1230, Dave thanks Vaha for his hospitality and gives him an envelope with a donation for the church. With that, we find our way down the hill to the dinghy and Dave rows back across the lagoon. When asked for money during our travels, we're very aware that we have no understanding of community norms and are always concerned about doing more harm than good. In this situation, we decided to make a donation equal to what we'd spent at Club Hunga the night before.

CHAPTER 17

Island Hopping

We were able to sail through open water to Hunga, but now motor to other anchorages, following routes across reef-dotted shallows and through passes marked by buoys. With the sun high in the sky, Dave takes the helm, and I keep watch at the bow, scanning the waters ahead. We then anchor in turquoise waters beside white-sand beaches on palm-clad islands.

Anchorage #16 at Vaka'eitu Island is our next stop, as there's supposed to be a good snorkeling reef nearby. Leaving *Windy Lady* safely anchored, we cross the bay in our inflatable and are surprised to find the water quite choppy. A high surf then tosses the dinghy about roughly before dumping us onto the beach. After walking down to the end of the island, we just stop and stare.

Thunderous waves pound the shoreline and the ocean pours in over the reef that extends across a narrow gap to the next island. With a high tide and strong onshore winds, we won't be doing any snorkeling now. Even swimming inside isn't an option, as the sand is so stirred up.

Winds are still strong next morning, but the day warms up nicely and we return to the gap at low tide. The reef, which extends out about 100 feet from shore, is now covered with knee-deep waves, and we wade part way across before stopping to put on our snorkeling gear. Despite buffeting by wind waves, Dave has no problem pulling on his gear, then disappears over the side.

I'm still struggling to put on my second flipper when a wave knocks me down. Unable to get back on my feet in the surging water, I'm dragged back and forth over the coral.

After a few minutes, I bang into a chunk that is big enough to hang onto and desperately grab hold. When the waves subside, I pull off my flipper, stand up, and make my way ashore. Shedding a few tears of relief/frustration, I discover numerous coral cuts on my bottom and thighs. Deciding I've had enough surf for the day, I walk back to the inside of the reef, figuring there has to be something worth looking at there.

Visibility is poor, with fine sand suspended in the water, but I can see the bottom, about fifteen feet down. The wall of the reef then rises steeply in front of me, and it's covered with white branch coral. Peering closer, I see streaks of color as schools of small fish dart through the branches. Colors range from brilliant blue to aquamarine, yellow, and even black and white, and I'm fascinated. Dave later reports that the reef's outer wall plunged down a long way and he saw some very large fish.

For the next two days, the weather is gorgeous, exactly what you'd expect on a tropical island. We even have the place to ourselves for 24 hours. With warm sunshine and a 10-kt breeze, we spend our time on the beach and in the sea, searching for shells and snorkeling. Dave again swims on the ocean side of the reef, but I am content to stay inside. I learn that, with a rising tide, ocean waves push in the very warm water on the top of the reef. Cooler seawater then follows, bringing refreshing currents that are pleasant to swim in and draw all manner of small fish into the humps and fissures on the face of the reef.

Before leaving the anchorage, we visit an eco-resort situated on a hill across the bay. The small, low raft that serves as their dock is anchored 200 feet off the beach and bringing the dinghy alongside is a challenge, as ropes lead off in all directions. Wind waves also break along one side, throwing up a salty spray. A rickety catwalk, several feet above the water, leads to shore, where we stop to inspect a dugout canoe pulled up on the sand. We then follow a broad path through the trees and up the hill. The buildings on top occupy an idyllic spot, with scenic views of an ocean channel on the outside.

As we wander about, we pass several small sleeping huts (fales), then come to a restaurant, bakery, and outside bar. The resort buildings have been constructed using native materials, so have grass-mat walls and thatched roofs. The only person we see is the bartender, an Austrian named Hans. After talking to him for a while, Dave asks if we can get a meal. Hans shakes his head, saying, "You need to book and it's too late for today." He then disappears momentarily and returns to announce, "I've talked to the cook and she can have a meal ready at 1830."

We return to the boat for a few hours and climb the hill again at sunset. As we're early, I sit on a swing outside the bakery, watching the light leave the western sky while darkness creeps across the ocean channel below. The evening quiet is then disturbed as a colony of fruit bats flies through the trees. A few minutes later, a young boy appears and calls us to dinner.

He leads us into a room lit by kerosene lamps and furnished with wooden tables and benches. Austrian music plays briefly and then the room falls silent; we are the only customers. The meal is delicious with a main course of tapioca root and mahi-mahi in garlic sauce, and a salad of lettuce, tomatoes, and carrots with a tasty dressing.

After dinner, we visit with Hans and his Tongan wife, Melee, who is the cook. We take the opportunity to ask about the political situation in Tonga, and in particular, the king. Melee responds, "We have a good King and people are generally satisfied with the government." Hans then adds, "Every male child receives eight acres of land upon reaching maturity, so as long as land is available, people will probably be satisfied." Having very much enjoyed the food and conversation, we pay $10 each for the meal, then make our way down the hill with the aid of a flashlight.

Overnight, the winds back to the north, and by morning, the sky is hazy, the water cloudy, and bits of debris float around the boat. The haze increases as the day progresses, and by late afternoon, the sun is an angry red disk on the horizon. By then, we've returned to Neiafu, where we prefer to spend stormy weather.

When the weather settles a few days later, we head for Lisa Beach, anchorage #10. This small cove doesn't have much of a beach, but we return here often as it's quiet and provides good shelter for *Windy Lady*. It's also near a snorkeling site on Mala Island, and on a day when winds are light and waves in the channel low, we load our gear into the inflatable and motor half-a-mile across to the island.

With the sun high in the sky and the tide low, we anchor the dinghy off the end of the island, then snorkel in the passage alongside it. The warm, crystal-clear water is five to six feet deep, and the white sands on the bottom are covered by a beautiful underwater garden. I've never seen anything like it, and the next two hours are the highlight of our visit to Tonga.

The coral comes in every shape and color imaginable, including yellow, blue, white and pink. There is blue-tipped branch coral, white branch coral, yellow fan coral, brain coral, table coral, and coral heads. The fish are just as fascinating, some in solid shades, others with stripes, bands, or dots, and their colors range from black and white to pale yellow, deep orange, brown, aquamarine, brilliant blue, and silvery white. Dave finds a large conch shell here, and later, at Lisa Beach, finds a smaller tiger cowrie shell.

We return to Lisa Beach on another occasion, after spending several days of inclement weather in Neiafu. We check out two anchorages on the way by, but give them a pass as we think the weather still unsettled. Three boats float peacefully in one of them, including a beautiful black sloop named Scaramouch. We've seen it before and were told that the forty-eight-foot Swan was of Danish registry and leased to a group of five men. All of them are sitting on deck, playing cards and drinking beer as we go by.

We're on our own at Lisa Beach and spend the afternoon and evening quietly. About 2200, well after dark, the roll of thunder reverberates through the cabin. Going up to the cockpit, we watch spellbound for half an hour as a storm moves in. Sheet lightning flares behind the cliffs on one side of the cove, providing a magnificent light show to accompany the deep drum rolls of thunder. As the storm advances, the occasional flash of fork lightning splits the darkness opposite the cliffs with an intensity that is almost blinding.

We only go inside when rain starts to bucket down, and although we don't notice the wind, *Windy Lady* turns and turns on the anchor chain. At daybreak, she is barely fifty feet from a cliff face, but still in deep water, and the dinghy holds a foot of rain.

As usual, we tune in the cruisers' net after breakfast, and that morning the words leap from the radio with a life of their own. "You probably know that Scaramouch was lost last night. The boat went up on a reef during the storm, rolled onto its starboard side and was holed. The crew is safe, and villagers and other cruisers worked with them throughout the night to salvage what they could."

As the words echo through the stillness of the cabin, we can only stare at each other in disbelief. The boat hadn't been anywhere near a reef when we saw it! Later, I go up to the cockpit and stand, looking around the bay. The morning is gorgeous, with bright sunshine and sparkling waters. *What a difference a few hours could make!* In my mind's eye, I picture the events that had occurred while we sat outside, watching the storm. Wind and waves battering the Swan, the anchor dragging, the reef grinding on the hull, and a desperate crew.

We learn that the men were planning a trip south to the Ha'apai Islands. Wanting an early start, they crossed through the barrier reef near the southern island of Ovaka, then anchored on the outside. The boat was thus exposed to the full fury of the storm. A high price had been paid as a consequence of their actions, but there seemed to be an inevitability to the tragedy, as if events had taken on a life of their own.

Our longest trip, four hours, takes us from Neiafu to Kenutu, anchorage #30, on the eastern edge of the archipelago. As we wind between the islands, a few buoys marking passes are missing, so I'm pretty tense. We then cross an underwater ridge and the water gets shallower and shallower. I keep my eyes on the depth gauge, and when it reads fifteen feet, I can't tear my eyes away; when it hits ten, I start holding my breath. Only at eight feet, with two feet of water beneath the keel, does the bottom level off. A few minutes later, we're in the sheltered waters of the lagoon.

Kenutu is a barrier island, and huge Pacific Ocean swells crash onto its windward side and onto reefs running between it and two adjacent islands. Behind the reef, in the sheltered waters of the lagoon, ten sailboats float serenely at anchor. We walk the beach here for hours, mesmerized by the sheer power on display, and at low tide, stroll across the scoured surface of the reef itself.

When the ocean pours back into the lagoon at high tide, we follow a winding trail up the hillside, walking in a soft, greenish light cast by sunlight filtered through the forest canopy. At the top, the ground is carpeted with needles, as evergreen trees grow on the windward side of the island. Looking out over open water from an elevation of 300 feet, we glimpse a wide coral reef extending off to the southeast, but my eyes keep returning to the spray flying high as waves pound the rocks below. The scenery is spectacular.

On our way back to Neiafu, we overnight at Port Morelle. Next morning, with sunny skies and calm seas, we dinghy down the channel to a local attraction known as Swallows' Cave. Swells sweep us in through a narrow fissure in the cliff face and we find ourselves in a large cavern. I first notice the rich colors, the oranges, greens, purples, and golds that coat the walls above and below the water's surface. I then study the high domed ceiling and hanging rock sculptures edging the perimeter. Smaller, semi-circular rooms are located at either end of the main chamber. Reportedly, another large room behind them has a floor above sea level and a hole in the ground that admits light. It's said to have been used for ceremonial purposes in times past.

What most fascinates me is the quality of the light in the cavern. It comes from below and is filtered through water that is crystal-clear and incredibly blue. Looking down, I wonder how deep it is, then something far below catches my eye. Peering closer, I see a flash and make out the fluorescent markings on the fins and wetsuits of four divers. Other than the markings, I see only their outlines and figure they are down about forty feet.

The divers are off a trimaran anchored in the bay outside, and as they proceed, a trail of small bubbles rises to the surface. Soon after, a giant bubble comes off the sea floor, rises steadily to the surface, where it forms a boil about two feet in diameter. I have no idea what causes it, but several more follow.

As cruising season draws to an end, boats start leaving Vava'u and one of the first is *Byjingo*. A few days before they depart for Australia, we join Dave and Maree for dinner on their boat. We're in Neiafu, but anchored half a mile apart, so dinghy down just before sunset. Heavy, dark clouds then move in and the night is pitch-black when we say our goodbyes.

I have no idea how Dave finds *Windy Lady* that night. Anchor lights float above the boats like dim stars, seemingly disconnected, and I only see a boat when it looms out of the darkness as he steers around it. About the time I'm wondering if we'll ever find her, he turns the bow twenty degrees and there she is.

CHAPTER 18

The World Intrudes

I n early October, we try a new anchorage, dropping the hook beside a white sandy beach on the edge of a broad expanse of turquoise water. We spend the afternoon snorkeling over coral heads in a nearby channel, then stroll down the beach, splashing in warm water and admiring the views. When strong winds stir up the sand that night, we spend the next day doing chores.

The following morning, a sudden, loud rapping on the hull at 0845 signals the end of our idyllic existence. The raps are repeated, conveying a sense of urgency, and Dave rushes up to the cockpit. A woman sits in a dinghy alongside and he recognizes her as being off *Southern Cross*, one of two boats anchored nearby. She hands him a piece of paper on which is written a message sent to us over the HAM network. We later learn that the message originated with Peter on the Triple D net in Victoria and was picked up and relayed by three boats, *Cabezon, Kiley,* and *Hope II*.

The note reads, "Phone home immediately, Mrs. Janitsky very ill."

The weather is deteriorating as we pack up the boat, and by the time we anchor in the lagoon at Neiafu, winds are up to 20 kt. We have a very wet dinghy ride ashore, then walk a half-mile down to the Communication Center. Joining a line at the counter, I give the details of my call to a clerk and wait in a closet for the phone to ring. Everything now has an unreal quality, and feeling terribly alone, I numbly focus on a column of ants climbing the wall beside me.

The conversation with my dad is difficult, made more so by a delay in voice transmissions that causes us to talk over each other. But the message is clear; if I want to see my mom and say goodbye, I need to go home immediately. I know that isn't possible and had reconciled myself to that fact before leaving Canada. Unhappily, I now have to convey that message to the folks back home.

That night, gusty winds howl through the rigging, and rumbling noises echo underwater as *Windy Lady* pulls and twists on the anchor chain, dragging it across the bottom. Next day, 25-kt winds push up high waves and we don't even go ashore. I make two more calls home in the following days, and we then move to a more sheltered cove near the entrance to the lagoon.

We anchor near a charter boat, and as the light fades from the sky, Dave notices a dinghy drifting silently away from its stern. Giving chase in our dinghy, we return it before the crew even notices it is missing, thus passing on the good deed done for us by Bob on *Adios* in Hilo.

We visit with the crew a while and learn that they are part of a group of 29 Brits, who chartered five boats for periods from two to four weeks. Their reservations were made eighteen months in advance, and one woman is very unhappy about the stormy conditions. I sympathize, thinking I probably wouldn't be happy either, if the previous week had made up half my vacation. Fortunately, we aren't on holiday, and from our perspective, whatever happens is just part of the journey.

Actually, aside from the occasional storm system that tracked through, we'd found the weather fairly comfortable. Afternoon temperatures are now in the mid 80's, and I'd recently started pulling up a blanket during the night. What we do find tedious is the constant use of the word *fine* in weather forecasts, as the sun often disappears after a few hours, leaving the day cloudy, windy, and often rainy.

Yachtees planning to spend the South Pacific cyclone season in New Zealand now start meeting and comparing notes. That's when many of us first hear of the Queen's Birthday Storm. The memory is recent enough to have left a deep impression on those who know about it, and for the rest of us, the story is an exploding bomb.

Two years earlier, at the end of May, 1994, thirty-five boats left New Zealand heading for Tonga. Reports indicate that trade winds were well established on June 2 and sailing conditions almost perfect. On that same day, however, a small area of low pressure between Fiji and Vanuatu began to deepen and move southward. It moved rapidly, expanded quickly, and by June 4, gale and storm force winds were spread over a 900-nm radius.

Many of the boats were then in an area south of Minerva Reefs. They couldn't avoid the storm and were battered by 50-60 kt winds and high seas. When it was over, one yacht was lost, along with three crewmembers, and seven boats had been abandoned. Rescue efforts were coordinated by New Zealand and involved ships of four nations.

The impact of the story is palpable, and cruisers turn to their friends to talk it through. Unfortunately, the more they talk, the greater their anxiety grows. It becomes a vicious circle, with everyone feeding off everyone else, and a couple of doomsayers in the group keep the pot boiling. The rhetoric becomes so bad that some yachtees talk about spending cyclone season in Fiji, or hiring someone to sail their boat to New Zealand, or maybe just selling their boat.

As if that isn't enough to deal with, other stories circulate that play on our fears and further erode confidence. One story concerns a cruising couple, who ran into trouble a few days out of New Zealand. The man fell overboard during the night and the wife found him next morning, dragging behind the boat by a tether attached to his harness. She couldn't get him back onboard, so had to carry on until close enough to call for help.

I tell myself that these stories don't change anything. We will prepare as best we can, then go to sea and deal with whatever happens, when it happens. But I know my confidence is being undermined when the old specter of a storm at sea returns to haunt me. Dave is impervious at first, saying only that the dithering is painful to listen to, but finally it gets under his skin too. In exasperation, he groans, "You'd think no one ever made the crossing to New Zealand before!"

We hadn't worried much about weather up to that point, simply picked a day to leave, maybe waited for stormy weather to clear, then left. In fact, during our crossing of the Pacific, we'd gone without weather forecasts for weeks at a time. But we don't know much about weather patterns in the South Pacific, and when a few cruisers organize a weather seminar, I persuade Dave to attend. Unfortunately, they only talk about weather windows and strategies, so we don't learn much. But we do talk to two couples who'd made the crossing numerous times, and they assure us that their passages were always pretty normal.

I am also able to buy a copy of a weather manual prepared by meteorologists in New Zealand, and it proves very helpful. I start monitoring HF weather broadcasts from Hawaii and New Zealand, and as I copy down information, I slowly rediscover the shorthand that I hadn't used in twenty-five years. Knowing where to get weather information while at sea boosts my confidence, but there is still one problem, as radio transmissions over long distances can be garbled.

Dave finally has had enough and suggests we go to Nukualofa, Tonga's capital city, which is an overnight trip to the south. As it's also the jumping off point for the passage to New Zealand, we get busy and finish our maintenance work. Two days before we're scheduled to leave, we return to the boat and hear the bilge pump running. A fitting on the salt-water strainer (part of the engine cooling system) is leaking, and we need a three-inch-long piece of threaded ¾-inch copper pipe to repair it.

We have nothing suitable in our inventory and there are no hardware or marine stores on the island. We check at a plumbing supply store, but they are no help. We then talk to several people, and one chap suggests we try Carter Johnson, the owner of the Paradise International Hotel.

The hotel is located halfway down the lagoon, and Carter is out back, tending to his garden. Actually, he's standing over some severely damaged tomato plants, berating himself for having confused imperial and metric measurements when mixing up some bug spray. He takes the time to politely listen to our tale of woe, then leads us over to a small shed. Directing Dave toward a bin full of galvanized fittings, he tells him to have a look. Within minutes, Dave finds exactly what we need, for which we pay one pa'anga, about $1 US. Elated, we return to the boat and Dave replaces the fitting.

This is the third time that equipment has failed just as we were heading out to sea. The pad eye broke on the boom off Cape Flattery, the winch flew apart in Palmyra, and now the cooling system has sprung a leak. All of them could have made life difficult if they'd occurred at sea. Having pondered over *Scaramouch's* fate, I'm starting to think that maybe the captain's luck transfers to the boat. I'd always thought Dave was lucky and wonder whether that might be something to consider, if you were thinking about crewing on a boat.

We need a clearance document to sail between Vava'u and Tonga's southern islands, so clear with Customs and Immigration on Friday, October 18. A trough moves in that night, bringing southerly winds of 30 knots and rough seas. It's cold and rainy, with winds on the nose, and we now sit and wait a week for winds to shift. We then move the boat to Hunga Lagoon, where we can get an early start next day.

CHAPTER 19

Nukualofa

We pick up a mooring buoy in front of Club Hunga, then put out jack lines and safety harnesses and double check that everything is properly stowed. My fiftieth birthday was the day before, but given that Tonga is twenty hours ahead of Canada, we now go ashore and celebrate with a few beers. I only have two, but when Dave rousts me out at 0530 next morning, I'm conscious of a dull ache behind my temples. *Maybe it hadn't been such a good idea.*

It's still dark when we motor across the lagoon, and we're out raising the mainsail in the greyness of early dawn. As soon as there's enough light to see, we transit through the reef. With winds steady at 20–25 kt from the east, we put two reefs in the mainsail and one in the headsail. We also raise the staysail for the first time, which increases boat speed by half a knot.

With a course of 195 degrees, eight-foot swells now break along the port rail, sending spray flying into the cockpit. We have to hand steer as Otto is immediately overwhelmed, but figure we can manage for 24 hours. Winds then increase to 30-kt, pushing up even higher swells, and *Windy Lady* heels sharply when they sweep beneath the keel.

A small pod of humpback whales appears when we're an hour out. They're about 200 feet away and I watch spellbound until they disappear. It's a rare treat to see these creatures in their natural environment, but *Windy Lady* seems a little vulnerable when they're this close. Most adults are at least as long as she is and more than double her weight, and incidents between whales and yachts are not unprecedented.

By mid-afternoon, we're in the lee of the Ha'apai Islands and seas are noticeably quieter. We discuss stopping for the night, but are enjoying the passage and decide to carry on. By dark, we've left sheltered waters behind, and winds now veer to ESE and settle at 15–20 kt, with seas about five feet. A full moon then climbs above the cloud lining the horizon and lights up the sky for the rest of the night. The hours pass quickly as *Windy Lady* races on, and at 0730, we log 150 nm in 24 hours, something of a record for us.

We're now at the GPS waypoint marking the start of the channel into Nukualofa harbor, but other than a couple of small islands in the distance, we're surrounded by open water. With not even a buoy marking the spot, we're slightly confused, but start the engine and drop the sails. For the next three hours, we follow headings, plot our position, and study the color of the water. On three occasions, the depth gauge flashes a reading of eight feet, although we're actually in 100 feet of water. Dave reacts each time by shoving the gearshift lever into reverse.

After motoring for 14 nm, we arrive at the small boat anchorage off the harbor in Nukualofa. Boats are stern-tied to the seawall, and with only a few empty slots and 20-kt winds, backing the boat into position poses a challenge. But as soon as we've dropped the hook at the edge of the channel, three inflatable dinghies appear and push the stern around. Once again, fellow cruisers come to the rescue.

Before *Windy Lady* has even settled in place, the young man who took our mooring lines is knocking on the hull and asking if we want crew for the passage to New Zealand. We don't, have never considered it, and now learn of the floating population of young people, men and women alike, who travel around working on sailboats. As positions or people became available, notices are posted on bulletin boards outside ablution blocks at major departure points.

When we meet our neighbors, Pete and Camille on *Sojourner*, we learn more about the chap who knocked on our hull. A few days earlier, two young men had approached them, looking for positions. Both were working on the same boat and desperate to jump ship, saying that the skipper was unqualified and they didn't trust his judgment. *Sojourner* had already taken on a crewmember and had room for only one of them; the other was the man who talked to us. The tale becomes more complicated in the days that follow, with reports of unpaid wages and missing passports; eventually the local police have to sort it out. (Apparently, a captain is responsible for anyone arriving on his boat, so he'd kept their passports.)

Eight inches of rain fall in three hours next morning, setting a record, while winds of 30–40 kt are reported outside the harbor and visibility is down to a quarter mile. When the rain ends, we walk downtown, splurge on greasy hamburgers, locate our mail, and check out the wet market. After another day of rain, the weather improves and we start exploring the city.

Although we never take the same route twice, we pass many schools and are amazed by the number of children we see. We even catch a glimpse of the Tongan king on the main street. He passes in a small procession made up of two motorcycles and three cars. We share that experience with Leo, an American single-hander, who is thrilled at this glimpse of royalty.

At the National Cultural Center, we learn that Tonga is the only country in the South Pacific that was never under foreign control. The first Europeans to make contact were the Dutch, followed by the English. Captain Cook named them the Friendly Islands when he arrived in 1776. The mutiny on the *Bounty* took place just off the Ha'apai Group in 1789 and resulted in Captain Bligh and eighteen men being put adrift in an open boat. With only a sextant and pocket watch to guide them, they'd made their way 3,618 nm to Timor, a feat that I find incredible.

We meet several cruisers while in Nukualofa, some of whom show their own brand of courage. Leo, the American, is a small man, slightly balding, and at 74 years of age is sailing the oceans long after most folks have thrown in the towel. Within minutes of meeting him, he's told us his whole life story. He'd circumnavigated the globe two and one-half times, lost a yacht on a reef in New Guinea, and had a prostate operation. In our numerous encounters, Leo never stops talking, not even to take a breath, and it's almost impossible to get a word in edgewise. He apologizes, saying he can't help it; he's just making up for all those days and nights alone at sea.

We also meet a couple from New Zealand, who are about our age and have been cruising for seven years. Graham and Jillian lost the self-steering on their boat when five days out of Nukualofa, so took turns hand steering until they were safely in port. What makes that so remarkable is that Graham is virtually blind. He has detached retinas and can't see the bow of the boat from the cockpit but could see the compass well enough to hold a heading. When Dave asks Jillian why they didn't seek medical treatment before starting the passage, she shrugs her shoulders and explains, "We were in India when the first symptoms appeared and didn't trust the doctors." They chose instead to make the long passage home before seeking treatment.

I, on the other hand, can't bring myself to phone home. I'd sensed my mother's passing in the dark hours before dawn during our crossing from Vava'u and now can't deal with it. Several days go by before I make the phone call, and I break down in sobs when my sister, Pat, confirms her death. Standing on a quiet backstreet in front of the small communications building, I weep into Dave's shoulder. I feel like I've lost my entire family.

CHAPTER 20

Passage to New Zealand

W
ith the coming of November, sailboats start slipping out of Nukualofa harbor one by one. We're not in any rush, thinking that it's still cold in New Zealand, but now boats begin arriving from the north and the endless discourse about weather windows resumes. Everyone is so busy consulting with everyone else that many can't make the decision to leave, which Dave describes as a perfect example of *paralysis by analysis*.

I'm not immune to the constant agonizing and start fretting about not being able to pick up weather broadcasts at sea. Dave then learns that the American yachts that sailed from the US east coast will be receiving daily weather briefings over HF radio all the way to New Zealand. He finds out the frequency and call sign, *Night Music*, and we're able to register with them.

On November 7, we clear with Customs and Immigration, intending to leave the following day, then realize that would have us leaving port on a Friday. According to an old maritime adage, that's a bad day to start a voyage. While telling ourselves that we're not superstitious, we see no good reason to ignore maritime custom and certainly don't want to jinx our good luck. We wait until Saturday and are one of four boats to depart that morning.

Our route takes us through Egeria Channel, then south for 50 nm to clear local hazards. At that point, we'll steer SW for 1,000 nm to a waypoint north of New Zealand, where we'll turn SSE to Opua on the North Island. This dog-leg approach at the end will give us a better angle to cut through any storm system that might be sweeping eastward across the Tasman Sea from Australia. We expect to be at sea ten days.

It's noon by the time we're clear of the channel, and the sky is overcast with light rain. Winds are from the NNW at 15 kt when we raise the sails and shut down the engine. Three hours later, winds are from the north at 20–30 kt, and *Windy Lady* is making 7 kt in a six-foot-high following sea. As Otto can't handle the conditions, Dave is steering but is also having trouble controlling the boat. We drop the mainsail and furl in most of the headsail, leaving out only enough to provide steerage.

When I take the helm at 1600, the roar of the sea is deafening, as breaking waves accompanied by spray and foam sweep past on either side of the boat. The sky then darkens as clouds grow heavier, and seas grow higher as the wind strengthens. Soon, twelve-foot-high waves pushed by 35-kt gusts are thundering down around *Windy Lady.*

The first time she slews sideways while surfing down the face of a wave, the bow is easy to bring back and I'm not too concerned. But when it happens again, I belatedly recognize that we could be dangerously close to broaching. Horrified, I glance at the grey, turbulent waters racing past and desperately try to remember what I know about steering a boat in following seas. I then try to hold the bow at a slight angle to the waves as they roll underneath.

But the bow becomes increasingly difficult to control and once it starts to turn, I can't stop it. Holding the wheel loosely, I concentrate fiercely, trying to feel any change of pressure on the rudder. I'm successful for a while, but as the light fades, I hear a loud roar coming up behind, and despite my best efforts, *Windy Lady* again slews sideways. This time, she heels over so far that mast and sail are lying out over the trough, and I am looking down into the abyss. Then the wave sweeps underneath, the boat rolls back in the opposite direction—and my heart starts beating again.

Beyond terrified, I clutch the helm ever tighter and focus so intently on steering that I block out much of the noise around me. I hear only the wave coming up from behind and see only the one directly in front. I soon realize that if I hope to anticipate movement in the bow, I have to loosen my death grip on the wheel. I stand at the helm for two more hours, holding *Windy Lady* in a delicate balance, sometimes, in a weird way, even relishing the challenge.

Darkness comes early because of the heavy cloud cover, and as the end of my watch nears, I start to think that maybe the worst is over. But within minutes, another loud roar comes out of the darkness behind me; it grows and grows until it sounds like a freight train coming down on top of us. Not daring to look around, I tighten my grip on the wheel, sure that we are about to be pooped. I don't know how I know but seconds later, a wall of water arcs over my head and falls into the cockpit and companionway. I emerge unscathed, wet only from spray, while a foot of water surges around the cockpit sole, then escapes out through the scuppers. Fortunately, Dave closed the top of the companionway hatch when he went off watch, so not a lot of seawater goes below.

When he takes the watch at 2000, we're close to our first waypoint and he turns the bow to the southwest. Although north winds continue to gust from 20–30 kt and waves are ten feet high, we no longer have a following sea. Winds then back to NNW during my midnight watch, putting *Windy Lady* on a beam reach, and waves breaking along the rail send an occasional shower of spray into the cockpit. Not a lot of water comes aboard, only a cupful at a time, but each one hits me in the face.

A front passes over just after daybreak, bringing rain and a wind shift of 120 degrees, then the wind dies and we sit and rock. Dave starts the engine at 0900, and at noon, we log 107 nm for Day 1. After plotting our position on the chart, I check the numbers from my wild ride the night before. I made almost 26 nm during that watch, and when adjusted for boat speed, the 37-kt gust that turned the boat sideways would have been closer to 45 kt. I'm just thankful for the 8,000 pounds of lead in the bottom of *Windy Lady's* keel that kept her upright and safe.

A 6-kt breeze rises out of the SSW early that afternoon, teasing us into raising the sails; it dies three hours later. Leaving the sails up, we motor-sail for the next 48 hours. The days are sunny and warm, winds light and variable, and the sea calms, becoming almost flat. The moon is dark and brilliant stars fill the night sky, the brightest reflecting on the quiet waters. Our berths are now as comfortable as any bed ashore.

We spot a pod of humpback whales just before noon on Day 3, this time maybe a dozen animals. They are closer than those we saw previously, and I'm filled with admiration and wonder. I can't help thinking, *so far from land, so much at home!* We log 87 and 103 nm for Days 2 and 3.

When an 8-kt breeze rises in the NNW shortly after midday, we start sailing again. With winds on the beam and a three-foot swell rolling silently beneath the hull, *Windy Lady* cuts smoothly through the water for the next ten hours. Otto works well, leaving us free to bask in the warm afternoon sunshine, and the silence is broken only now and then by the soft swish of a wave curling off the bow.

At change of watch at 1600, I turn slowly through 360 degrees, studying the perfect, unending horizon, where gently rolling blue waters meet a pale blue sky. Later, I watch the golden globe of the sun drop down to the edge of the world and disappear. When I search the sky, looking for stars, I feel a cool breeze on my face, much cooler than it's been for a long time.

An hour later, *Night Music* issues its first weather warning, advising boats to stay north of Latitude 25S. We're only 40 nm away, so have difficulty taking the advice seriously. I dig out my notes from a forecast I'd picked up that morning and see nothing that would justify such a strategy. Dave is concerned about the amount of fuel we'd be using and protests, "We can't just sit out here motoring. We're still a long way from New Zealand!"

As darkness settles over the ocean, the breeze drops away, leaving the sails hanging limply and the boat rocking gently in swells. Dave starts the engine two hours later. By midnight, winds are on the nose at 8–15 kt from the WSW, bringing dark clouds and driving rain. The autopilot now quits working, so I stand out in the rain and hand steer. Meanwhile, the boat is pushed southward and we cross Latitude 25S just before 0400. An hour later, the breeze drops below 10 kt, the sea calms, and the rain stops. Dave now fixes the autopilot and continues to motor with winds on the nose.

I listen uneasily when *Night Music* repeats their warning that morning, but Dave just shrugs and responds, "If we don't go south, we'll never get to New Zealand!" We cross the International Dateline (180 degrees of longitude) at 1028, and at noon, log 90 nm for Day 4.

Winds now increase to 10–12 kt, and we're again pushed southward. Feeling like we're wasting fuel, we go back to sailing, and also raise the staysail in the hope that it will help us steer closer to the wind. Even though we're not going in the right direction, the sailing that afternoon is extraordinary. There's hardly a cloud in the sky, and as we relax in warm sunshine, *Windy Lady* glides effortlessly through quiet, rolling seas at 4 kt. The magic continues into my sunset watch, when the sun drops over the edge of the world and the night sky fills with brilliant stars.

Winds now veer to the west and drop to 8 kt, and by 2000, we're able to make our course. But an hour after midnight, they veer a bit more and increase to 15 kt, putting them abaft the beam. For the first time ever, I roust Dave from his berth, and we drop the staysail and put a second reef in the main.

By the end of my watch at 0400, winds are again on the nose (WSW) at 15–20 kt with a five-foot westerly swell. At 0800, we tack and steer WNW, beating into six-foot seas as we try to make some westing. Two hours later, the winds back 20 degrees and we're able to steer straight west. We log 85 nm on Day 5.

The winds then slowly back another 20 degrees, to SSW and ease a bit. During the afternoon, we have no problem making our course, but seas are rough and Otto needs help. That evening, *Night Music* is advising boats to stay north of Latitude 30S. While Dave seems able to ignore these warnings, they are getting to me. All I wanted was weather briefings, not someone telling us what to do!

By midnight, winds are down to 10 kt and they're then light and variable for the rest of the night. With seas still about three feet, I struggle to keep *Windy Lady* moving forward and spend most of that shift watching the lights of a sailboat motor past to the south. Dave reluctantly starts the engine again at 0800. We log 85 nm on both Days 5 and 6 and are now halfway to New Zealand.

During the warm, sunny afternoon that follows, we motor through calm seas with long, high swells that most resemble a rolling mirror. We continue under a night sky filled with stars, and about midnight, the wind stirs out of the west. After running the engine for eighteen hours, we raise the sails at 0230. Winds are steady at 12 kt at change of watch at 0400 and are up to 15 kt by noon. We log 107 nm for Day 7.

Winds are soon on the nose again, coming from the WSW at 18–25 kt. The sky is now grey and overcast, and for the next twenty hours, we push into five-foot-high seas. As we begin to lose some of the westing we made the previous day, we hold the bow close to the wind, trading boat speed for direction. The winds back a little overnight, but by noon, they're again from the west at 15 kt. We log 95 for Day 8.

The warnings from *Night Music* are now more urgent. "Stay north of Latitude 30S! A low-pressure center that's been building over Australia has started to move across the Tasman Sea!" After five days of listening to this nonsense, I can no longer ignore it. All the stories I heard in Neiafu are again swirling around in my head, with special emphasis on terms like *gale-force winds, knockdown,* and *lost-at-sea.*

I'm not a happy camper when Dave and I stand in front of the GPS that afternoon and watch it change as we cross Latitude 30S. In fact, I'm dreading the days ahead and take little comfort when he confidently observes, "We're only three days away from making landfall."

The temperature now drops and we start wearing long pants and shoes for the night watches. With the breeze steady from the west at 15–20 kt, we put in reefs or shake them out at every change of watch, trying to get the best speed for sea conditions. By noon next day, winds are gusting up to 25 kt, seas are over six feet, and we have three reefs in the main and one in the headsail. We log 105 nm for Day 9.

When *Night Music's* warning is repeated that morning, I decide that enough is enough. I have to figure out exactly what's going on. After plotting our position on the chart at noon, I dig out a pad of graph paper. The storm front had been approaching the east coast of Australia and was now over the Tasman Sea; it had deepened from 996 to 979 mb. The forecast was calling for 35-kt winds in an area stretching north 360 nm.

I now plot the storm's noon positions for the last two days, then add our own, and feel a huge weight drop from my shoulders. I'm sure we'll be in the lee of the North Cape before the storm front closes on New Zealand. No doubt we will face stormy seas, but we'll avoid the worst of the weather. Secure in that knowledge, I'm able to push the turmoil out of my head and concentrate on enjoying the rest of the voyage.

Conditions ease a bit over the next eight hours, with winds steady at 20 kt and six-foot seas. *Windy Lady* handles it all well and Otto provides yeoman's service. We talk about making a beeline for the Bay of Islands but stay the course, as Dave wants to be a little farther west before turning toward Opua.

By nightfall, winds are strengthening and seas have grown higher. The center pressure of the low is now 973 mb and the forecast calls for 40-kt winds extending north for 500 nm. During Dave's 2000-watch, winds increase to 25 kt and veer from 270 to 300 degrees. At midnight, the clear sky reveals a spectacular night sky, and seas have grown to eight feet. Winds increase to 30 kt during that watch, and I put a second reef in the headsail.

Next morning, the low has a center pressure of 970 mb and 40-kt winds are forecast for an area 600 nm to the north; the huge storm now spreads across 1,200 nm.

The storm front is moving across the Tasman Sea at a speed of 30 kt, bringing rain to an area 60 nm in front, and is now approaching the North Island. When I update my graph, it highlights how slowly we are moving compared to the storm, but there is no doubt that we will beat it to the North Island.

When I enter the cockpit for my 0800 watch, the roar of the sea is deafening and the view mind-blowing. The pale-blue sky is filled with brilliant sunshine and long, regular rollers pushed up by 40-kt winds stretch in every direction. The sun glints off breaking waves that are ten feet high, and the wind rips long skeins of foam from the crests and carries them away.

We now turn the bow to 170 degrees, just slightly east of south, and head for the Bay of Islands. We seem to have the perfect angle for the westerly swells, and *Windy Lady* soars across the waves in what will prove to be the most exhilarating ride of our lives. About 1000, the winds back to 270 degrees and swells grow to twelve feet.

The troughs in between are deep and steep-walled, and occasionally, a strong gust blows the tops off the swells and flattens the water, but they quickly build back up again. With a triple-reefed main and just a bit of headsail, our ride is absolutely smooth. We could have rested easily in our berths when off watch, but powered by adrenalin, we stay in the cockpit. At noon, the Signet records 136 nm, but because of our change in course, the GPS shows less. We log 123 nm for Day 10.

The winds now back to 240 degrees, and winds continue gusting over 40 kt, with twelve-foot seas. Through it all, Otto performs flawlessly. It's after midnight before we start to draw into the lee of the North Cape, and after sixteen hours of gale-force conditions, winds then drop to 20–25 kt and seas to eight feet.

With the dawn comes our first view of the low hills of the North Cape, by which time winds are down to 15 kt and seas to three feet. We wait for better light off the channel to the Bay of Islands, and at 0500 start the engine, drop the sails, and motor through the entrance. At 0845 on November 20, under a grey, overcast sky, we raft up to a charter boat at the Customs Dock in Opua and clear in with authorities.

After eleven days at sea, our rhumb line course of 1,083 nm has stretched to 1,192 nm. For the 24 hours ending at 0400, we logged 162 nm, for an average speed of 6.7 kt. On our fastest watch, we logged 31 nm for an average speed of 7.75 kt.

We're able to leave *Windy Lady* on the dock for a half-hour, so walk down the long pier to the Post Office. We'd been told that information about available berths is posted there. After the intensity of the past few days, even that simple task has a dreamlike quality. When Dave now hears someone call his name, he turns and sees a familiar face standing only a few feet away and is momentarily bewildered.

The face belongs to a former client, who scheduled a stop in Auckland while flying from Tahiti to Vancouver. With time on his hands, he'd driven up to the Bay of Islands for the day. We can't stop, as we need to move the boat, and when we walk on, Dave ponders over how it was possible for someone from our hometown to be walking up the dock at precisely that moment.

At the Post Office, we learn there are no marinas nearby, but a mooring buoy is available just across the inlet. Having no desire to anchor out, we take it without a second thought. After returning to *Windy Lady*, we motor over to the buoy and settle into what will be a six-month stay in New Zealand.

For the first week, we sit and watch as more boats arrive from Tonga. Some fifty sailboats make the passage and most are at sea between two and three weeks. The fastest takes ten days, the slowest twenty-three. A few boats

are becalmed, others stop at Minerva Reefs to wait out weather, and several
run out of fuel and end up being towed into port at Opua.

CHAPTER 21

On the Hook in Opua

Our mooring buoy is a ten-minute dinghy ride from the dock at the Opua Boat Club, where we have access to an amenities block, bar/restaurant/lounge, and potable water. The village also has a post office and marine repair and supply facilities, but no grocery store, so on our second day in port, we walk into Paihia, following a trail that winds below the cliffs lining the inlet. The day is pleasant, the views scenic, and we very much enjoy the six-km hike, as it's been weeks since we've had much exercise. But our backpacks don't hold much in the way of fresh fruit and vegetables, and a few days later, we're bumming a ride with a local woman into the town of Kerikeri.

As more cruising boats arrive in port, we're kept busy connecting new faces to the names and voices that we've heard for weeks on VHF radio. Yachtees are identified by first name and boat name, so amongst couples like ourselves, there's Pony and Sylvia on *Rassamond*, Ivan and Trish on *Lancia II*, and Ken and Pat on *Iron Butterfly*. There's an older couple, Bill and Gail on *Bright Wing*; a family with a young lad, John, Kim and Alex on *Moonshadow*; and single handers, Skip on *Wild Flower*, Don on *Sourdough*, and Leo on *Valkyre*. The boats are mostly American, with a few flying Canadian or European flags.

It's quickly apparent that anyone staying here for very long will need a car, so there's a bit of a rush on used vehicles. When Dave hears one advertised on the cruisers' net, he quickly contacts the local owner and is soon driving around in a 1979 Datsun sedan. In the process, we learn a little about the local banking system (transferring funds from Canada), as well as registration and insurance requirements.

Having a car gives us access to shopping in the nearby towns of Kerikeri and Paihia, as well as in Whangarei, a larger town about an hour's drive south. Generally, except for meat, prices are more expensive than in Canada. In early December, Pony and Sylvia join us for a trip to Auckland to check out marinas. We don't see anything we like better than where we are, but they eventually move down to the city.

On those first trips, I am dismayed by the hundreds of dead opossums that litter the highway; there are just too many to count. We later learn that 'possums are an introduced species, have no natural enemies, and are now a problem. More sobering are the dozens of white crosses beside the road that mark traffic fatalities. They don't seem to cause drivers to reduce speed or quit cutting corners though, and we're soon of the opinion that Kiwis are the worst drivers we've ever seen.

In all fairness, they seem to accept with equanimity the annual influx of yachtees who clutter up their roads, especially as many of us have never driven on the left side before. Driving a car with a right-hand drive means manipulating the gearshift lever with the left hand, while windshield wipers and signal levers are reversed on the steering column. More importantly, the driver's perspective on the space occupied by the vehicle is very different.

Accidents happen and a local woman rear-ends a yachtee when he stops for traffic at a one-lane bridge on route to Auckland. Jumping out of her car, she cries accusingly, "You could have made it!" As she has no insurance, he has to find $600 in his cruising budget to pay for repairs. Without the repairs, he would have lost the Warrant of Fitness, without which he couldn't sell the car. Fortunately, nobody is hurt.

On Christmas Eve, a van disappears from the boat club parking lot, where all the cruisers leave their vehicles. When it turns up a few days later, thieves have tried to strip it of everything of value, including the air-conditioning. Dinghies also go astray, and it isn't unusual to find them at the high tide line on the opposite shore.

In mid-December, a small boat on the mooring buoy next to us seems to be getting closer, and we wake up one morning to find it barely six feet away. At the time, *Windy Lady* is pulled right back on her mooring line and the other boat is riding up on hers. We report this to our landlord, and he has the boat moved.

The following morning, a work barge appears at the neighboring buoy. The crew lower two stabilizing legs, then pick up the buoy and winch it aboard, bringing in the end of a very large, heavy chain. The diesel engine now growls loudly as something heavy is lifted off the sea bottom. We later dinghy across and talk to the operator, who tells us that the weight is a two-ton cement block, and he used GPS to find and reposition it. He also reports that there is a back eddy in this part of the bay that is affecting lighter boats more than usual.

It's comforting to know the buoys are well secured, although we don't recognize the significance at the time. That changes on December 29, when the early weather forecast includes a cyclone alert. To say we're flabbergasted is putting it mildly; we thought we'd left cyclones in the tropics!

Cyclone Fergus is poised to track down the east coast of the North Island within 24 hours. Winds are forecast to be 80-kt at the center and 60 kt for 180 nm around it, with a *phenomenal swell*. The cyclone had been moving southeast between two weather systems, then the high-pressure area in front stalled and a low-pressure area behind pushed up against it. Caught in the squash zone between them, Fergus turned and headed straight south.

We already have 20-kt winds, heavy rain, and limited visibility, but everyone with a boat in the inlet now prepares for the worst. Dave and I bring the dinghy up on deck, secure everything above and below decks, and add a second line between bow and mooring buoy. Boats on the hook set out additional anchors, trying to anticipate the wind shift when the storm passes overs.

Winds increase to 30 kt during the afternoon, and I now listen to weather updates and conversations on VHF radio until my stomach is in knots. We decide to keep a watch overnight, as forecasted winds could be disastrous. I take the first shift, and swells are surging down the inlet when Dave relieves me at 0200. Soon after, winds begin to ease as the cyclone heads southeast again. He goes back to bed, and by morning winds are down to 15 kt.

Still, the storm causes problems. A few boats drag their anchors, running into other boats and fouling anchor lines, and torrential rain turns campgrounds filled with Christmas holiday campers into muddy pits. Long queues form at the local laundromat as people wait to dry out their gear.

Another cyclone warning is issued ten days later, on January 8. Cyclone Dreena is tracking south-southeast toward the west side of the North Island and has a center pressure of 945 mb. It has the potential to do a lot of damage. By the time it hits on January 10, the pressure is 983 mb and maximum winds are 60 kt.

At 0900, winds are gusting up to 25 kt and visibility is poor in heavy rain; an hour later, they're hitting 30 kt. When we go out on deck at 1100 to check the boats around us, winds are at 40 kt. Waves break over the bows as boats strain back against their mooring lines, but all appear to be riding out the storm safely. Shortly after noon, we record a top wind speed of 42 kt. At the long dock across the channel, the three-masted tall ship, *Spirit of New Zealand*, records a top speed of 55 kt.

The winds ease for a few hours that afternoon, but are back up to 20 kt by 1800, with heavy rain and gusts up to 35 kt overnight and into the morning. The only damage we hear about is from Leo on *Valkyre*, who reports that a motor launch passed close by and cut his anchor rode. He had another anchor ready to deploy, but lost the first one along with 40 feet of chain and 100 feet of nylon rode.

Bad weather traps us onboard for up to five days at a time during our first two months in Opua, and the need to take a dinghy ride every time we step off the boat becomes tiresome. Even when it isn't raining, winds blowing over tidal currents create high waves in the channel between us and the boat club, so we start using the hard dingy, as it's drier than the inflatable.

We keep the dinghy tied up alongside and bail out buckets of water two and three times a day. Occasionally, we have to winch it up on deck, as high waves racing down the channel cause it to buck like a bronco, with the bow rearing up almost level with the upper lifeline, six feet above the water. When we go ashore, we hear the dinghy dock moaning and groaning long before we reach it, as waves surge underneath. Dave then pushes his way through two or three rows of jostling boats and motors in order to tie up.

Our only real distraction comes from regular morning visits by a family of ducks. The mother quacks loudly to announce their arrival and brings six ducklings on the first visit. Dave crouches in the dinghy, feeding them oat flakes, and soon one that is solid brown is sitting in his hand. Two of the ducklings are missing on their second visit, and the last time we see the family, two more are gone, including the brown one.

We spend a lot of time reading, as we have a large number of books onboard. Dave also takes to baking cinnamon buns and becomes adept at tying knots, laboring for days over a Turk's Head. On an early visit to Whangarei, he'd purchased a transistor radio and now discovers talk radio. It seems to be very popular with the locals and gives us a window on the country that we wouldn't have had otherwise.

Primary topics concern national politics and crime, particularly theft, but nuclear testing and nuclear waste are hot button issues. The environment itself doesn't seem very high on the agenda, even with a hole in the ozone layer. Lotteries, along with horse and dog racing, seemed to take an inordinate amount of money out of people's pockets, while sports are embedded in the national psyche, including rugby, America's Cup sailing, and any new activity that provides a thrill.

The thrill seeking is reflected on the nation's highways, with fifteen dead on a three-day weekend in a population of 3.5 million. There are frequent reports of people in need of rescue as boats capsize, kids drift out to sea on air mattresses, and hikers get lost. In between, commercials promote bee pollen, deer velvet, and other home health remedies.

When the weather improves, we start exploring by car, at first following paved, two-lane roads through the countryside to see where they go. The roads are narrow, with no shoulder between ditch and pavement, and bridges have only one lane. Thousands of sheep and cattle graze in fields where gum and kauri forests once grew, and the yellow scars of access roads show up clearly on the ridgelines. Some of the land has now reverted to bush.

We visit Haurau Falls and admire a panoramic view of the Bay of Islands from Bledscoe Lookout. We spend an hour with the locals in the park at Whangarei Falls and enjoy ocean views while driving along the Tutukaka Coast. I take particular pleasure in the large, showy blossoms of flowering plants that edge the roads, and in the brilliant red blossoms and dark green foliage of the pohutukawa trees dotting the seascapes (known as Kiwi Christmas trees.)

One day, our car breaks down on the highway, leaving us stranded in the countryside. We have no idea which way to go for help, so I start walking north and Dave stays with the car, which he'd pulled off onto a side road. With his usual good luck, a farmer arrives at the nearby gate and offers to phone for a tow truck. A garage is located a few miles to the south, and a mechanic soon arrives and fixes the fuel pump, which is the problem. Dave then realizes he doesn't have his wallet, but convinces the chap that he will return next day and pay the bill.

I walk for half an hour, self-consciously sticking out my thumb, before a vehicle stops beside me. When I turn and peer into a van, my first instinct is to keep walking. I don't know what I expected, but it certainly wasn't to be looking into the face of a very large, very black man. I then notice a boy, maybe ten years old, sitting in the passenger's seat, and a whole load of oranges covering the back of the vehicle. In the next moment, I am explaining our predicament to the driver.

As I climb into the back seat with the oranges, he responds, "I saw the car back away with the hood up, so wasn't surprised to see you walking down the road." I now learn that the driver of the vehicle is a recent immigrant. He and his family came from Tonga, and he'd spent the morning picking oranges with his son.

After driving ten km into the next town, he drops me in front of a garage. I locate the mechanic and we return up the highway in a tow truck. Of course, the car is gone when we get there, and we catch up with Dave at the edge of town. I pay my mechanic $30 for his trouble, and next day, we return and pay Dave's mechanic $40.

Another day, on our way to the island's west coast, we see a sign advertising *The Old Monarchs*, so stop to check them out. I'm especially interested, as the largest kauri trees are said to be forty to fifty feet around the base and produce multiple tops over 100 feet high. But the boardwalk leading into the site takes us through a scrub forest of willow-like saplings and small trees, and the few mature trees we then see are not exactly majestic. The experience is not improved by the clatter and chatter of visitors, who stand around on the boardwalk because barbwire has been spread on the ground around the trees to protect feeder roots.

Occasionally, we climb the low hill next to the anchorage and visit with our landlord; Tony and his wife Mary live in a very comfortable house overlooking the bay. We make the six-km trek into Paihia several times and twice walk a similar distance along a lightly traveled country road to the small, historic town of Russell. We climb Flagstaff Hill on our second visit and watch the Tall Ships' Race. It's a beautiful, sunny day, but very windy and not that warm. The views are splendid, however, with boats sailing down the channel and the village nestled in green hills around a small bay.

When a stretch of good weather settles in, Ivan off *Lancia II* persuades Dave to enter a Fun Race, going from Opua to Whangaroa, forty miles up the coast. When race day arrives, all sunny and warm, there's not a breath of wind. After motoring all day, we anchor in the harbor near the Game Fish Club.

Going ashore, we stroll along the waterfront near the club, where officials are weighing in an incredible-looking sailfish. Weighing in at 210 pounds, the fish is close to nine feet in length from the tip of the bill to the end of the tail fin. We now meet up with Ivan and Trish, have a few beers, then pool our resources and return to *Windy Lady* for a late supper. Trish brings the mince, Dave cooks spaghetti, and we spend the evening enjoying each other's company.

Next morning is bright and clear, and we're slow getting started as we plan to stay the day. Then, about 0900, I notice a parade of sailboats leaving the harbor. Tuning in the weather broadcast at 0930, we learn that strong, southerly winds are pushing up the coast. They're expected to reach 30–40 kt by evening and will last for two to three days. The harbor is surrounded by high, steep hills and can be very squally in stormy weather, so we make the decision to return south.

We immediately get underway and Dave steers the boat down the inlet, while I scurry around below, securing everything in the cabin. Once in open water, with the sky bright and sunny, we raise the sails. Half an hour later, winds are on the nose at 20 kt; a few hours later, they're at 30 kt. We initially try motoring inshore, but end up fighting high swells and strong currents, so shut down the engine and tack out to sea.

An hour away from the entrance to the Bay of Islands, winds are hitting 40 kt, and we stop and put a second reef in the main and partially furl the jib before making our last tack into the inlet. In the grey twilight at the entrance, we see *Lancia II,* their dinghy bouncing along behind them at the end of a towline; it turns turtle soon after. It's fully dark when we pass the marker buoys off Russell, at which point the swells begin to ease but winds continue to howl down the channel.

Somehow, Dave homes in on our mooring buoy, but with waves tossing the boat in one direction and the buoy in another, I'm not able to snag it with the boathook. After making three attempts, we give up and drop the anchor. It's now 2315. Next morning, 30-kt winds still make it difficult to pick up the buoy, but we succeed on the third try. Strong winds then keep us onboard for the next two days.

On a pleasant summer afternoon near the end of January, we take *Windy Lady* out for a sail, then stop at the fuel dock on our return to fill water tanks and scrub down the deck. A sailboat is tied up to pilings nearby and two young lads are climbing and swinging on the heavy ropes strung between them. The boys are maybe nine and twelve, and we stop to watch, enjoying the sight of kids being kids. One of those *boat moments* now occurs. The younger lad's glasses slip from his face, falling into the water. The father's reaction is extraordinary; he dives after them so quickly it seems he will grab them before they hit the surface. Of course, that doesn't happen, and he later explains that they stayed just beyond his fingertips.

CHAPTER 22

Land of the Long White Cloud

Early in February, we pack up the car and set off to explore farther afield. We drive south to Auckland, then follow the west coast down to New Plymouth, arriving there just as the setting sun lights up the perfect cone shape of Mount Egmont. Next day, we drive to Wellington, where dark clouds sit low on the hills, and it's rainy and windy. We thought we'd be able to stop wherever the spirit moved us, but quickly learn that if we want a room, we need to make a reservation.

We stay in Wellington for a day and spend most of it at the Maritime Museum. While the exhibits are all interesting, the story of *the Wahine* is particularly memorable. In 1968, this large, modern, inter-island ferry ran headlong into tropical cyclone Giselle and foundered almost within sight of the city. Reports of the heroic efforts made by local citizens to rescue the 734 passengers and crew are riveting.

Next day, we board a ferry to cross to the South Island. The weather starts to improve as we leave Wellington harbor, and seas are flat as we cross the notorious Cook Strait. By the time we sail down Queen Charlotte Sound and disembark at Picton, the day has turned very pleasant. We drive to Nelson, then around Tasman Bay to Golden Bay, where Abel Tasman came ashore in 1642. He named it Murderers Bay after four of his crew were killed by Maoris.

We spend a few days driving down the South Island's west coast, first crossing the saddle to Greymouth, where we see evidence of serious flooding caused by torrential rains a few days earlier. Wide, shallow riverbeds cut the highway as we proceed south, all spanned by long, narrow, one-lane bridges, and seascapes change around every corner, as swells rolling across the Tasman Sea crash onto the shoreline.

With the weather sunny and warm, we stop frequently and begin to relax, strolling along sandy beaches and hiking into both Franz Josef and Fox Glaciers, as well as Paparoa National Park. Somewhere along the way, I notice a forest of superb tall trees, surrounded by heavy undergrowth. Turning inland at Haast, we drive to Wanaka, where we stop for the night and stay a week. Perfect weather turns it into our ideal playground.

We climb through fog to the top of Mount Roy and are enchanted when the mist lifts, revealing spectacular views of Glendhu Bay and Lake Wanaka. We hike up Mt Aspiring and into Rob Roy Glacier, then swim in the glacial waters of Lake Haura after hiking the Sawyer Burn Trail. At the end of each day, we sit and barbeque steaks on a grill outside our motel room.

Only an early morning phone call from the manager on a Friday, telling us that the motel, including our room, is fully booked for the weekend prods us into moving on. Then, when we stop for gas on the way out of town, the attendant tells Dave that we are lucky, because normally the summers are cloudy, windy, and rainy.

We stop in Dunedin on the east coast and visit a cold and windy albatross sanctuary. We learn that adult birds practically need gale force winds to become airborne. At Turtle Rocks, we inspect large, round rocks strewn along a sandy beach; most are about three feet across and their cracked surfaces do resemble turtle shells. As we drive north, much of the eastern plains appears to be under cultivation, and I wonder if they have the same problem as in Opua, where fertilizers leach into streams and end up in the ocean.

A flat tire going into Christchurch on a Saturday results in a two-night stay in that beautiful city, as we can't get it repaired until Monday. The Flower Festival has just ended, so we're able to admire the displays as we walk through the downtown. We tour the Air Force Museum and Antarctic Center on Sunday, racing to and from the car through driving rain.

After two more nights on the road driving up the east coast, we catch a fast ferry out of Picton, cutting the travel time across Cook Strait by one-half. But arriving ahead of schedule in Wellington is a problem; we can't find a place to stay. By 2100, all motels have posted *No Vacancy* signs, and we end up spending a very uncomfortable night in the car. Next day, when we see signs promoting Rotorua, we heave tired sighs and keep on driving. In fact, *get-home-itis* has set in and we arrive back in Opua the following afternoon.

We feel very comfortable traveling in New Zealand; not surprising I guess, given our shared history of British democratic institutions and common law. But we are intrigued when we learn that the Kiwis had recently changed their electoral system from first-past-the-post to multi-party-proportional. We don't know why the change was made, but have front row seats to the consequences.

The first election incorporating the change was held on October 12, 1996, six weeks before we arrived in the country. No party won a majority of the seats, and leaders of three political parties haggled over power-sharing arrangements for the next three months. The leader of the third-place finisher, with 13% of the popular vote, then called a press conference and announced that his party would form a coalition government with the National Party, who heard the news along with everyone else.

The coalition had only a one-seat majority in the legislature, and according to talk radio, the junior partner dominated government policy. During the six months that we follow events, the shenanigans of the political class take priority over the running of the country, and the government just stumbles from crisis to crisis.

Dave and I take our responsibilities as voters seriously, so make an effort to understand the changes that were made in the guise of electoral reform. Previously, the legislature had 90 seats, each filled by a candidate elected by voters in an electoral district. The number of seats had been increased to 120, but only 65 seats were now filled by voters in an electoral district.

The remaining 55 seats were supposed to be allocated to political parties based on the percentage of popular vote they won in a separate ballot. (The parties provided lists of candidate names in advance.) But for some reason, that was not how it worked out. When I study the results, I see that two parties ended up with eleven list seats; one had 28% of the popular vote and the other 13%.

We have no idea what arguments were used to convince voters to turn over 45% of their seats to list candidates, who would be loyal to political parties, not voters. To us, the new system was hardly a success. It was more complex, less transparent, and resulted in an unstable government.

CHAPTER 23

A Sailor's Life Ashore

I f I thought life in New Zealand was going to be a holiday, I was wrong. The cruising season took a toll on *Windy Lady* that went far beyond normal wear and tear, and we seem to spend a day doing maintenance on shore for every day that we were at sea. Most of the work we do ourselves, as we went well over budget when outfitting the boat. While the responsibility falls mostly on Dave's shoulders, there's more than enough work to keep us both busy.

We start by wrestling the mattress from the port berth up on deck. While I scrub down the saltwater stain on its side, Dave traces the leak to a deck drain, not the porthole, and seals it. As salt air was driven into every corner of the cabin, we scrub down walls and shelves throughout and oil the teak trim. The settee cushions in galley and salon are permanently damp, so I buy a spray cleaner and spend hours brushing them, only stopping when my wrists ache.

The bright work in the cabin needs attention, and Dave sands and varnishes the sole in the salon (three coats) and the sides of the companionway (five coats). Meanwhile, I clean and grease our six winches, drawing sketches so that I know how to put them back together, then pull the anchor chain up on deck and use flagging tape to re-mark it in twenty-five-foot sections. We reseal the galley hatch, replace a few fittings in the hydraulic steering system, and fix the strobe light on the mast. Dave then cleans hoses and fittings in the head, and tries to free the pin on the beak of the whisker pole, which is frozen shut.

He takes the dinghy ashore every three weeks to scrub silt and barnacles off the bottom, and when the diesel engine overheats, he finds barnacles plugging the thru-hull in the saltwater cooling system. For my part, I regularly balance in the dinghy and pull myself around the boat as I scrub down the hull. Barnacles and algae grow rapidly in the inlet, as streams emptying into it carry sediment and fertilizers (nitrates) from the fields. On a couple of occasions, after days of heavy rain, the water turns brown and smells like a barnyard.

In between chores, we visit boatyards and talk to yachtees about hard dodgers and RIBs, two expensive items on Dave's wish list. We can't afford both, and while a RIB (rigid-bottomed inflatable dinghy) would have been nice, Dave deems a dodger essential. He likes the design and workmanship of several built by a local farmer, Warren Patterson, and engages him to build one. We've already had dealings with Warren, as he sold us the car, and he is prepared to let us help with the grunt work.

On a blustery, grey day near the end of January, Dave dinghies over to the fuel dock and picks up Warren and his gear, which includes a small generator, a skill saw, a tape measure, two sheets of 9 mm plywood and some pieces of timber. While *Windy Lady* fidgets at the end of her mooring line in gusty 25-kt winds, the two men start cutting and fitting a framework together. When they're done, we take the boat over to the fuel dock and load the structure they've built onto the back of Warren's pickup.

A few days later, we drive out to Warren's farm, prepared to go to work. He's glued the pieces together and the structure now sits in an old shed. Another sheet of plywood is held in clamps nearby; it's for the roof and has been curved to a drop of one inch for every three feet. We sand the glued surfaces, then begin laying fiberglass. Warren cuts and places the matting, Dave applies the resin, and I roll out the bubbles. After working most of the day, we complete the outside of the frame and the top of the roof; next day, we complete the inside.

The following morning, another grey, windy day, we take *Windy Lady* over to the fuel dock and meet Warren for a fitting. The men position the dodger on the cabin roof and set the curved roof on top, and Warren checks it one last time. They then load it back on the truck, and we return the boat to the mooring buoy. We spend the afternoon at the farm, sanding and putting on a coat of bog (filler). The next day, we sand off most of the bog, and that is it until we return from touring the South Island.

When we re-appear at the farm in early March, the roof is on the dodger and Warren has cut the openings for the windows, reinforcing them with pieces of kauri timber. We work for the next six days, fiberglassing and bogging, and by the time the dodger is ready for its final fitting, we've put in a total of 93 hours.

We again meet Warren at the dock, and the final adjustments don't take long, but putting on the "doublers" that hold the dodger in place is a fiddly job. It's late in the afternoon when he finishes, and we then drop the dodger off at Doug's Boatyard for painting. Next morning, we return to the boatyard to have *Windy Lady* hauled out.

The day is grey and miserable, and a super high tide covers the boatyard dock, leaving only the tops of posts visible. We then stand about in steady rain for six hours, waiting through one equipment failure after another. When *Windy Lady* is finally propped up in the yard, she leans over on her supports, with an uncomfortable tilt to the deck. Living on the hard is never something I enjoy, and this makes it worse.

We spend the next 24 days camping on board, and our living space is soon limited to the galley, as tools and supplies are piled all around the salon. Dirt on our boots tracks up the ladder and onto the deck, where it grinds into teak and fiberglass, and as we have no water, I haul dishes up and down the ladder once a day.

Dave first wet sands the bottom of the hull and covers himself in blue, ablative bottom-paint in the process. He then removes the paint from the propane bottles, as they've started to rust. He repaints them with one that is supposed to be rust inhibiting (but isn't!). I spend six days standing on scaffolding, applying wax to the hull above the water line. It takes six coats, all rubbed in by hand, before *Windy Lady* again resembles the boat that left Victoria.

The thru-hull beneath the galley sink is badly corroded and needs to be replaced, as do the zincs and the galvanized fitting we put on in Tonga. We also sand the dodger between applications as Doug puts on primer and two coats of two-pot paint.

Dave wants to apply a non-skid paint on the foredeck, as it's just too slippery, and we spend backbreaking days on our knees, sanding deck and cockpit as we prepare the surfaces. We then apply masking tape around windows and deck trim. Doug does the actual painting, but is slow getting started, and by the time the two-pot paint is dry, the masking tape has been on too long. It comes off in bits and pieces and is a terrible job to remove. We re-tape the deck before he applies the thick non-skid paint, then stand by and pull it off before the paint dries.

As we're running out of energy, we have Doug replace the black Sikaflex between the narrow teak boards on benches and sole in the cockpit, and he does a beautiful job. He then sprays on the new bottom paint. Dave now spends a morning preparing the cockpit, then he and Warren hoist the dodger up fourteen feet in the air and place it in position. After attaching it to the coach house roof and doing more bogging, Warren installs an opening hatch in the front. The following morning, a crew from Aqua Glass install the windows and the job is finished, except for touching up the paint.

Shining like a newly minted penny, *Windy Lady* goes back in the water that afternoon. But there's still one more task, as Dave's concern about the gel cells overheating when we left Hawaii was valid. Both were dead when we returned from our trip to the South Island, and he decided to replace them with lead-acid batteries. We now make the exchange, which is a real struggle. Each battery weighs 130 pounds, and we have to move the old ones up the companionway and off the boat, then bring the new ones onboard. At the end of a long, tiring day, we return to our mooring buoy.

Three days later, Dave drives down to Auckland and catches a plane to Canada; he'll be away three weeks. I stay behind, as we don't want to leave *Windy Lady* unattended on a mooring buoy. We've heard too many stories about boats being vandalized; one even had a windlass cut from the foredeck. Besides, there's still a lot of work to do before we leave for the tropics.

As I wave goodbye to Dave in the parking lot, my mind is already on the dinghy. I'm pretty sure the engine is going to be a problem. Returning to the dock, I stand looking down at it dubiously, but for now, it roars to life when I tentatively pull on the starter cord. As soon as I'm back on the boat, I start on the next challenge. I'm to run the diesel engine for two hours every day and record the charging data. Dave is already unhappy with the new batteries. I turn the key, engaging the glow plug momentarily, and the engine throbs to life.

I'm still charging the batteries at 1400, when Doug arrives to touch up the paint. He sits in his dinghy, looking up at the dodger, and glumly observes, "That primer coat hadn't been sanded!" I stare at him guiltily because we hadn't even thought of it in the rush to prepare for Dave's departure. Being Doug, he just shrugs his shoulders and says, "The paint's mixed and won't keep, so where's your sandpaper?"

We set to work and when we're done, I clean up the dust and he starts to paint. When he's finished, he comments unhappily, "The paint doesn't cover the primer very well, so you may want to repaint below the windows in a year or two." Turning, he now looks around the cockpit, touches up a spot in front of the propane locker, and then freezes. Staring at the floor below the seats, he cries in disbelief, "Has somebody been grinding metal?"

Uncertainly, I reply, "Uh, Dave did file down the dinghy oarlocks."

"Well, you'd better get busy with Comet, or something similar," he responds icily, pointing to the yellowish-red specks in the gutter and on the coaming.

I spend most of the next day on my hands and knees scrubbing the deck and cockpit with comet and scrub brush. I then scrape glue and paint off the coaming and dodger windows with a razor blade. The sky grows darker as the afternoon drags on, and I realize that rain is coming. Remembering that the dodger roof is designed to catch water, I attach a hose to one of the downspouts and set up a bucket on the side deck.

A few minutes later, I hear a scraping noise, accompanied by a gust of wind, and turn to see my bucket settling in the bay. Staring at it with actual dislike, I debate where or not to retrieve it, then reluctantly decide to do so. The blue bottom of the pail is moving away quickly in the outgoing tide, so I chase after it in the dinghy. As I can't grab onto it with just one hand, I have to maneuver the boat into a position where I can reach out over the stern with both arms and pull it in.

When I get back, I tie the bucket handle to a lifeline. The dodger roof proves very effective at collecting water, and by morning, the two downspouts each produce a bucket of clean rainwater. A few days later, I collect three buckets in half-an-hour.

On the first calm morning, I climb the mast and spend a half-hour examining halyards, fittings, and welds on the steps, looking for anything that seems different from the last time I inspected them. I repair the jib halyard, which is badly chafed near the shackle end, and reposition the sheets through the deck organizers and guides in the new dodger, wondering if they will chafe.

When it rains, I'm forced to confront the chaos below decks, where chart table, settee, and starboard berth are still piled high. We'd shoved tools and supplies back into lockers helter-skelter when *Windy Lady* went back in the water, and now it's time to pull the lockers apart and re-stow everything.

I continue charging the batteries daily and start puzzling my way through the brochures we'd accumulated in our file, trying to make sense of the data I am recording. When I fax it down to the dealer in Whangarei, he responds that the batteries are fine and will have to be cycled thirty times before they reach maximum capacity.

My days aren't all work, however, and I'm grateful to friends who ask me over for dinner or meet me at the boat club on movie night. In particular, there are Len and Pam on *Kapalua II*, Ivan and Trish on *Lancia II*, and Ken and Pat on *Iron Butterfly*.

Then, one day when I'm ashore, my fears come true; the dinghy motor won't start. Unhappily, I pull out the oars and start rowing, but my progress is slow as waves are sweeping down the channel. It doesn't help that the oars are short, so don't give much bite to the blades, or that the weight of the engine hanging off the stern causes the bow to sit high in the water. I'm about halfway across, when Pam off *Kapalua II* comes along and takes me in tow.

The carburetor has been the most frequent problem, so I dig out the operator's manual and read through the instructions. I don't want to try lifting the engine up into the cockpit, so plan to work on it in place, but waves are jerking the dinghy back against the painter. I wait awhile, then grow impatient and climb down into the dinghy.

Removing the engine cover, I start checking switches, sparkplug, and fuel filters. I'm nearly finished, when a large wave pops the bow of the dinghy up into the air, sending me face first into the engine. Realizing that the next wave could put me in the inlet, I finish up as quickly as I can. I'm not surprised when the engine still doesn't run, as I'd found only a bit of grit in the tank outlet.

As luck would have it, I'm having dinner at the boat club with Len and Pam that night; they are anchored nearby and pick me up. Over dinner, I tell them my tale of woe and ask Len for advice. After listening patiently, he suggests, "If you want to try again, I'll lift the engine onto our deck in the morning and supervise your efforts. But I'm in the middle of my own work," he warns, "so I can't do it for you."

I jump at the offer, as I really want to figure out the problem. By late afternoon next day, however, I am bitterly regretting that decision. I had taken the engine apart four times, even stripped the carburetor down to its smallest component, and it still wouldn't run. I'm tired, frustrated, and feeling dreadfully guilty for having wasted hours of Len's day.

Next morning, Len and Pam pick me up on their way ashore, and I glumly walk over to the outboard engine shop and talk to Charlie, the mechanic. After explaining the problem, I ask, "Do you have time to take a look?"

He responds, "Sure, but you can probably fix it." He then explains, "It's probably the kill switch. They frequently malfunction on Suzuki motors and you don't really need it because the engine can be stopped with the choke."

Leading me over to a nearby engine, he points to three wires near the handle and explains how to disconnect the live wire and secure it out of the way. He ends by saying, "If that doesn't work, bring the engine in."

Len again invites me to work on their foredeck but I hesitate, feeling like I've imposed too much already. But I don't want to work on the engine in the water either, so compromise and suggest, "I know you've got things to do, so why not get on with them. If you have time later on, call me on the radio and I'll row across."

Pam calls me on the VHF about 1600, and soon after the Suzuki is again sitting on their foredeck. It takes me only a couple of minutes to find the wires, disconnect the hot one, and wrap it with black electrical tape. We then lower the engine down to the dinghy. With some trepidation, I pull on the starter cord—*and it runs!*

I am so pleased to have it running again that I start going for rides just for fun. The dinghy becomes my new best friend. But after celebrating for a few days, the engine quits again, leaving me adrift in the middle of the bay. This time it's my own fault. I'd read in the manual that the fuel switch should be turned off when the engine wasn't in use, and I forgot to switch it back on. I then sit there, cursing my own stupidity and pulling on the starter cord.

I see a dinghy approaching, and when I recognize Len and Pam, I come crashing down from my high. I would have preferred to sit there all afternoon, rather than be rescued yet again. Len quickly points out, "You've flooded the engine, so hold the throttle open while you pull on the cord." I follow his instructions and the engine starts immediately, leaving me feeling even more inept.

Trying to hide my humiliation and embarrassment, I stammer, "You truly are a knight in shining armor, coming to my rescue once again." Regrettably, that is not a good thing to say to someone else's husband. Pam takes offense and that is the end of that relationship.

I now spend three days canning thirty-six jars of meat and vegetables, which is a long, tedious process. With Dave due back the following day, I sit back and look around the cabin, which sparkles almost as much as the outside did when we put the boat back in the water. I then remember the Velcro strips we'd bought for the settee cushions. Sewing one side to the cushion backs and screwing the opposing side into wood, my hope is that they stay in place during the next passage.

CHAPTER 24

The Second Season

Although still early in the cruising season, a few boats have already left for the tropics when Dave returns from Canada. Two days later, as we're making our final preparations, he breaks a tooth. The dentist tells him he needs a root canal and a crown, and his appointments span the month of May.

On May 2, we stand by and watch enviously as a small flotilla of twelve boats heads down the inlet. Several are back in port a few days later, establishing a pattern that continues all month. A few boats return from every group that leaves, and one yacht starts out five times. The problem is weather, with cyclones near Fiji and strong winds, or winds on the nose, closer to New Zealand. Boats with schedules to keep press on, but others see no reason to battle the seas.

Rumors circulate about the difficulties yachtees are encountering, with most reports coming from far away HAM networks. We start listening to a local Ham operator, Des at Russell Radio, as many boats leaving from Opua check in with him. We'd tuned him in a few times on our way to New Zealand, but only now, as regular listeners, do we come to appreciate his knowledge and commitment.

Des transmits twice a day, reading the area forecast and calling a roll. At his busiest, he speaks to more than forty boats and takes over an hour to go through the list. Many skippers, their voices strained, ask for advice, and with endless patience, he provides all the information he can. After reviewing their options, he always ends by saying, "The decision is yours." For a boat in difficulty, his voice is a lifeline, always reassuring but never sugarcoated. (Two years later, we have personal experience of that.)

When we tune in on May 9, boats had been battling 30-kt winds and rough seas for five days. Crews are tired, and I hear relief in voices reporting that winds have started to ease. The skipper of *Kemo Sabe* is one of those voices, but his day is about to be turned upside down. Des relays a message from Search and Rescue; they want him to go to the assistance of a yacht in trouble. An emergency locator beacon (EPIRB) went off that morning from a position 60 nm south of the yacht.

To the skipper's credit, he takes only a few minutes before agreeing to turn back. However, he stipulates that he will need a fuel drop, as the boat will be punching into wind and he'll have to motor. Many sailboats have small fuel tanks and lash jugs of fuel on deck to provide a margin of safety during a crossing, so his request is not surprising. At the end of the broadcast, Des confirms that authorities have agreed to a fuel drop, and *Kemo Sabe* turns around.

When the captain calls in twelve hours later, the boat has made maybe 30 nm. Des now relays another message; the promised fuel drop has been cancelled. We listen in shocked disbelief, and at the end of the conversation, the captain turns his boat around again. News of the cancelled fuel drop has Opua buzzing for days, as people try to learn what happened.

I find the whole business extremely disturbing. Just finding a boat in those seas at that distance would have been a challenge for us, and how much help would we have been? Rescues in rough seas were hazardous and we had no training. I have to wonder, *was a second boat put at risk with little chance of accomplishing anything?*

We learn the rest of the story when we meet George and Sarah on *Kemo Sabe* a few months later in Vanuatu. New Zealand authorities picked up an EPIRB signal from a location southwest of Fiji and sent up an aircraft. The crew located a sailboat and saw someone wave, but weren't able to determine whether help was needed. Authorities then contacted Russell Radio and asked Des to deliver a message.

When the emergency signal suddenly went silent the following morning, another aircraft was sent to the area. The crew dropped a VHF radio and spoke to the sailor, a single-hander. He was okay, but his boat had been knocked down and rolled. The rigging was damaged and his radio didn't work, but he had the engine running, which was why he switched off the EPIRB. He was on his way to Minerva Reefs.

Dave and I believed, as this sailor apparently did, that we were on our own at sea. That message had been reinforced during our crossing of the Pacific. HF weather broadcasts had occasionally concluded with a *Notice to Ships*, advising anyone near a given location to be on the lookout for a yacht in distress. We didn't think that message of much help, given how few ships we saw. (Although a high-tech racing boat did bring the Australian Navy steaming 1,500 nm into the Great Southern Ocean.)

We'd also faced the grim reality that neither of us would be able to rescue the other from rough seas. Privately we joked, only semi-humorously, about throwing a Canadian flag into the sea if such a thing happened. The longer we were on the boat, the more convinced we became that our safety depended on staying onboard in the first place. Anything else was a waste of time and money.

In the days that follow, reports continue to trickle in from far away cruisers' nets. One boat is abandoned and three crewmembers are airlifted to Fiji. Another boat loses its rudder and is making its way north under sail. An American boat named *Ora* goes up on North Minerva Reef and is lost, but yachtees anchored inside the lagoon rescue the crew. Two acts of piracy take place in Papua New Guinea. One involves an American yacht in the Louisiades; the other, a fishboat near Bougainville, where a man is killed.

Boats now begin making landfall, and Leo on *Valkyre* is the first. He checks in to Cairns, Australia, on May 15. Skip on *Wild Flower* reaches Hawaii five days later, and two boats arrive in Fiji the same day. This causes a flurry of activity in Opua, and Des adds at least thirty boats to Russell Radio's roster in the next three days.

When we're finally able to run a capacity test on the batteries, the results come in at 325 amps, nowhere near the 480-amp rating. The data we've submitted now produces results, and we go from talking to the dealer in Whangarei to the supplier in Auckland. The company agrees to replace the batteries, stating that they appear not to have been properly *formed* before being shipped.

Dave is now having second thoughts about the lead-acid batteries, as they produced a corrosive emission during the charging process that had set off the propane alarm in the engine compartment. He disconnected it, but worries about the effects of the emissions on GPS and EMON, both of which are closer. After re-studying our battery information, he decides to go back to the gels.

He waits until May 20 before placing a *For Sale* sign in the car window, then frets as the days go by with no inquiries. The cruisers he's talked to who've sold vehicles have taken a bath. He then receives one phone call, and that's all it takes. He gets $450 less than he paid for the car, which he thinks a fair price for six months use, and we're able to keep the car to the end of the month when he agrees to renew the Warrant of Fitness.

When beautiful fall weather settles over the Bay of Islands, we take *Windy Lady* out for three days. There isn't enough wind to sail, but we check our equipment and brush up on our anchoring skills. We then top up our supplies, and soon *Windy Lady's* lockers are bulging again. On the last day of the month, we make a day trip to Ninety Mile Beach, where we walk down the sands and watch waves roll in across the Tasman Sea from Australia. When we return to Opua, Dave turns the vehicle over to the new owner and heaves a sigh of relief as he pockets the cash.

We're now awaiting delivery of a weather fax from West Marine. I'd researched alternatives for getting weather at sea and decided that it provided the best solution. Dave had taken some convincing, however, and didn't order the unit until May 13. The shipment was then delayed two weeks, but we'd received a notice saying that it was shipped on May 30.

We're still monitoring Russell Radio, and as the anniversary of the Queen's Birthday Storm approaches, weather at sea deteriorates and so do tempers ashore. An overseas cruiser calls in while Des is reading the area forecast and tries to give his own weather briefing. The chap then breaks into the roll call, telling boats that a *bomb* is headed in their direction. Recalling how unsettling I'd found *Night Music's* advice the year before, I don't envy the boats at sea. When the weather improves a few days later and no *bomb* has developed, broadcasts return to normal.

The Safety Inspector comes aboard and pokes about for half an hour as he does the mandatory inspection required by New Zealand authorities. After asking many questions, he signs our report. The following day, we take delivery of 450 liters of diesel fuel and exchange the lead-acid batteries for two new gel-cells. Dave reprograms the EMON, then prepares a chart of *Do Not Exceed* charging rates for higher temperatures.

We're still waiting for the weather fax when the weather deteriorates, bringing NE winds, heavy overcast, and rain. Morning temperatures are down to fifteen degrees in the cabin, and heavy condensation covers the windows. The morning of June 11 is even colder, and Dave starts the furnace for the first time since leaving Canada. By noon, the temperature inside has risen six degrees, but it's still too dark to read.

Next morning, the sky is bright and sunny, and we hurriedly contact Doug at the boatyard and ask him to have the fax machine sent on to Fiji. We then move *Windy Lady* over to the Customs Dock. Soon, we're motoring down the channel for the last time, and as I study the picturesque inlet, I think of the people who'd touched our lives.

Colleen at the Post Office had been a treasure, providing information to newcomers with endless patience and good humor. Our landlords, Tony and Mary Watson, had welcomed us into their home, and while working on the dodger, Warren and Jillian Patterson had provided us with a different perspective on New Zealand. Contact with others had been briefer, but the memory of many kindnesses has endured.

CHAPTER 25

Passage to Fiji

We pull away from the dock at Opua just before noon on June 12, and two hours later are clear of the inlet with batteries fully charged. Suva and the island of Viti Levu lie 1,050 nm due north, but we expect SE trade winds to push us westward during the latter part of the voyage and will try to make some easting early on. We anticipate being at sea ten days.

Thankful that the long wait is over, I look around contentedly as we raise the sails. Conditions are close to perfect with a bright, sunny sky, SW winds of 12 kt, and a two-foot swell. Dave brings up the vivid, red sail for the hydrovane, and soon Otto is doing the steering, leaving us free to relax and soak up the sunshine. When the hills of the North Cape begin to fade on the horizon, I realize that I have no qualms this year about leaving land behind.

The temperature drops quickly as the sun nears the horizon, and we dig out our cruising suits for the night watches. By 2000, an icy SSW wind blows straight into the cabin, and for only the second time since leaving home, we close the companionway hatch. Dave sees the lights of two ships before midnight and tracks them on radar. One is 2 nm to starboard, the other 4 nm, and they're an hour apart.

Just after midnight, a slim, crescent moon slips down into the sea, and as its light fades, the heavens fill with brilliant stars. Winds stay steady at 10–15 kt overnight but veer to WSW. With clear skies, the morning brings a long, slow dawn, and by 0800, winds are down to 10 kt from the SW. We're now able to make some easting, and at noon log 124 nm for Day 1.

When winds back to SSE early that afternoon, we set the sails wing-on-wing, poling the headsail out to starboard and easing the main out to port. With 10–12 kt winds, *Windy Lady* then rolls comfortably through three-foot seas for hours. As night falls, southerly gusts of 15 kt begin to overpower Otto, so we reset the sails to their normal configuration.

Winds are steady at 10 kt for much of the night, and *Windy Lady* makes 5 kt in a two-foot swell. Our watches are long and cold, but the boat motion is so smooth that we should have been able to sleep. I can't; the exhilaration of being at sea hasn't yet worn off. The winds start moving with the sunrise, and by noon are gusting from the SSE at 10–20 kt and seas are about six-feet. We log 123 nm for Day 2 and make 59 nm of easting.

Unbeknownst to us, the winds now begin a journey around the compass. By mid-afternoon, they're coming from the east at 10–15 kt, and *Windy Lady* charges into five-foot swells on a beam reach. They gust up to 25 kt overnight, and we babysit Otto for twelve hours. Dawn brings overcast skies and a stormy sunrise, then the breeze drops. We run the engine for four hours to charge batteries, and at noon log 133 nm for Day 3.

We start sailing again with six-foot seas and east winds of 6-8 kt. Squalls bring 25-kt gusts and rain showers throughout the afternoon, and Otto needs help. By 2000, winds are steady at 15–20 kt and Otto is working flawlessly. At midnight, Dave writes in the journey log, "A sleigh ride, I didn't touch the helm once!"

The winds now move forward of the beam and 30-kt gusts from the NE send *Windy Lady* racing through a rainy, pitch-black night at six kt. Otto gives up entirely and we hand steer through the next two watches. By 0800, winds are gusting from 15–25 kt in rough, six-foot seas, and the boat has become hard to control. We put another two reefs in the mainsail and still make 25 nm during that watch. We log 142 nm for Day 4, but use up 37 nm of our easting.

When the winds take a breather that afternoon, Dave optimistically shakes two reefs out of the mainsail, but two hours later, ENE winds are gusting from 15–25 kt, and *Windy Lady* tosses and twists as she plunges into eight-foot swells. Soon, the windows are leaking again, dispersing saltwater throughout the cabin. We also close the thru-hull in the head, as seawater pushes through it, filling up the toilet bowl and spilling over the rim. A ship crosses in front of us at sunset, and I keep track of the lights for thirty minutes, catching sight of them only when we ride up on a swell.

We put a second reef in the main at 2000, which proves fortunate because winds are howling out of the NE at 20–30 kt before midnight. With *Windy Lady* beating into eight-foot seas, squall after squall then sweeps out of the darkness. The boat takes a pretty good pounding, and our watches are long, cold, and wet. By daybreak, we've lost all of our easting.

A few hours later, winds back to the NNE (025 degrees) and settle at 20–25 kt. With *Windy Lady* crashing into swells, the best I can now steer is 350 degrees. At noon, we log 124 nm for Day 5. I now have to admit that the hard dodger was one of Dave's better ideas. The roofline is still directly in my line of vision, which I'd objected to, but it keeps a lot of rain and spray out of the cockpit.

The sky grows darker as the afternoon progresses, and seas begin to ease. The wind dies an hour into my 1600-watch, then the clouds open up and rain pours down. When it stops an hour later, a 12-kt breeze rises out of the north, and with three-foot seas, I'm only able to steer 300 degrees.

Overnight, a squall line brings 20-kt winds from the NNE, with periods of rain, and we're now steering 320 degrees. We put in reefs and take them out, and occasionally, I catch a glimpse of the stars. We're both very tired, as it's impossible to rest with all the rocking, rolling, and banging going on.

At 0800, winds are steady at 20 kt with five-foot seas and Dave is concerned that we won't make Suva. By noon, winds are gusting from 20–30 kt in eight-foot seas, and he's talking darkly about making landfall in Vanuatu. We log 89 nm for Day 6 and are now 59 nm west of our course line.

The winds finally resume their journey that afternoon, backing to the NNW and settling at 20 kt. With hope renewed, we tack and turn to a heading of 045 degrees. Four hours later, winds are down to 12 kt. A warm front then passes overhead, bringing light rain and SW winds of 8 kt (a wind shift of 115 degrees), and *Windy Lady* now wallows uncomfortably in six-foot seas. We hand steer through the night, struggling to keep wind in the sails and the boat moving in the right direction.

Just after 0800, winds increase to 10–20 kt, blowing away the clouds and pushing up even rougher seas. We put a second reef in the mainsail and now Otto starts working again. At noon, we log 104 nm for Day 7 and have recovered much of the easting we'd lost.

Dave runs the engine for the next four hours to charge batteries, and when we start sailing again, winds are steady at 10 kt from the south. We set the sails wing-on-wing, and with a rolling three-foot sea, *Windy Lady* rocks gently from side to side as she cuts smoothly through the water at five kt.

During my watch that evening, I relax for the first time in days. Sitting in my usual rear seat, my body swaying with the motion of the boat, I listen to the soft swish of water washing against the hull and watch the sun slip down a cloudless sky and drop into the sea. Minutes later, a magnificent full moon peeks over the eastern horizon. It quickly climbs up into the night sky, and by 2000, moonlight reflecting off water has turned night into day.

Winds are steady at 10-15 kt throughout the night, but by the time we cross the Tropic of Capricorn (Latitude 22S) at 0400, seven-foot swells are pushing against the stern and Otto needs help. By daybreak, winds have backed to the SE, and Dave takes down the whisker pole and resets the sails.

The winds bring scattered clouds and warm, dry conditions, and two hours later, seas are easing. At noon, we log 117 nm for Day 8.

By 1600, winds have increased to 10–20 kt and seas are about five feet. Four hours later, winds are at 15–25 kt and seas are ten feet. By midnight, *Windy Lady* is tossing and twisting erratically in twelve-foot seas, and we put another reef in each sail. It's now a challenge to move about the boat, both inside and out, and we're mindful of the climber's rule, always keeping three secure points of contact.

The morning brings bright sunshine with a few scattered clouds, and by 0800, winds have backed from SE to E and are gusting from 10–25 kt. Seas are down to six feet but are still very rough. At 0850, we spot the southern-most headland on Kandavu Island, 40 nm away. It shows up as a lump, barely visible above the rough surface of the ocean, then slowly grows on the horizon. For Day 9, we log 128 nm.

Seas are then pushed up to ten feet by 30-kt gusts, and even with three reefs in each sail, *Windy Lady* crashes through the waves at 6 kt for the next four hours. When we turn into the lee of the island, I'm hopeful that the worst is over. Not wanting to arrive in Suva in the middle of the night, we now ease out the main and partially furl the jib, slowing the boat to 4 kt. Half an hour later, we're making 5.5 kt, so drop the mainsail and furl in all but three feet of the jib, again slowing the boat to 4 kt.

That works until midnight, when we emerge from the lee of the island and are hit by ESE winds gusting from 15–25 kt. We're soon making 6.5 kt in a seven-foot-high following sea. There's nothing I can do to slow the boat, as the little bit of headsail still up is needed to provide steerage. I concentrate on watching for traffic and keeping the boat in the center of the channel, well away from any reefs.

Winds are soon steady at 30–35 kt, and *Windy Lady* races through the water, surfing down southerly swells and rolling in easterly wind waves. Half an hour later, the winds finally start to ease, dropping to 15–25 kt, but the night is not yet over. Twice in the next three hours, a lull in the storm drops the winds below 10 kt, and I barely have control as *Windy Lady* wallows in the swells.

Dave starts the engine at 0400, as he wants the batteries fully charged when we arrive in harbor. We both keep watch on the way in and arrive off Suva just at daybreak; we're unbelievably tired, as we haven't slept in 24 hours. The rising sun streams into our eyes through a break in dark clouds sitting over the island, and unable to see directly ahead, we anxiously study the surrounding waters. Eventually, we spot the leads and follow them in through the reef. We drop the anchor at 0819 on Sunday, June 22. We'll be in quarantine until Customs opens next day.

After putting the boat to bed, we relax in the cockpit, relieved to be safe and secure in port. During our ten days at sea, we logged 1179 nm, for an average speed of 5 kt. Seas had been rough, which wasn't unexpected, but the weather hadn't warmed up until we were halfway across. I'd worn my winter underwear beneath my cruising suit and then under my raingear. I'd worn the raingear even when the rain stopped because of spray. The dodger had been well christened, and I have no doubt that the passage would have been most uncomfortable without it.

The following excerpt from Dave's personal journal best sums up his thoughts: "A year ago, I would have dreaded it and just wanted it to be over. Now it wasn't that bad. You put in your watch, do your chores, and try to get some sleep. There isn't the same concern over bad weather because you've had some and coped reasonably well. While it's a bit uncomfortable at times, you tell yourself that this too will end—and it does."

CHAPTER 26

A Month in Suva

Both tach and alternator quit working on our way into Suva harbor, but Dave is too tired to give them more than a cursory look. He worries though, as he's never considered the possibility of the alternator failing at sea. He now decides to go through the entire charging system as soon as he's had some rest. Next morning, he calls Customs on the radio, explains the problem, and is given permission to come alongside in the dinghy. That makes me happy, as I'd been stewing about bringing *Windy Lady* alongside another high wharf.

He's ashore for two hours, dealing with Health, Immigration, Customs, and Port Authority. The paperwork is endless, and he fills in forms in triplicate, with no carbon paper. When he returns, we dinghy over to the Royal Suva Yacht Club (RSYC), about a fifteen-minute ride away, and tie up at a small dock out front.

We climb up a few stairs into the grounds, and a minute later are in the clubroom, which appears to be a large, enclosed veranda. We'll spend considerable time here in the weeks to come, as the comfortable chairs and big, overhead fans make it a gathering spot for yachtees, a place to renew old friendships and make new ones over a jug of beer.

We buy club memberships at the office, which also provides mail and fax services, and pay $30/week for use of the dinghy dock, clubroom, laundry room, and ablution block. A restaurant and bar are also located on the premises. We then walk downtown, as we need some local currency. Thirty minutes later, we're in the busy financial district, where we track down an ATM with a cirrus logo.

With cash in hand, we continue on to the Port Authority office at King's Wharf and pay our port fees. Inadvertently, we leave the dock through a gate used by cruise ship passengers, and three Fijian men rush over to greet us effusively. We quickly explain that we're not off a ship, but no matter. Any tourist will do.

Shaking our hands, the men engage us in conversation, asking our names and where we're from. One of them shoves two carved masks into our hands, while the other two step back behind us. I just happen to glance over Dave's shoulder as one of them puts a small knife to a piece of wood now sticking out of the long, paper-wrapped package he carries. Turning away, I start screeching, "No! No! No!" and flee across the narrow, deserted lane. Dave is right behind me. The men are con artists and we'd read about them in our cruising guide. They carve your name into the handle of a wooden sword, then insist on payment, sometimes not very pleasantly.

Next day, after a good eight hours sleep, Dave digs out the information we'd accumulated on the charging system. After studying diagrams, he checks connections and performs self-tests, but finds only what might have been a loose field ground on the high-output 105-amp alternator. After carefully re-fastening the wire, he starts the engine and monitors the charge going into the batteries. Everything seems to be working normally, so we raise the anchor and leave the Quarantine Area.

We take a quick tour through the anchorage, looking for the right spot to call home, but the depth gauge quits working as we approach several catamarans at the head of the bay and *Windy Lady* runs aground. Fortunately, the bottom is soft mud and Dave has no problem backing her out into deeper water. Referring to a chart, we then drop the hook near a shoal just off the RSYC.

The weather in Suva is very pleasant. In fact, when I compare it to the heat and humidity in Hilo, or the cold temperatures in New Zealand, I find it pretty close to perfect. Rain showers are generally light, although one night I collect two buckets of water off the dodger roof. A layer of cloud sitting over the island seems to be responsible, as I feel the sun burning my arms when it infrequently finds a hole in the clouds.

We spend most of the first few days tending to business. The weather fax, which we thought would be waiting, hasn't arrived. Doug, at the boatyard in Opua, tells us that he hasn't seen it and offers to contact West Marine and have it sent directly to us. Our mail, which was supposed to have been airmailed from Canada ten days earlier, is also missing.

Dave contacts Signet in the US about the depth gauge and is told that it will have to be sent to them for assessment. That's a non-starter because the process would take a month, even using airmail, and we don't intend to be in Suva that long. He then contacts a marine store in Canada and orders a spare alternator, but when weeks pass without a word, we just forget about it.

He becomes thoroughly frustrated when trying to place an order for spare parts with Hydrovane in the UK. The fax won't go through, although he tries at different times over several days. He finally phones them, which requires dinghying ashore in the dark because of the twelve-hour time difference. After placing the order, he complains that he'd been unable to send a fax. The fellow at the other end just laughs and says, "Oh, we only have our machine on during office hours!"

We now start walking about the city, first following a narrow, paved road that winds along the shoreline from the RSYC. Within minutes, we pass a small prison, where we look curiously at any inmates that happen to be outside. After twenty minutes, we near the central bus terminal, where the warm air is heavy with the smell of diesel and exhaust fumes from all the taxis and buses on the road. Crossing through the terminal is an adventure on its own, with dozens of buses coming and going. They don't stop and don't signal, so it's necessary to watch them closely and move quickly.

After another ten minutes, we're downtown, where narrow streets curve along the shoreline, frequently changing name, and traffic moves so fast that I run across the intersections. We then branch inland, following streets that wind up and around low hills through older sections of the city. The narrow storefronts here are crammed together, sidewalks are crowded with pedestrians, and streets are chock-a-block with vehicles.

Native Fijians all smile and say hello when we meet them on the street. A few even call out "Boolah!" from across the road. If we pause uncertainly on a street corner, or look at a map, someone always stops and gives us directions, whether we want them or not. I find myself admiring the women, who are tall, well built, and confident, with thick, fuzzy hair standing out six inches from their scalps.

Dave discovers cabin crackers when we're checking out the stores and buys a 5-kg can, then develops a life-long passion for them. We happen to walk by a Cinema 6 theatre as people are entering, and when we learn that movies change frequently and prices are cheap, we become regular visitors.

The wet market is in a huge building near the bus terminal and is without doubt the most impressive market we see anywhere. Rows and rows of produce are piled high on tables that stretch down the main floor. Wandering through. we have our pick of bok choy, cabbage, tomatoes, chili peppers, green beans, carrots, eggs, coconuts, bananas, oranges, papaya, and pineapple.

Potatoes, onions, and other unusual items are sold in stalls on the upper floor, along with a huge variety of bulk spices. Many of the stalls also sell kava root, and a small kava bar occupies a corner. (The local drink is reputed to have a sedating effect.) At the back of the building are two small shops that sell fresh fish, and a roofed-over area with concrete floor, where locals sit with their catch of the day amid hordes of flies.

On Fridays and Saturdays, the market expands outside, taking over the sidewalks as well as a large open area down one side of the building. Tarps are strung overhead, and roots, leaves and other produce are piled high on pieces of cloth laid on the ground. Half the population of the city seems to come to shop. Fijian women look neat and clean in colorful, flowered shirts and dresses, and Indian women stand out like exotic birds in beautifully tinted saris.

One day, we find our way to a fascinating two-block area on Cumming Street. The shops here cater to the Indian population and several sell beautifully fashioned jewelry, much of it 22-carat gold. Some pieces are so finely crafted that they look to be spun gold. Other shops are draped with saris of varying styles and in such a rainbow of colors that I can't help but stop and admire them.

Outside, the crowds on the sidewalks ebb and flow around stalls that sell jewelry and watches, providing a kaleidoscope of color and sound that is irresistible. I try taking pictures but am not able to capture the essence of the hustle and bustle around me. I begin to suspect that it's the flashing eyes and generous smiles of dark-skinned faces, the gleaming ripple of muscle in arm or leg as passersby dodge one another that I find so fascinating.

Small, slim Indian men with straight black hair slip purposefully through the crowds, while their bushy-headed Fijian counterparts, clad in shirts and sulus, stop and chat, then amble on. Most of the Indian women wear saris, and a few Fijian women are in long skirts, but others wear western apparel, including fitted dresses and long pants. A few tourists, like me, sport shorts. Flitting around the edges are Fijian schoolgirls in uniforms that are probably intended to be shapeless, but actually highlight their slim bodies and young breasts.

I'm especially intrigued by the Indian women, their delicate features and dark skins accented by gold jewelry and the striking shades of their garments. Some are so small and fine boned that they appear fragile. When I come across some beautifully tinted saris, I'm tempted to buy one, but know intuitively that I could never wear it with the natural grace of those around me.

In early July, we refocus our attention on the RSYC, as a flurry of cruising boats arrives in port. Among the new arrivals are Tony (*Dandelion Days*), Del and Joanne (*Limbo*), Bill and Gail (*Bright Wing*), Charlie and Janette (*Quark*), and Ed and Fran (*Aka*). It's now impossible to walk through the clubroom without being caught up in discussions about equipment, cruising areas, or weather. It turns out that Ed has the expertise needed to fix our depth gauge, while we have the spare manual water pump that Tony needs. Charlie is the mechanic who showed me how to disconnect the kill switch at the outboard engine shop in Opua.

A few families also show up in the clubroom, and I'm finally able to satisfy my curiosity about kids on sailboats. They all seem healthy and reasonably well behaved, and one day I watch in admiration as several youngsters take turns shinnying four or five feet up a veranda post. It's apparent that life is life, however you live it, and these families just happen to live it on a boat.

One boat, *Three Daughters*, has four children onboard, with the youngest being a little boy, maybe four years old. He frequently seems to try his dad's patience because he can't stay away from a cat that hangs out near the clubhouse. In all fairness, I think the cat is as much to blame as the boy because I never see it except when the youngster comes ashore, and then it is front and center.

On our eighteenth day in Suva, the weather fax finally arrives, and we spend half a day following the tedious procedures necessary to claim it. First, we go to the Fed-Ex Customs Depot downtown and pick up the paperwork, which has to be taken to the Customs Office. After Customs have approved it, we return to the depot and pick up a large box, which we take to the Custom's

Boarding Officer at King's Wharf. The box is not that heavy, but awkward to carry, so Dave balances it on his shoulder as we parade through streets in the heat. The boarding officer checks our documents, ensuring the shipment is going onto an offshore boat, then signs the form, leaving us free to walk the mile back to the RSYC.

The next day, Dave secures the fax machine to the chart table and attaches a splitter to the HF antenna, so the signal can be directed to either the radio or the fax. I start listening to daily weather forecasts, then compare the information to the maps I'm able to print, learning how to interpret them.

The weather changes during the second week of July, when a mass of warm, humid air moves over the island. Sudden squalls bring clouds, rain showers, and gusty winds and a few boats drag their anchors. Strong southwest winds also push swells up into the harbor, causing boats to roll uncomfortably.

We now start working on maintenance. The car on the whisker pole track that runs up the mast broke during the crossing and has to be spot-welded, the head has developed a slow leak, and mold is growing on a few surfaces in the lockers. On a dry day, we clean the cabin windows, then run a bead of silicon around each one, both inside and out.

I regularly scrub down deck and cockpit, re-using the rinse water after washing clothes. The harbor is actually very dirty, with smoke and exhaust residue settling on the boat at night. One morning, there's also a layer of black grit from a freighter that offloaded a cargo of coal. Diesel spills are common too, and large pools of streaky water send fumes wafting into the cabin as they drift about with the tide.

One day, we make an hour-long hike across town to the Suva Museum. We now learn that, in traditional villages, men had started their day by attending a *yoqona ceremony*, where a priest drank kava and articulated messages from the gods. Men's bodies had carried many scars, most of them self-inflicted, and women's were heavily tattooed from waist to mid-thigh and around the mouth. I'm initially appalled by exhibits dealing with cannibalism, but something about the matter-of-fact style of their presentation manages to pique my curiosity. I then read about *human meals* and how they were prepared, and study the *cannibal forks* used to eat the brain.

The last exhibits turn out to be the most surprising, as we learn about a coup d'état that occurred in Fiji in 1987, some ten years before. One month after a general election, the prime minister and his entire cabinet were kidnapped during the opening session of parliament. We're stunned that such an event occurred in a country with a history of democratic governance similar to our own. Even more troubling is the fact that we'd never heard about it, although we both followed news broadcasts faithfully.

The unrest is said to date back over a century, to a time when the British brought laborers from India to work in the cane fields. Native Fijians were then protected from forced labor and only they could own land. But since then, the Indo-Fijian community had increased in numbers, wealth, and influence, and their success at the ballot box in the 1987 election is cited as the reason for the coup.

A new constitution that highly favored native Fijians was adopted in 1990; it mandated that the prime minister be one. Thousands of Indo-Fijians then left the country, even though government exchange controls limited their ability to take their wealth with them.

In fact, when we arrived in Suva, legislators were debating a constitutional amendment, one that was touted as creating more equality between the races. We now read in a newspaper that the bill has passed. Politicians are very pleased with themselves and busy congratulating each other. There is even talk of reapplying for membership in the British Commonwealth, as the country was forced to withdraw after the coup.

The editorials aren't reassuring, however. At least one claims the amendment will not change anything, that clauses appearing to address specific issues are overruled by clauses maintaining the status quo. Some residents bitterly claim the whole process is too confusing and bureaucratic, and that leaders are only interested in their own futures.

(When we return to Suva two years later, in August of 1999, continued political uncertainty has noticeably disrupted the tourism industry. Two more coups rock the country before the end of 2006, and it isn't until 2014 that the situation begins to stabilize. Reports indicate that the economic cost of the conflict was immense.)

CHAPTER 27

The Rains Come Down

As we approach the end of July, a big, black cloud settles over Suva and rain pours down endlessly. I collect buckets of water off the dodger roof and we bail out the dinghy two and three times a day. When I do laundry, clothes never dry outside, and I have things draped all over in the cabin. Sudden squalls cause boats to drag their anchors, and occasionally one runs afoul of a neighbor's anchor chain. Southwest winds then push swells in through the reef, causing *Windy Lady* to rock and roll for hours one night.

We defer trips ashore as the ride in can be miserably wet, and the return trip often worse. One afternoon, we sit in the clubroom for two hours, waiting for a deluge to ease. But we do like our fresh fruit and veggies and make an effort to get to the wet market. We also make a weekly trip with two 22-liter jugs to haul fresh water from the RSYC. We filled up the tank when we first arrived and that keeps it topped up.

When time starts to drag, we bake bread and cookies, trying to use up some of the supplies we brought from Canada. Otherwise, Dave keeps busy cleaning the bilge, monitoring batteries, or some other such chore. I start studying cruising routes through the islands and am reminded that malaria is endemic on some. We've decided not to take anti-malarial drugs because of the side effects reported by cruisers, so the next time we're ashore, we track down a dry goods store and buy yards of mosquito netting.

The only flat working space inside the boat is a small area on the salon floor, and working with all that material is a bit difficult, but I have my small portable sewing machine and figure things out as I go. Dave suggests using a bit of rope or bungee cord to hold them in place and that works well. We end up with voluminous seven-foot-long curtains for the companionway and two billowy hatch covers that successfully keep the mossies out as long as we're on the boat.

Eventually, the Hydrovane order arrives, as do two packets of mail, neither of which are the one we've been expecting. Dave phones our mail forwarding service in Canada and discovers that the first batch of mail was sent surface and will take at least two months to reach us. At that point, we decide to leave on the next sunny day.

We now obtain our Australian visas, which we need before entering that country, then purchase a cruising permit that covers most of Fiji. After clearing with Customs on August 1, we wait for weather. Two days later, the outboard engine dies and Dave can't fix it. Rowing ashore, he loads it into the trunk of a taxi and takes it to a dealer on the far side of town. Another two days go by.

When we're downtown on August 6, we run into Ken and Pat off *Iron Butterfly*. They were heading for Niue when they left New Zealand, and we now learn that headwinds caused them to divert to Tonga. Cyclone Kelly had limited their activities there, and then the crossing to Fiji was very rough. We don't see them the next day, as a storm with 40-kt winds tears through the anchorage, and the following morning, Ken has devastating news.

A yacht named *Camelot* was lost the previous day; it went up on a reef at the entrance to Bligh Water on the north side of the island. Apparently, the autopilot had been doing the steering and the boat was making 7 kt when it went aground. As seas were calm at the time, the skipper decided to wait for the tide to turn before attempting to refloat the boat. One of those fierce, fast-moving squalls found them first, and half an hour later, the boat started to break up. The crew, carrying little more than their passports, were taken aboard another cruising boat.

The clubroom is abuzz with the news when we stop by the RSYC. The report has a chilling effect on us all, a reminder of just how quickly life can change. We then find a message waiting from the marine store in Victoria; they shipped an alternator three days before. It's been six weeks since Dave talked to them, and when he checks the invoice, he lets out a roar that can be heard across the anchorage. It includes shipping charges of $336. Initially, he wants to send it back, but then realizes he'd be paying the same amount for the return freight. Besides, he really does want it.

We wait another four days for the alternator to arrive, then follow the same tedious procedures as before. This time, however, a guard challenges us as we enter the main gate at King's Wharf and asks to see our paperwork. We then continue on to the office, where the Boarding Officer signs our document. We leave through a different gate as it's closer to the RSYC and wave to the guard as we go by.

Two blocks down the road, a vehicle comes roaring up behind us, then cuts across the sidewalk in front of us. Two uniformed Customs officers jump out, demanding to see our parcel and paperwork, then check everything carefully. After exchanging a few words and shrugging their shoulders, they hand the stuff back, return to their vehicle, and drive away. Somewhat bemused, we assume that we should have checked with the guard when we left. Apparently, procedures have changed since our earlier visit.

Next morning, sunshine pokes through a few holes in the clouds. It is now August 13 and we've been in Suva seven weeks. In unspoken agreement, we go ashore to dispose of garbage and fill up water jugs, then prepare the boat for sea. When we can't raise the anchor, we don't think twice about using the weight of the boat to break it free. It's 1000 when we motor out through the reef, and we then head for Beqa Lagoon, 37 nm to the southwest. With unsettled weather in the forecast, we've decided to limit our sailing to the waters around the island of Viti Levu.

Although I'm expecting sunny skies with winds on the stern, seas are actually very rough and *Windy Lady* bounces about unpleasantly. Surf then pounds the reef on either side of Sulphur Pass when we enter the lagoon. With help from the GPS and a cruising guide, we make our way safely down to an anchorage on the west side of Yanuca Island. By 1600, we're anchored in calm waters near two other sailboats.

Glad to be out of the city, we relax in the cockpit, enjoying the tranquility of the lagoon as we watch the setting sun. The evening is extraordinary, with bright stars filling the sky and a warm breeze caressing our faces. By morning, however, swells are creeping in around the end of the island, causing the boat to roll.

We're underway at 0730, exiting the lagoon through a deep-water channel known as Yanuca Passage. With clear, sunny skies, the morning would have been perfect if only we'd had some wind. Staying two miles off the coast, we motor westward and manage to acquire decent sunburns before the clouds move in. At 1600, after traveling 44 nm, we anchor in Natadola Harbor.

I'm not happy with the anchorage right from the start, but it's too late in the day to go farther. The wide entrance opens to the southwest, and if the wind shifts, I figure the swells will push right up to the top. Rain starts to fall just after we go to bed, and by midnight, swells have reached us and the boat rolls from side to side. As the swells grow higher, the boat rolls farther, and we sleep less.

Next morning, the forecast is calling for winds of 30 kt by midday. Anxious to get underway, we're up on deck at first light, then stand in stunned silence. *Windy Lady* is enshrouded by low, grey cloud and rain, and not a foot of shoreline is visible. When the cloud begins to lift an hour later, we start the engine.

We're hit by 30-kt winds as we motor out the entrance, and high, rough seas then toss *Windy Lady* about like a toy. She rolls far over on her sides when we make the ninety-degree turn to the west, but settles down quickly once wind and waves are coming from behind. We stay a mile offshore for the next two hours, navigating through a grey, shadowy world, where clouds lift and re-settle on hillsides, and passing rain showers reduce visibility to zero.

The sky starts to lighten as we near Navula Passage, and with binoculars, I quickly spot the buoys marking the edge of the reef. The water calms as we enter the channel, but 25-kt winds follow us inside. We drop the hook at 1235 in a nearby, all-weather anchorage, finding good holding in eighteen feet of water. After a sleepless night and an anxious three-hour passage, I'm happy to be behind the barrier reef again.

We're now in the lee of the island and next morning set off on the three-hour trip to Musket Cove. With an overcast sky, we can't see into the dark waters, so cautiously motor around rocky shoals and small islands. We then miss the channel into the resort and have to plot our position on a chart. Retracing our route, we're able to identify Black Rocks, on the north side of the entrance.

Dave is at the helm and I keep watch at the bow as we start down the long, twisting channel into the resort. The route is well marked, but the dark waters on either side reveal no sign of what's beneath them. All goes well until the resort comes into view, then Dave unconsciously steers toward the boats he can see at anchor. I have to repeatedly warn him to keep to port.

He turns the helm slightly one last time, then sees the depth gauge shoot from sixty feet to forty and immediately corrects his course. But it's too late, the stern might be in forty feet of water but the bow is over the reef. I can clearly see the coral beneath my feet, and in my head hear the keel grinding harshly upon it. Luck is still with the captain, however; there is just enough water over the reef to keep the bow afloat.

Close to forty boats are squeezed into the small anchorage, but Dave finds a hole on one side and we drop the hook in fifty-five feet of water. We then winch the dinghy over the side and motor ashore. We run into our friends off *Limbo* on the beach, and after discussing the reefs we'd seen on the way in, or rather not seen, Del admits, "Yeah, we went up on one this morning. But it wasn't serious as another boat was nearby and pulled us off."

The afternoon is hot and muggy, and after wandering about the resort for a couple of hours, we return to *Windy Lady*. The barometer starts to drop as dark clouds move in, and the temperature inside the cabin is almost unbearable when we go to bed. The hatches are both wide open and we talk about closing them, but decide against it after Dave points out, "We're a boat, aren't we? A little water won't hurt us!"

He has cause to rethink that statement about midnight, when we wake up to the sound of rain drumming on the deck. Crawling from his berth, he goes forward to close the two hatches. I'm not far behind, and as he closes the one in the galley, I see the teak floor shining wetly. He then swears softly as he steps into ankle-deep water in the head. After closing that hatch, he gropes about on the floor and removes the plug to the holding tank, letting the water drain in. Meanwhile, I find a basin and start mopping up in the galley. Together, we wipe up four full basins.

Come morning, we wipe down the floors again, as well as the surrounding walls, but it takes two full days in a hot sun before the seat cushions dry out. The dinghy is full of water too, with seats awash and low waves threatening to run over the transom. According to the weather report, eleven inches of rain fell overnight.

The next few days are sunny, but winds are mostly strong, gusting from 20–25 kt. I spend a couple of hours the first day tracking the boat movements on the GPS, making sure the anchor isn't dragging. Dave sits in the cockpit and studies the cove as more and more shoals are exposed by an ebbing tide.

He finally shakes his head and wonders aloud, "How did we manage to find our way in through all that!"

We spend some time on the beach the following day, and Dave buys a membership in the Musket Cove Yacht Club. I think it's something he's wanted to do ever since reading that member and boat names were carved into the beams of the clubhouse. It's then a very wet ride back to *Windy Lady*, with winds hitting 30 kt.

The next day brings a respite from the wind, and we put on our snorkeling gear and swim over to a nearby reef. There's not much to see, as the tide is high and sand is still suspended in the water. Next morning, the winds are back, and by noon, half the boats in the anchorage have moved on.

We leave for Lautoka the next day, and with the sun high and bright, it's easy to see the shallow water lying over the reefs that line the narrow, winding passageway. When again in the lee of the island, we set the autopilot and motor through calm, blue waters, relaxing in warm sunshine and enjoying the views of white sandy beaches and palm-clad islands.

Four hours later, the wind picks up as we enter Lautoka harbor, making it difficult to anchor. A mud flat extending out from the dock also makes for a long dinghy ride ashore. Next morning, *Windy Lady* rolls in swells pushed up by a 20-kt wind, and when we go on deck to let out more anchor chain, I look about in disbelief. The top of the boat is completely covered with a layer of black soot from the sugar mill, so I start the day by scrubbing the cockpit.

We dinghy ashore about midday, the wind making for a wet ride, then check out a nearby marina, which is under receivership. The facilities are in tough shape but the toilets work, and Dave is able to find a telephone. He calls the yacht club in Suva and learns that our missing mail has arrived, so arranges for them to forward it. A couple of days later, we pick it up downtown. There is absolutely nothing of interest in it.

We walk into town on each of the five days we're here, passing through a small village on the way in. We then wander up and down streets for hours, but never see a big smile or hear a cheerful, "Boolah!" At first, I think that's because the city is a modern industrial town, with many people working in the sugar mill and newer stores that are large and impersonal. But everybody on the sidewalk seems to be preoccupied, and we start to wonder whether racial tensions are closer to the surface here.

The winds bring another ten boats into harbor, making a total of twenty-three. We visit with some of the newcomers on the deck at the marina and learn that stormy conditions in the outer anchorages had limited their activities for much of the season. We then stroll through the adjacent hardstand, where a few people work on boats. Other boats rest on the grass, their keels hidden in holes in the ground, giving new meaning to the term *hurricane hole*.

We had hoped to visit the Yasawa Islands in the far west of Fiji, but given the winds, there doesn't seem much point. As we're running out of things to do, and cruising boats are starting to depart for Vanuatu, we decide to move on also. We clear with Customs and Immigration and depart the following day.

CHAPTER 28

Passage to Vanuatu

The morning is clear and bright when we raise the anchor at 0800 on August 27, and it seems like a good day to start a passage. We're not anticipating any difficulties on the 542-nm crossing to Port Vila. We'll be heading due west, with SE trade winds on or abaft the beam, and expect to be at sea for five days.

We start off by motoring for four hours through sheltered waters to Malolo Passage, the westernmost pass through the barrier reef. With the autopilot doing the steering, Dave and I relax in the cockpit, enjoying each other's company while we have the chance. When *Windy Lady* suddenly veers off to starboard, I jump up and grab the helm, while Dave goes below to check the autopilot. It's malfunctioned a time or two before and taken the boat in a large circle. We don't know why. He sees nothing obviously wrong now, but fiddles with the controls and it starts working again.

A light breeze ruffles the water's surface when we stop near the pass to raise mainsail and staysail. Dave then steers *Windy Lady* toward the entrance, and I sit on a cockpit bench, admiring the view of sparkling surf breaking outside. Seconds later, all hell breaks loose. I guess we leave the lee of the island as we motor through the pass because *Windy Lady* is suddenly tossed in all directions by rough, five-foot-high waves, while the sails are pummeled by 15—25 kt southerly winds.

Dave has his hands full trying to keep the helm under control until we're far enough off the entrance to safely turn the bow on route. We then pull out the headsail and shut down the engine, but *Windy Lady* continues to crash through the humps and hollows in the water in front of us, and Otto doesn't even try to work.

This is our introduction to reinforced trade winds, which move between south and southeast at 25—30 kt for much of the passage. They are accompanied by a SE swell that surges relentlessly against the port quarter and grows to heights we've never before seen. As we are heading due west, these forces conspire to turn the bow southward and overwhelm Otto.

When I come on watch at 1600, I stand at the helm and hand steer, trying to adapt to this new reality. Dave then pokes his head out the companionway and calmly announces, "The GPS isn't working and I don't know what's wrong with it."

Staring at him in disbelief, I respond icily, "In that case, I think we should turn around and go back to Lautoka and get it repaired. I don't want to start a voyage with a sick GPS!"

He turns away without answering, leaving me scowling as very black thoughts flash through my head. *We follow the GPS blindly when at sea! How will we ever find a small island in that vast ocean without it?*

Half an hour later, he pokes his head outside again and says with forced cheerfulness, "The GPS is working now, so everything's going to be fine." Of course, he knows that I know that in spite of whatever he's been doing, he has no idea why it quit, or why it started working again.

Even with the new hard dodger, we wear our foul-weather gear on watch that night, as so much spray is thrown into the cockpit. We then don't get any sleep, as the boat movements are rough and erratic, but I probably wouldn't have slept anyway, I'm much too worried about the GPS.

By morning, Windy Lady is making 7 kt in 30-kt winds. She charges across the ocean, rolling, pitching, and twisting, sometimes quite viciously. It's now essential to hang onto the boat when moving even a few feet. But, on the bright side, the windows aren't leaking, and I'm also too busy steering during my 0800 watch to do much worrying. At noon, after 24 hours at sea, we log 150 nm for Day 1.

I don't even try to sleep that afternoon, instead sit in a rear cockpit seat with my legs braced to hold myself in place. Dave stands at the helm, hand steering, and scowls in the direction of a sailboat about a half mile to port. The boat is *Limbo*, with Del and Joanne aboard. They came through the reef an hour behind us and have been slowly gaining ground ever since.

The other boat moves constantly in relation to *Windy Lady*, sometimes it's off the bow, sometimes it's abaft the beam on the port side, or it can be anywhere in between. It's just a visible indication of the twisting and turning that *Windy Lady* is doing in extremely rough six-foot seas. We smooth out a little of the roughness by putting a second reef in the mainsail at change of watch at 1600, although that slows the boat a bit, to Dave's chagrin.

By nightfall, winds have backed to the SSE and dropped to 25 kt, but waves now grow higher and are over eight feet when Dave takes the watch at 2000. In spite of all my pillows, I can't sleep, as the berth continuously rolls and bounces beneath me. I then have to force myself to get up at midnight and ache all over from the constant twisting and jolting of the boat. I guess Dave feels much the same because when I step into the cockpit, he immediately starts below. He then turns and tells me, "The GPS quit working two hours ago."

Standing at the helm, trying to hold the bow on course, I stare out into the darkness and bleakly wonder how we will ever find our way into Port Vila. But now that I've calmed down and am able to think about it, the answer is simple. Thanks to Dave's decision to maintain a journey log, we have a starting point.

Our last recorded position was made two hours before the GPS quit working. Since then, we've steered a course of 270 degrees, and the Signet log has measured the distance the boat traveled through the water. We also have pilot charts that show the average speed and direction of currents in the area. The only unknown is the effect of swell pushing against the port quarter, and I figure that's a minor problem.

Before long, I've convinced myself that it won't be that difficult, and as my confidence returns, I look forward to the challenge. Feeling quite cheerful, I even tell myself, *if we happen to miss Vanuatu, we're bound to run into Australia.*

Dave, meanwhile, lies awake in his berth; he's also thinking about the GPS, but his thoughts are a little more practical. He'd performed a self-test earlier that indicated an internal problem. But when he entered a new waypoint, the unit had recalculated course and distance, suggesting the antenna was the problem. The more he thinks about it, the more convinced he is that the unit isn't picking up satellite signals.

So, when the sky brightens during his 0400 watch, he takes a closer look at the small, mushroom antenna clamped onto the push pit rail. Wondering whether it could have moved, he releases the clamp, repositions the unit, and re-secures it. When he checks the monitor a few minutes later, the screen is lit up brightly, showing boat position, as well as distance and course to destination.

When I come on watch at 0800, there is good news all around. The GPS is not only working, but for the first time, winds are down to 20 kt. Otto is even trying to steer the boat, although still needs help. As the sky is clear, I decide to make a serious attempt at taking a sun shot at noon and ask Dave if he'll come on watch half an hour early. I want to see how close I can come to our GPS position.

By mid-morning, seas have grown to eleven feet, and the boat is bouncing around so much that I'm wondering whether there's any point in bringing up the sextant. But when Dave shows up as agreed, I feel obliged to try. The first challenge is finding a place to stand where I won't have to hang on, as I need both hands to manipulate the sextant. With the deck heaving and rolling, there's only one possible spot, and that's forward of the binnacle along the centerline of the boat. By leaning back against it and bracing my legs, I can absorb the movement of the deck with my knees, giving me a fairly stable base.

Raising the sextant to my eye, I adjust the various settings and use the mirrors to bring the sun down to the horizon. The first readings vary far more than normal, and it takes me a few minutes to realize that the rolling motion of high swells in the distance actually causes the horizon to move up and down. I take a few more readings, trying to compensate for that problem, and then the sun disappears behind a cloud. I stop to change the lens, and just as I raise the sextant again, a wave rears up behind me and dumps half-a-bucket of saltwater over my head. I manage to keep the sextant dry, but admit defeat. The sun is almost at its zenith and I've run out of time.

We log 141 nm for Day 2 and after plotting our noon position, I check the stats for the ten-hour period we were without the GPS. The Signet log reveals that the boat traveled 60 nm through the water, but according to the GPS, we covered 66 nm over the ground. So, currents were stronger than the .5 kt/hr shown on the chart. We also drifted a mile south of our course line, which doesn't surprise me. But even with two days to go, I'm confident we could have found our way into port.

By midafternoon, winds are gusting over 30 kt for up to ten minutes at a stretch, making it ever more difficult to stay on course. At 1600, when I take the watch, we estimate swells to be twelve feet high. These aren't the long swells that we saw on route to New Zealand, but small mountains of water that loom high over the port quarter, then surge beneath the hull, causing the deck to roll and pitch beneath our feet.

I'm uncomfortable standing with my back to them, so steer from the other side of the wheel, looking out over the stern. Its just as easy, and I can then study the line of swells rolling toward the boat from the southeast. As I watch, the swells grow higher and higher, until I actually feel intimidated. I try to estimate their size by comparing them to the dodger roof and radar mast, and my best guess is twenty feet. After half-an-hour, these huge swells gradually begin to subside. By the end of my watch at 2000, the swells are back down to twelve feet, but I've furled in most of the headsail.

Winds back to the SE about midnight and settle at 20-30 kt for the rest of the night. Seas now begin to ease, and by 0400, swells are down to eight feet and Otto is making efforts to steer the boat. Four hours later, swells are down to five feet and Dave has shaken three reefs out of the headsail. At noon, the breeze is steady from the SE at 15–20 kt, and we log 127 nm for Day 3.

The winds remain at 15–20 kt, with occasional gusts to 25 kt, during the last twenty-four hours into Port Vila. Seas are over six feet for about eight hours during the night, and we again hand steer. When Dave relieves me at 0400, we are right on course and expect to be in sight of land by daybreak. As we want two sets of eyes on watch going into harbour, I stay in the cockpit.

As the sky begins to lighten, I search for signs of land, but see only waves stretching to the horizon. My first thought is that the GPS had failed again, which wouldn't have surprised me in the least. A few hours later, the southeast corner of Efaté Island comes into view; it's low and flat, with only the treetops showing above the horizon. As usual, we motor the last few hours into port, charging batteries.

Dave contacts Port Vila Radio about 1000, giving them an ETA of 1200. Immediately after, *Limbo* comes up, advising they've just anchored. Once in harbor, we notice inconsistencies between the chart and the GPS, and when I plot our GPS position on the chart, it shows us on land. The chart it turns out is in error by almost two miles in both latitude and longitude.

We anchor a fair distance from the dinghy dock, as many cruising boats are crowded around it, then flake the mainsail and wipe up some of the salt spray in the cockpit while we wait for the authorities. They're busy clearing in new arrivals, even though it's Sunday. Customs give us 30-day visas, while

Agriculture takes the few vegetables we have, leaving only a couple of onions. After the officials are done, we finish putting the boat to bed.

We arrive in Port Vila at noon on August 31, having logged 564 nm in 100 hours, for an average speed of 5.6 kt. Strong, gusty winds and lumpy seas tied us to the helm for most of the crossing and prevented us from sleeping when off watch. Although the first three days had been warm and sunny, we wore our foul-weather jackets because of the amount of spray thrown into the cockpit. At night, we pulled on long pants and I wore a sweater, as the temperature dropped after sunset.

After supper that night, Dave fiddles with his transistor radio while I relax with a book. He can only pick up one station and it is in French. As he plays with the dial, we hear the words *Princess Diana* and *morté*. We can't understand anything else, but those words are repeated constantly. Obviously, something significant has happened.

CHAPTER 29

Port Vila and Efaté Island

When we walk through downtown Port Vila next morning, the street is very quiet. I peer inside a few of the restaurants and bars as we pass and see native staff members standing in front of TV sets. Entering a facility called the Office Bar, we sit near one of three large-screen TVs tuned to CNN and learn of the car crash in Paris that took the life of Diana, the Princess of Wales.

The coverage continues for days and Ni-Vanuatu, as local people are called, spend their lunch hours watching CNN, seemingly mesmerized by a story that is repeated over and over. I find it strange that they are so absorbed by the death of a woman they couldn't have known much about. When I read that the islanders only gained their independence in 1980, I find their reactions even more unsettling; it's almost as if they'd been re-colonized.

We later learn that people in cities around the world responded in much the same fashion. The only connection seemed to be the international media, whose stories had captured the hearts and minds of millions of people.

The 82 small islands that make up Vanuatu have a long history of isolation. They are spread out over 700 nm of open water, so were isolated even from one another. The inhabitants originally spoke 113 different dialects, and on larger islands, villagers living on one side couldn't speak to neighbors on the other side. That only started to change in the late 1800s, when laborers from Vanuatu and other Melanesian countries were working in sugarcane plantations in Australia and Fiji. They developed a pidgin language known as Bislama, which is now the second language of the majority of Ni-Vanuatu.

The first Europeans to visit the islands were the Portuguese; they landed in 1606 but didn't stay. In 1768, De Bougainville claimed the northern islands for France, and in 1774, Captain Cook claimed the southern ones for England, naming them the New Hebrides. Each country then ruled using its own language and customs, and missionary schools taught one of the languages to their students. (When the country became independent in 1980, it recognized three official languages, French, English, and Bislama.)

In 1906, Britain and France agreed to manage the islands jointly through the British-French Condominium, which formalized the duplication of all government services, except for a joint court. As Canadians, Dave and I lived with our own French-English tug-of-war for years, including a divisive national referendum only five years before. We can't begin to imagine the bureaucratic nonsense that must have existed under this administration, but hear it described as pandemonium.

As a result, we have a natural empathy for the islanders, and our interest in the country differs somewhat from other cruisers. Most visit dive sites or relive events of WW II, and a few head for traditional villages where unique customs have developed. We tend to simply be curious about how people live.

When we start exploring the city, the first thing I notice are the flowers, which are blooming everywhere. I recognize hibiscus, bougainvillea, and frangipani (plumeria), and the fragrance of the latter follows us up and down streets. We've soon located a supermarket and then the wet market, which occupies a large, open-sided building. Piles of coconuts, roots, and leaves are set out on long tables, but vegetables are scarce. Several varieties of lap-lap are for sale (food wrapped in leaves and cooked in an underground oven).

Vanuatu became a tax haven in the early 1970's, and the financial center in Port Vila is located in the middle of the tourist area. At least, women work at computer terminals in several small offices beside the souvenir shops, restaurants, and travel agencies. Not far away, villagers sit on the ground alongside the main thoroughfare, with trinkets and shells displayed on dirty sheets of cloth in front of them.

Women are far more visible in government offices than was the case in either Fiji or Tonga. They aren't just supporting jobs either, as one issues our inter-island cruising permit. When we run into a Kiwi with a charter boat, he explains that only Ni-Vanuatu can work in the country. Non-native people have to apply for permits, which are only approved if local people can't do the work.

In general, Ni-Vanuatu are slimmer and shorter than Fijians, with the tight woolly hair and broad noses of SE Asia (Melanesian). The women wear knee-length, shift-style dresses with short sleeves, lace trim on the front, and foot-long ribbons flying off the shoulders. Some people wear flip-flops, others are barefoot; some meet my eyes and smile, others simply walk blindly past.

Even as we explore the city, *Windy Lady* remains our first priority and we inspect her from top to bottom on our first full day in port. The bilge pump is coming on three or four times a day, and Dave traces the leak to the rudder-stock, which comes through the hull beneath the port berth. We drag the mattress into the salon, and after removing the cover over the access port, he finds that both the inner nut and locking nut on the rudderstock are loose.

I dig out the large wrenches, but as soon as he sees them, he knows he has another problem. The long handles will be difficult to use in the confined space of the access port. Not saying a word, he just sets to work, but soon a steady stream of loud, ill-tempered cursing is turning the air blue. I hide out in the galley, as there's nothing I can do to help. His frustrated ranting goes on for an hour, only stopping after he's made the last turn on the lock nut.

We haul fresh water from shore in order to wash the salt from our foul weather gear, as well as from deck and cockpit, and he replaces the Racor fuel filter, which is filled with black gunk dislodged from the bottoms of the fuel tanks. He also cobbles together a light for the cockpit, as we happened to anchor near a traffic lane, which we only realize when a large vessel squeezes between us and two other sailboats after dark. Putting together the light doesn't take long, but the electrical outlet in the cockpit is badly corroded and he patiently spends hours reaming it out. The effort is worth it because the light also makes it easier to find *Windy Lady* on a dark night.

Toward the end of the first week, Dave runs into Del and Joanne (*Limbo*) during an early morning visit to the wet market. They invite us to join them on a day trip to Cascades Waterfall, a local attraction not far from the city. While the day starts off warm and sunny, clouds are building in the sky when we meet them at the bus stop. We're then too busy visiting to pay attention to business and fail to confirm the fare when we board the small van. It's too late to argue when the driver overcharges us at the other end. He demands even more to return and pick us up, so Del tells him not to bother; we'll find our own way back.

We now see two men standing at a kiosk near the trailhead and are told that we have to pay to hike the trail. That's not something we're used to doing, but it becomes a little more palatable when one of the men offers to come with us. Robert looks to be in his early twenties and is taller than Dave, with a muscular build, very dark skin, and a mat of black, curly hair covering his head and jaw.

Speaking softly in English, Robert informs us that we'll follow a stream up the mountainside and cross it numerous times. When we arrive at the first crossing, Del, Joanne, and I remove our shoes, then carry them. As Dave has on sandals, he just wades across. The stream is about thirty feet wide, the water ankle deep, and rocks on the bottom are smooth and slippery.

We follow a winding dirt path through the jungle, then come out on the bank of a large pool. A curtain of water spills over limestone rocks on the lower side, and we cross near the edge, where the current has washed away the mud.

There are four such pools along the trail, complete with freshwater fish, and water spilling from them drops between eight and twelve feet.

A gentle rain begins to fall as we climb and turns into a downpour lasting half an hour. Robert cuts off large, broad leaves to use as makeshift umbrellas, but mine barely keeps my glasses dry. Intermittent showers then continue for another two hours. Fortunately, being wet in this climate isn't a problem.

Robert identifies pineapple and mango plants growing beside the trail, then grapefruit and banana trees. He also points to water taro plants as we go by a spring. Farther on, he climbs a palm tree and cuts down three drinking nuts; slashing the end off one, he hands it to Dave for the four of us to share. He cleans up the other two and later gives them to us to take home.

The source of the stream is a spring that gushes out of rock on the mountaintop, and from the last pool, we're able to see several waterfalls high above, leaping off the top of a cliff face. Falling in long, lacy veils, the water drops onto an outcropping of rock, then tumbles down in long cascades to a deep ravine, where it pools and overflows. It's a gorgeous spot, and I have trouble tearing my eyes away as I wade across the edge of the pool.

We follow the streambed for another ten minutes, then climb up steps scoured into the rock, pushing against the rush of water spilling down. Savouring the moment, we stop and take pictures of the spectacular scenery. Having thoroughly enjoyed the climb up, I reluctantly turn back when the others start down the trail.

In no time at all, we are crossing the stream for the last time. We then sit, putting on our shoes, and watch as small groups of villagers emerge from the jungle and wade across in front of us. They've been foraging in the forest and carry wood, leaves, and roots. One group includes three women and half-a-dozen young children, while the older kids appear in twos and threes and seem to be on their own.

After saying goodbye to Robert at the trailhead, we walk down the road towards the sea. We soon came to a black-sand beach with a beautiful view of an island resort; I take note, thinking it could be good spot to anchor. The rain ends as we approach a bus stop, and after a brief wait, we board a bus, paying only a normal fare for the ride back to town.

It turns out that Del and Dave are both curious about kava, the local drink, so the four of us visit a kava bar next day. A cab driver downtown directs us toward the lower level of a modern-looking building, where we enter a large, bare room. Kitchen-type chairs are placed in a row across the long back wall and down the two end walls. A small bar is located on one side of the entranceway, and a low, narrow sandbox stretches down the base of the wall on the other.

A few men sit in the corner opposite the bar, so Joanne and I sat down on chairs in the middle of the back wall, while Del and Dave stand. As we take in our surroundings, one of the men gets up, walks over to the counter, and hands over 100 vatu (about $1 US). Picking up his drink, he strolls over to the sandbox, stands for a moment facing the wall, then downs the contents and immediately spits into the sand. Returning his glass to the bar, he takes a swig from a water bottle and spits again. A few minutes later, another man gets up and repeats the routine.

When I see the bartender swishing the glasses back and forth in a tub of water, I decide to pass on this experience. I've already learned that my system doesn't tolerate local bugs very well. I believe that Joanne has one drink, Dave four, and Del has even more. He tests his reflexes after each one, saying that he doesn't feel a thing. Dave describes the drink as tasting like chemically treated wood, and later adds that his lips feel numb.

Del and Joanne return to the dinghy dock before us, as we have some shopping to do, and we don't see what happens next. I understand, however, that Joanne has trouble getting Del into the dinghy and back onboard *Limbo*. He reportedly stays pretty close to the settee the following day.

During the bus ride back to town, I confessed to Joanne that small ants had taken over the boat and were driving me crazy. They had a trail across the back of the settee and sometimes ran over my hand, arm, or even the back of my neck. We figured they came aboard with the stock of bananas that Vaha gave us in Tonga and then multiplied over the winter. She now leaves a small bottle of some product in our dinghy, and it quickly brings them under control. (It might have eliminated them altogether, but I suspect the cockroaches that came aboard in Australia also played a role.)

A steady stream of cruising boats passes through Port Vila, with most staying only a day or two before setting off for other islands. It is here that we meet George and Sarah off *Kemo Sabe* and learn more about the aborted fuel drop. We also meet Don and Mimi off *Silver Cloud;* they rescued the crew from *Camelot* when it was lost on the reef off Viti Levu. Don tells us that a Kiwi boat from the Bay of Islands, *Rock Steady*, was also lost on a reef at Black Rocks, near Musket Cove.

CHAPTER 30

Vanuatu's Chain of Islands

U nlike Fiji and Tonga, the islands of Vanuatu do not lie behind a barrier reef. They are volcanic in origin and are scattered across open water in a Y-shaped archipelago. We need a cruising guide to safely navigate the waters, as all we know about the country is that it has many active volcanoes and malaria is endemic in coastal areas. We can't find one anywhere. Other cruisers have similar problems, and those with charts and guides are soon sharing them. The local print shop is then kept busy making photocopies.

After obtaining the necessary cruising permit, we leave Port Villa at 1100 on a Tuesday morning, crossing the large bay on which the city is located, then following the coastline around to the west and north. We motor-sail, charging batteries, and five hours later enter Havannah Harbor, on the island's north side.

This large, sheltered bay was a staging point for US forces during WW II, and as we cross it, I try to picture what it then looked and sounded like. My imagination fails. We see only a single sailboat anchored on the far side as we motor through calm waters to the eastern end, where we anchor in a small cove.

After we've put the boat to bed, I stay at the bow, soaking up the quiet solitude as lengthening shadows spread across the water. The early night sky then fills with stars, and soon a half-moon climbs up out of the sea. The air is cool, reminding me of late summer evenings at a lake near home, and I wouldn't have been surprised to hear the call of a loon. But the silence is broken only briefly by sounds carried on the wind; the distant putter of an engine, the faint cry of a human voice. The three nights we spend here are gorgeous.

While eating breakfast in the galley next morning, we hear the soft murmur of voices and rush up on deck. A dugout canoe carrying a man, woman, and two small children sits just off the port lifelines. The man greets Dave and wants to trade fresh vegetables for tinned meat or fish. He doesn't have any vegetables but promises to bring some next day. Looking at the small family, Dave decides to risk a can of corned beef—and we never see them again.

An hour or so later, some twelve to fifteen canoes cross the bay, and about half of them stop to check us out. One is paddled by a young man whose loud singing arrives long before he does. They live on nearby Moso Island and are crossing to the main island to tend gardens located beyond the mangroves.

The young men stop again on their journey home that afternoon, and a youth hits Dave up for a liter of petrol. He refuses as we carry only what we need for the dinghy. Another youth sits in his canoe a few feet off the starboard rail and chats comfortably with Dave, seeming to be in no rush. His name is John; he's twenty-one years old, unmarried, and invites us to visit his garden.

More canoes visit next morning, but most stop only briefly. John lingers on, however, then asks if he can see inside *Windy Lady*. When Dave gives permission, he calls to two of his mates, who quickly paddle over. Tying their dugouts to the toe rail, the three men climb over the lifelines. Dave takes them below and answers their questions, then they return to the cockpit and climb back into their own boats.

John repeats his invitation to visit his garden, and we made a quick decision to go with them, doubting that we'd find it on our own. Dave rows the dinghy ashore, tying it up in the shade of the mangroves near a sturdy-looking outrigger canoe. John has already started down a well-defined trail into the jungle, followed by a young man named Alex. Dave and I quickly fall into line, and two more youths bring up the rear.

Keeping to an easy pace, we follow a path that winds through sun-drenched grasses and beneath shady trees. The four men carry machetes, and I watch as John swings his blade up and slashes at certain trees along the trail, noticing that his mates do likewise. Watching the blades flash in the sunlight, I am reminded that the ancestors of these young men had eaten *long pig*, they'd been cannibals. And it's not hard to picture a man tied to a pole slung over the shoulders of natives following this very same trail. Telling myself that was a long time ago, I quickly re-focus on the countryside. Actually, it wasn't that long ago, as the last recorded cannibal feast in Vanuatu was held on the island of Malakula in 1969.

We walk for about twenty minutes, passing several intersecting trails, and eventually arrive at a large clearing in the jungle. Family members, including three women and six older children, are already at work, but stop and come over to visit and have their pictures taken. John, meanwhile, proudly shows off their crops, from huge heads of cabbage to a pile of ripening tomatoes, as well as lettuce, corn, green peppers, and yams. He explains that most of the vegetables are cash crops that they take to market in Port Vila on a weekly basis; they also grow bananas and papayas for their own use.

As we walk around the garden, he tells us that villagers initially burnt off the bush, then dug up the soil with shovels. Crops are replanted in the same area each year, except for yams, which are relocated every second season. Individual family members are responsible for their own plots of ground and hand-water the young plants until they're big enough to make it on their own. For much of the year, they draw fresh water from a narrow well, about eight feet deep, dug beside a small stream nearby. In the dry season, they catch a bit of rainwater but haul drinking and cooking water from a stream farther around the harbour.

Feeling privileged to have spent the morning with this family, we reluctantly say goodbye and leave them to their chores. Carrying a few tomatoes, lettuce and a yam, we find our own way back to the harbour. That night, John asks for some fishhooks and swivels as he paddles by on his way home.

Next morning, a clear, bright sky beckons us onward. and we have the anchor up before 0800. I stay at the bow as we motor across to a pass called Little Entrance, taking a long, last look at the quiet beauty of the harbour. The water in the pass is clear, with a minimum depth of thirty-five feet, and then we're outside, surrounded by quiet waters that sparkle under a bright, sunny sky.

After raising the sails, we steer NNW, and powered by a 15-kt breeze from the NE, *Windy Lady* cuts smoothly through the water. We pass near an active volcano on Nguna Island, but see no sign of steam above the cone. When we leave the lee of Efaté Island, winds veer to the SE, bringing whitecaps and swell for over an hour, but with Otto doing the steering, we're free to relax and enjoy a sparkling day. Six hours later, four dolphins escort us into Sesake Bay, an open roadstead off Emai Island, where a high, steep volcano rises into the sky on the western end.

We drop the anchor in 25 feet of water about a quarter mile off the island, and I study the beach through binoculars but see no sign of a village. I then sit and soak up the incredible view, but before long, my musings are disturbed as *Windy Lady* starts to roll slowly from side to side. The low swell creeping in from the channel grows higher overnight, and the rolling becomes much worse, waking us frequently. Dave then has to gimbal the stove to cook breakfast.

At 0730, we're out on deck raising the mainsail, then pull up the anchor, pull out the headsail, and are sailing. It's a beautiful morning with winds below

10 kt. Farther out in the channel, winds increase to 10–15 kt, bringing some cloud and a few whitecaps. By mid-morning, a line of squalls is passing behind us, sweeping across the sea from the west. I watch, fascinated, as storms swallow up islands for thirty minutes at a time and then move on. The islands emerge from the mist like in a dream, and the sky again fills with sunshine.

The breeze is up and down throughout the day and Otto handles it all, but I prefer to stand at the helm and hand steer during my watch. The sea flattens out when we draw into the lee of Epi Island, and after sailing for eight hours, we drop the hook in the picture-postcard setting of Lamen Bay. Noticing that the three sailboats already anchored are rolling noticeably, we tuck in as close to shore as possible. As we relax in the cockpit, enjoying the last hour of the day, Dave points to a number of outrigger canoes that are just visible in the dusk; they are crossing the channel to Lamen Island.

Our rest is disturbed for a second night by swells rolling the boat, and we again gimbal the stove to cook breakfast. We go ashore a few hours later and are caught by surprise when a three-foot-high surf tosses the dinghy about roughly, then dumps us abruptly onto a black-sand beach. Leaving the dinghy well up on shore, we stroll down the beach, which curves around a large bay.

The day is sunny and warm, with a gentle breeze stirring the air, and it's really very pleasant. The surf roils the water out for about twenty feet, and before we reach the end of the beach, a steep, 10-foot-high bank of white coral rubble blocks our path. Seeing a similar pile across the bay, we assume that it washed up out of the sea.

Circling inland, we cross a flat, grassy meadow that we recognize as an airstrip only after Dave picks up a discarded boarding pass. We see no one in the village on the other side, so continue on to a restaurant sitting off on its own near the beach. It's closed, so we have to be satisfied with admiring the immaculate grounds, which include a tree fern carving and a tam-tam (slit drum).

We then walk in the direction of a large building visible in the distance, and before long see half a dozen figures crossing a field towards us. We stop and wait, watching as the figures turn into young women, probably in their mid-teens. Fortunately for us, they speak English and we're able to satisfy each other's curiosity. They want to know about our travels and where we're from, then explain that they are students. The large building is a high school, or more accurately, a boarding school.

Some 150 young people attend the school, many of them coming from the Shepherd Islands to the southeast. After completing a four-year program, students earn a grade ten certificate. Impressed by their fluent English, we ask them what other languages they speak. Each first learned the language of her village, then Bislama, followed by English, and now a little French. At which point, Dave interjects, "Parlez-vous francais?" Something about his accent seems to tickle their funny bones because they all laugh delightedly.

Having thoroughly enjoyed our visit with these young people, we return to the beach. The swells are now higher, but we have no problem launching the dinghy into the surf. Coming alongside *Windy Lady* is another story, however, as she's rolling wildly. After studying her movements, Dave positions the dinghy so that I can grab the bottom rung of the rope ladder when the hull rolls toward us. I hang onto it as the hull rolls back, which pulls us in. When it starts toward us again, I launch myself up the ladder while pushing the dinghy away. I take the end of the painter with me, and once on board pull in the dinghy and Dave makes the crossing.

Limbo, with Del and Joanne onboard, are now anchored nearby, and when we later dinghy across to visit with them, the rolling has eased. But it returns, and after a third sleepless night, we decide to move on. I regret not having seen the resident dugong, but the early morning appearance of a large sea turtle more than makes up for it. The turtle swims in amongst the six anchored boats, rolling over onto its back and splashing about with large flippers.

The day is quite stormy, and with winds behind us, we sail up a wide channel between the islands using only the headsail. SE winds of 10 kt increase to 15 kt about midday, and a halo of clouds hides the top of the active volcano on Lopevi Island when we pass. We each take a turn at the helm during the six-hour crossing to Ambrym Island, and enjoy the day so much that we go by the next anchorage and have to turn back into gusty 25-kt headwinds.

The anchorage at Craig Cove is just a slight indentation in the shoreline, so we tuck into shore as close as possible, anchoring in forty feet of water. I suspect we're in for another bumpy night, but wake only twice when the boat rolls sharply. The shoreline here looks rather dreary, with dark jungle creeping out to meet black lava rocks that are scattered across the beach.

Not long after we arrive, a leaky outrigger canoe holding five young lads eases up beside *Windy Lady*. The boys are maybe fourteen to sixteen years old, and one of them bails constantly. They speak French. While Dave remembers a few words of his high-school French, I've forgotten all of mine. Our feeble attempts at conversation go no where, but one of the boys has enough English to sell Dave two papayas. Dave also gathers that there are no tomatoes because of new lava. The boys then sit alongside for the longest time, not even speaking amongst themselves.

When they leave, a smaller dugout canoe appears carrying three young girls. They're probably about the same age as the boys, and one holds a year-old baby on her lap. They also speak French and we sit looking helplessly at one another until they return to shore.

The next morning brings clear, sunny skies, with strong winds that again have white horses leaping out in the channel. We're anchored so close to shore that I monitor the GPS for a couple of hours, just to make sure we're not moving. While studying the shoreline through binoculars, I see a woman dump a basket of waste over the rocks at the water's edge.

We dinghy ashore just after midday, stumbling over lava rocks and across black sand as we carry the dinghy up from the beach. A cloud of flies buzzes annoyingly around our bare legs, rising from the garbage strewn about I assume. We now join forces with an Australian couple, who are also ashore; Bill and Judy anchored *Hacienda* nearby that morning.

We follow a dirt track towards buildings half hidden in the trees and soon enter a long, roughly finished structure displaying a Co-Op sign. A wide variety of goods are on the shelves, with a luggage set prominently displayed, which I find curious. About 20% of the space is allocated to soft drinks and liquor. The few small homes in the nearby village have neatly maintained grounds, thatched roofs, and woven-mat walls. A swarm of pre-school kids wander about, as do a few chickens, and several men load sacks of copra into a battered pickup truck.

I assume the women and older children are foraging in the jungle or tending bush gardens. There is no evidence of a school, so students probably have to leave home to obtain an education. I then spot three pickup trucks driving away from the village, each with several men sitting in the back. Earlier, I'd noticed a man in a small powerboat leaving the bay, but am starting to wonder what men do to keep themselves occupied.

We leave Ambrym Island the next day, and I feel depressed as I watch the shoreline recede. These young people seem trapped. I tell myself that maybe I'm wrong, maybe I'm over-reacting because we weren't able to talk to them. I then remember the girl in the canoe with the baby, and a wave of sadness sweeps over me. I saw her and the child loitering in the store, then later in the village, and assumed it was hers. I also recall the shelves of pop and liquor in the store and wonder who buys it.

From radio reports, we'd learned that the government's attempt to develop the economies of the outer islands ended in the early 1990's, when copra prices crashed. We also heard that some families could no longer afford to send their children to school. Ever since first hearing about government policies that made subsistent farmers dependent on cash crops, I'd wondered about the wisdom of it. *What happened if the programs didn't succeed? How did people survive? And now, what kind of life would their children have without an education?*

The teenagers we'd met the day before, sitting silently in their canoes, had been such a stark contrast to the girls on Epi Island, whose faces had glowed with confidence. But even those young women would have to leave their villages for larger centers, like Santo and Port Vila. *So, what would happen to the traditions and support systems of those small villages? Would they ultimately be lost? And where would that leave the next generation?*

CHAPTER 31

Malakula

With sunny skies and sparkling blue waters, the day is incredibly beautiful as we cross to the island of Malakula. We motor sail, as we're heading into southerly winds. Three hours later, we're approaching the entrance to the harbor at Port Sandwich and pay special attention to a shallow reef extending out on one side. Too much as it turns out because we almost run aground on the other side.

After entering the large, protected bay, we see a high, wooden dock with the word *SHARK* painted in large red letters across the front. Pretty sure that it's a warning, I lose all interest in going in the water. We drop the anchor at 1320, and for the first time in nearly a week, *Windy Lady* sits quietly.

We dinghy ashore, then walk down a narrow dirt track into the jungle. According to our guide book, it leads to the coastal village of Lamap. Alongside the road, the tall, slender trunks and green, leafy tops of coconut palms sway gracefully in a light breeze. Debris beneath them has been piled and burned, leaving only small circles of ash, and every so often, a sheet-metal-roofed copra dryer sits deserted. A few cows graze near the road, and we occasionally walk by an individual home, then come to a small village. The grounds around the homes are neat and clean and decorated with colorful shrubs, some bear flowers and others have variegated leaves.

When we return to the beach where we left the dinghy, a slim, middle-aged woman is working nearby. She responds to Dave's greeting in English, which is a relief, as we'd read that people in that area spoke French. A child about eighteen months old plays fitfully beside her, his small, naked body covered with sores that look a lot like chicken pox. She tells us that he's had a "slow" fever.

The woman's name is Mary and she lives in a metal-clad shed that sits about three feet from a copra dryer near the wharf. The shed is small, with one door and no windows, and she shares it with her husband, child, and an older woman. When Dave asks about fresh vegetables, she tells us she'll bring tomatoes and cucumbers the next day, so I assume she has a bush garden. I later notice that she spends all her time working outdoors.

As usual, I sit outside at sunset, enjoying the quiet serenity of the bay as light fades from the sky. An outrigger canoe now emerges from the shadows, and as it draws closer, the paddler calls out a greeting and asks if I speak French. When I confess that I don't, he continues in English. Coming alongside, he asks where we're from, and we talk for maybe ten minutes, mostly about the voyage from Canada.

I look at him closely, and decide he's maybe thirty years old. He wears red knee-length shorts and sits on a board placed across the gunnels of a very narrow dugout canoe with legs and feet jammed together inside. He sculls constantly with his paddle, causing muscles to ripple across his arms and chest, and as we talk, his deep laugh peals out freely, seeming to float across the water.

He's a very impressive individual, in both manner and appearance, and I find his laughter intriguing. But when I tentatively ask permission to take a picture, he just shakes his head. After he disappears into the deep shadows that have settled over the bay, I sit and wonder about his education, his obvious fitness, and especially his joie de vivre. *How did this man fit into a subsistence existence in Port Sandwich?*

Later, well after dark, I decide it's safe to take a sponge bath in the cockpit, so undress and start washing my hair. As I wipe the soap from my eyes, I hear a male voice call out a greeting and ask, "You want lemon?" Sinking to the floor, I crouch down behind the cowling and return the greeting as graciously as I can, adding "No, thank you."

We spend the following morning doing chores, and when we go ashore at midday, Mary and two other women are sitting on the grass under the trees. Beside them is a pile of bananas split in half lengthwise, and the women chat as they scrape out the pulp and throw it into a big pot. A large pile of folded leaves sits on the grass nearby, and Mary explains that they will wrap the pulp in the leaves and bake it underground. A fourth woman arrives at that point and says they are making lap-lap, or island pudding.

We set off down the dirt track once more, passing more coconut palm plantations, a men's meetinghouse guarded by two tree-fern carvings, and a sheet-metal-covered kava bar with pole benches inside. When we pass through a second village, we stop to take pictures of several children and their mothers.

At an unmarked fork in the road, we stay to the right, and after walking another half mile, we hear a man's voice call out. Turning in the direction of the sound, we see a native man working at a copra dryer about 100 feet off the road. As we walk beneath the coconut palms towards him, I see the blue haze of smoke rising up against green leaves, and then orange-red tongues of flame darting out below. The man cheerfully hollers again, "If you're going to Lamap, you've taken the wrong road."

Laughing wryly, Dave admits that we are, but shows an interest in the dryer operation and the chap seems happy to talk. Continuing to tend the fire, he explains that the coconuts are collected and husked after they fall from the trees. The nuts are split in half, exposing the white meat inside, and placed on a drying rack above the fire. (Thirty coconuts provide about ten pounds of copra, which is the source of coconut oil.)

The fellow, who is fairly husky and looks to be about thirty, now asks, "Are you thirsty?" He then quickly climbs thirty feet up the slender trunk of a nearby coconut palm and knocks down several green drinking nuts. After shinnying back down, he skilfully trims the end of one with a machete, then slashes straight across it with one cut, leaving an opening about an inch and a half in diameter from which to drink. He presents it to Dave and then prepares one for me. I'm in awe all the while, admiring both his physical dexterity and his skill with a machete.

We backtrack to the fork in the road, take the left one, and are soon in the old townsite of Lamap. The town was the center of French Administration on the island, so has been vacant since 1980. We now study shabby-looking buildings as we wander down streets in the process of being reclaimed by nature.

Eventually, we come to a large grassy area beneath a huge banyan tree, where a long, narrow boardwalk leads to a small building set back in the shade. At the entrance to the walkway, faces have been painted on two twisted pieces of driftwood, apparently identifying it as a kava bar. Continuing on, we arrive at a cliff top that overlooks a broad reef running along the shore and provides magnificent views out over the channel towards Ambrym Island.

As we hike back to Port Sandwich, we start meeting women returning from their bush gardens. Sometimes a woman is alone, sometimes two or three are together, and we come across several resting in the shade beside the road. They are loaded down with coconuts and/or corn, leaves, roots, and chunks of wood that they carry in dirty pieces of material thrown over their shoulders. One woman also carries a shovel. I now recall meeting a few women the day before when we returned from our walk.

I ponder over my impression that men and women live quite separate lives. The women seem to be away from the village most of the day, tending gardens or foraging in the bush, while men are most noticeable sitting in the backs of pickup trucks. They obviously look after the copra crop and probably fish, although we don't see much evidence of that.

Mary has fresh cucumbers, tomatoes, and a papaya waiting for us when we reach the harbour. Dave rows out to the boat and brings back two cans of corned beef for her. As things go, that is probably too much, but we have no use for the canned meat and feel the fresh vegetables are worth it.

Not long after we return to *Windy Lady*, we're visited by another canoe paddled by a young man. He also speaks English and tells us that he is picking up his wife, who spent the day working in her garden. His dugout canoe looks more finished than others I'd seen, with wooden strips added to the sides, raising the gunnels. What really catches my eye, however, is his paddle, it's a perfect teardrop in shape and nicely tapered.

Friday morning brings strong southerly winds, and we are content to spend the day onboard. We discuss moving to an anchorage eight miles away, as it's supposed to be safe for swimming, but I've heard several reports of shark attacks that season and am just not interested. Then, shortly after midday, a small inter-island freighter pokes its bow into the harbour and ties up at the dock.

For the next four hours, we watch a flurry of activity ashore, and some of my questions about what men do are answered. A crew of maybe a dozen men offload various bales and barrels, toting them from the deck of the freighter down the gangplank to the end of the dock. The goods are then loaded into the back of a pickup truck. When piled high, it disappears into the jungle, and a trailer pulled by a farm tractor takes its place. The two vehicles alternate about every thirty minutes until the supplies are gone. The ship's crew then loads sacks of copra and cacao, as well as empty barrels that wait nearby. (Cacao pods grow on small tropical trees, and according to Mary, are used in making both chocolate and coca cola.)

We are still sitting in the cockpit when an outrigger canoe appears out of the lengthening shadows. This time the paddler is a fairly small man with grey in his hair and not too many teeth. He's soon standing in his canoe, gripping the toe rail with one hand and talking to Dave. I have to wonder whether he stands in an effort to bring the level of his head closer to ours, which I'd read was a concern in some cultures. He also ignores me when I ask questions, making me suspect that I'm being rude.

He seems inclined to stay and talk to Dave, however, telling him that he has five children and the eldest lives in Port Vila. When Dave remarks on the fact that he speaks English, he nods and gravely states, "Yes, I live on the far side of the harbor and am Presbyterian." He goes on to explain that the people living on this side are "Catholics Roman", so do not.

With the shadows now deepening, he waves his hand toward a 5-gallon plastic jug in the bow of the canoe, and says that he is on his way to the freighter to get kerosene. I watch as he paddles over to the wharf, and a few minutes later see him climb back into his canoe and disappear into the night.

The freighter departs at 0530 next morning, passing close to *Windy Lady* on its way out. Disturbed by the throbbing of the diesel engine, as well as flashing lights and a bow wave that rocks the boat, we get up, make coffee and mull over our plans. The forecast calls for sunshine and southerly winds of 20 kt, but we believe they could easily strengthen. Deciding to return to Port Vila, we make plans for an overnight passage, as we'll be pushing into headwinds and want to cover the distance as quickly as possible.

CHAPTER 32

Port Vila Again

We're out on deck at 0730, lifting the anchor, and as the chain rattles aboard, I see Mary and another woman watching from shore. Minutes later, Dave is turning the bow toward the harbor entrance and I'm waving goodbye. After clearing through the entrance channel, we raise the sails, putting two reefs in the main.

We now sail east, and with 10–12 kt winds on the beam, the sailing is superb for two hours, then 25-kt gusts begin overpowering Otto. An hour later, we've cleared a point of land to the south, so tack and turn the bow southward. *Windy Lady* now plunges into lumpy eight-foot seas pushed up by 20-kt winds from the SE. The waves soon grow higher, and she starts falling off them. Each time she does, the bow smacks loudly against the water and a shudder runs through the entire boat.

Conditions ease for a while when we pass through the lee of an island, but then get worse. By 2000, 25-kt winds have pushed up ten-foot seas, and *Windy Lady* now hits the water so hard when falling off a wave that I feel the shudder in my own core. We reduce sail, lowering boat speed, but seas remain extremely rough overnight. We don't get any sleep, and the GPS quits working at 0200.

At 0430, we're nearing the western side of Efate Island. Seas are now twelve feet high and the wind is strengthening, so Dave starts the engine. We then inch along at 2.5 kt as winds hit 30 kt. At first light, we're nearing the SW corner of the island, but track too close to shore rounding the point into Mele Bay. Huge waves hit *Windy Lady* on the beam, pounding her brutally and rolling her over so far that I'm sure the higher waves hit the masthead. All we can do is hang on, while everything that isn't nailed down goes flying.

I don't know how long it takes to clear the maelstrom off the point, but two hours will pass before seas are noticeably calmer. We drop the hook in the harbour at Port Vila at 1100 hours, having logged 262 nm in fifty-six hours of local sailing. I am bone weary and ache all over, but sleep isn't an option. A layer of salt residue and dust coats everything inside the cabin, and while Dave checks equipment, I spend the afternoon cleaning. Next day, we turn in our cruising permit to Customs.

We now start on the repairs that need to be done before we leave for New Caledonia. The headsail has a small tear, so we find a sailmaker and drop off the sail. Dave looks for a service center for the GPS but can't find one, so orders a hand-held unit from West Marine. (We discussed buying one in New Zealand but procrastinated, and now pay $50 for a phone call, $60 for airfreight, and $150 for the unit, all in US funds, of course).

During the week we wait for it to be delivered, Dave locates a marine electronics store and takes the mushroom antenna in for testing. It checks out okay, but takes a long time to acquire satellite signals when he reinstalls it. After he's made numerous trips back to the shop, the tech makes a trip out to the boat and discovers that the pin inside the fitting on the end of the antenna cable is making only intermittent contact. He figures that someone or something must have yanked on the cable. While he doesn't have a replacement part, he is able to repair it.

We now learn that dancers from northern Ambrym Island are bringing their *Rom Dance* to Port Vila. The dance is normally performed in August, as part of an all-male, grade-taking ceremony on the island. Traditionally, the lives of men were governed by a hierarchy consisting of more than thirty grades. As best we can determine, a man rose through the ranks by holding parties and giving away all his wealth. Rumor has it that it was women's work that created the wealth.

The venue is within easy walking distance, and we pay an entrance fee of 1,000 vatu each (about $10 US). That gives us access to a wide, grassy field at the Chiefs' Nakuma and allows us to take still pictures. (It's 3,000 vatu for a video camera.) After strolling about the field, we stop near handicraft stalls where two pigs are tethered beneath the trees. The smaller pig is apparently the price paid for using the facilities that afternoon. These animals are highly valued in traditional culture, and a boar's tooth is a status symbol. One that makes a complete circle identifies the wearer as a chief.

Dave now turns to the woodcarvings on display, and as he examines them, more tourists crowd in around us. Deciding to get out of their way, I turn around and come face-to-face with a naked black man standing about a foot behind me. The man is slim, not much taller than I am, and wears only a penis cover. Totally discombobulated, I cast a desperate look for Dave but he's now hidden by a wall of people. I manage to slip out through the crowd, then wait off to the side, where I see several similarly dressed performers moving nonchalantly amongst the tourists.

Spectators now settle themselves around the edge of the field, and the performance begins with the beat of a tam tam (slit drum). A tight circle of dancers shuffles forward, accompanied by the chanting of male voices. At first glance, the performers look like moving haystacks, as their bodies, arms, and legs are hidden by costumes made from the long, dried leaves of banana plants. I then see the elaborate painted masks covering their faces, and the tall, bearded headdresses concealing their heads and hair.

Stamping their feet, the dancers move slowly out into the field, and a rattling sound comes from the long, funnel-shaped wands they carry. They spread out as they move forward, revealing a second group of men hidden in their midst. These men are the singers and they now dance forward, one of them keeping time by knocking two sticks together.

The singers are naked except for penis wrappers, which are attach to belts that encircle their waists. A few have leafy twigs hanging down their buttocks. The lead dancer, an older man with grey hair and beard, carries a spear and wears a boar's tooth bracelet on each wrist. A third tooth forming a complete circle hangs from his neck. (I took his picture earlier and he'd closed his eyes as he posed.)

After a time, the singers withdraw from the field and the masked dancers are again the center of attention. Whirling fiendishly across the grass, they shake their rattles vigorously to the beat of the tam tam. As their costumes rustle ever louder, bits of leaves fall onto the grass, where they're picked up by an errant breeze and sent dancing through the air with a life of their own.

The eerie, otherworldly quality of the scene now has my own scalp tingling, but the spell is broken by a flash of red shorts as a dancer twirls. Soon after, I notice a pair of Nike running shoes on the feet of another performer. It then becomes apparent that some of the dancers don't know the routine, as a couple of older men watching from the sidelines push them into position.

After about an hour, the focus shifts from the dancers to the larger of the two pigs we'd seen earlier. Using a long tether attached to a front foot, one man drags it out onto the field. A second man then approaches, and with one swift, powerful motion swings a club back, up, and down. I don't see or hear the club strike but close my eyes when the pig's squeals ring out across the field. The squeals continue as three different men strike it numerous times on the skull, then it falls silent.

Each dancer now comes forward and touches the body with the end of his wand. They then spread out across the field, sweeping away any spirits that might have lingered after the dance. Traditionally, costumes were destroyed after a performance, as it was feared they might retain the energy of the spirits represented by the dancers. But I've been shaken by the ritual killing of the pig, and my interest in the performance has fled. As people leave the field, everyone seems unnaturally quiet.

We return to the handicraft stalls, where the vendors have slashed their prices. Dave quickly makes a deal for a heavy, three-foot-long hardwood slit drum with a beautifully carved head. While carrying it back to the boat, he tells me about a native man who stood beside him for part of the performance. The man had turned toward him and casually observed, "Not that long ago, you'd have been lunch!"

I now study charts, pilots, and tide tables, preparing for the crossing to New Caledonia. We also discuss route planning beyond Australia, and with the British lease in Hong Kong soon to expire, we wonder whether policy changes will affect cruising boats. As the Chinese Consulate is within easy walking distance, we stop and inquire. It's not a question the Consul is used to, but he assures us that it will be business as usual, with the only obvious change being a new Governor. Our thirty-day visas then expire and we renew them for another month.

The day the GPS arrives, we clear with Customs and Immigration. The following morning, we go ashore for a few last-minute purchases and run into a couple who tell us that they've just returned to port after attempted the crossing. They assure us that they'd never turned back before, but strong headwinds and rough seas were more than they could stomach. Next morning, boats at sea are still reporting strong headwinds.

CHAPTER 33

New Caledonia

The crossing from Port Vila to New Caledonia takes us through a pass in the Loyalty Islands. In order to reach it, we need to maintain an average heading of 195 degrees for 48 hours, which won't be easy. We'll be beating into reinforced SE trade winds and expect the boat will be pushed westward. We then want to be at a waypoint off Havannah Pass at first light on Day 3, so we can go through the barrier reef on a flood tide. If all goes well, we'll be in Noumea that afternoon.

We have two reefs in the mainsail when we leave Port Vila on the morning of October 5, and within minutes, *Windy Lady* is beating into 20-kt winds from the SE. Charging into six-foot seas at 5 kt, she rolls, twists, and bobs, all at the same time, and right from the start, we drift westward. Three hours later, just after midday, the winds ease for a bit, then veer to the SSE and increase to 25 kt. She now crashes into waves at 6 kt. Her movements grow increasingly violent, and at 2000, we reduce sail, lowering boat speed by a knot.

By midnight, winds are up to 30 kt, and we're drifting off course at a rate of one mile/hour. At 0400, we tack and Dave sails east for four hours; he makes 15 nm of easting, but we're then 5 nm farther from our destination. When we turn back on course, conditions are extremely rough, with winds from the SSE at 20-25 kt and seas up to ten feet. *Windy Lady* careens into the waves at 5.5 kt, causing waves to wash over the bow and spray to fly high over deck and cockpit. It's hard on both boat and crew. At noon, we log 117 nm for Day 1.

Seas ease a bit during Dave's afternoon watch, then 30-kt gusts from the SE again push up ten-foot swells. Having drifted west once more, we tack at 1600 and sail east for another four hours. Before the end of that watch, I see the lights of a ship bobbing about on the horizon, and Dave tracks it on radar for thirty minutes as it passes 5 nm astern. When we turn back on course at 2000, we've again gained 15 nm of easting and lost 5 nm to our destination.

Sea conditions that evening are the roughest we ever experience. Dave is thrown across the galley as he's preparing supper and ends up sprawled on a bench at the table with a paring knife in his hand. It's my turn a few hours later, when I'm standing at the chart table filling in the journey log. The boat lurches violently, breaking my grip on the grab rail, and I fly backwards, do a back flip over the coffee table, and end up on the settee.

Sometime around midnight, the winds back a few degrees and drop to 20 kt. We take a reef out of the headsail, and as seas grow quieter, manage to get some sleep. When I come on watch at 0800, the seas sparkles beneath a bright, sunny sky, waves are down to three feet, and the sailing is superb. We log 116 nm for Day 2.

We arrive off Lifou, in the Loyalty Islands, just after midday and are through the island chain well before dark. With quieter seas, *Windy Lady* is now making 6 kt, and by midnight, we're trying to slow her down as we don't want to arrive at the entrance to Havannah Pass before daylight. I'm quite happy to do so, as I'm a little uneasy racing through reef-strewn waters in the dark, even if those reefs have flashing lights.

We reach our waypoint off Havannah Pass at 0612 and enter just after low tide, with the sun not yet over the horizon. The channel is notorious for cross currents and hidden shoals, but we're coming in under power at the best time. Still, my stomach knots up when currents cause the boat to slew sideways, then a rain squall reduces visibility to zero for forty-five minutes.

After steering us safely through, Dave sets the autopilot and we motor for the last eight hours, following GPS waypoints around islands and reefs for 40 nm into Noumea.

When we tie up at the marina at 1400, our rhumb line route of 320 nm has stretched to 382 nm. While the passage was difficult, the gorgeous, sunny skies and brilliant, star-filled nights were extraordinary. A pair of dolphins accompanied us briefly when we came in through the reef, reminding me of how little sea life we'd seen that season.

I stay on deck, cleaning up, while waiting for the Customs Officer to arrive. When I see him walking down the dock towards me, I can't help but notice the large handgun on his hip. He then stops beside *Windy Lady*, and I greet him with a cheery, "Bon jour!"

Beaming, he responds in kind and adds, "Parlez-vous francais?" When I shake my head and say that I don't, he grows visibly excited and exclaims, "But you are Canadian, surely you much speak French!" As I continue to shake my head, he mutters, "You should be ashamed! You are Canadian and don't speak French!"

After that exchange, the officer refuses to speak to us. He climbs aboard *Windy Lady* and stands beside Dave, rudely thrusting papers under his nose and pointing to whatever needs to be signed. When he has to ask a question, he uses such poor English that I can't understand a word. Fortunately, Dave is familiar with the routine and knows what is required. When the officer leaves, the Immigration and Agriculture Officers come onboard; he was white and they're both natives. Neither of them speak English, and while surprised that we don't speak French, at least they're not offended.

Our American cousins tell us that they have no problems dealing with the authorities, but we go through the same routine when we check out. It seems that in the international world of French-speaking countries, officials believe that Canadians speak French. I assume that's because the federal government promotes our country as being francophone, although less than 25% of citizens acknowledge French as their mother tongue.

The next day, we set off to explore Noumea, and as usual, our first stop is the wet market. I'm actually stunned by the contrast to Port Vila, where native people sat on the floor or ground beside piles of roots and coconuts, and oranges had just started to flood the market. Here, the tables are piled high with fresh fruits and vegetables, and there's also a bakery and a fish market. In an adjoining space, shells and trinkets are attractively displayed on tables, and a band is just packing up its instruments. Every person working in the complex is white.

We walk up and down the hilly streets for hours, but see only a few dark-skinned people and no sign of native dress. In fact, the city appears very European, with stores open from 0700 to 1800, and a lunch break that runs from 1100-1400. We end the tour with a late lunch at a French restaurant downtown, enjoying the novelty of a glass of wine as we discuss our first impressions of the city.

With the weather sunny and warm, we spend the next few days doing touristy things. We climb aboard *The Little Train* for a guided tour through the downtown, then spend an afternoon at the Botanical Garden. Here, we tour several aviaries and are introduced to a flightless bird called a Kagu. It's native to the country and a national symbol. But truthfully, we're tied up at a marina for the first time in seventeen months, and mostly we just enjoy the novelty of being able to step off the boat onto a dock.

When we're ready for some exercise, we make the long hike out to a small aquarium at Baie d'Citron. I'm fascinated by the exhibits, which include all sorts of colorful fish, as well as lobsters, seahorses, and sea snakes. One small fish, called *the bulldozer*, digs a nest in the bottom of the tank by sucking up mouthfuls of gravel and spitting them out to the side. Another species featured is the *Nautilus*, a large, deep-water mollusk that can reach eleven inches in diameter and uses jet propulsion to make its way through the water. It's described as a living fossil, dating back 500 million years.

I could have spent all day studying the phosphorescent corals on display in a darkened section of the facility. One of the corals has a dim, slender stalk with a bright button of light at the top; a second appears to be bathed in a silvery glow; a third resembles a display of crystal. Other corals are bathed in either green or orange hues coming from what looks like threads of colored light woven into their surface.

On the way back to the marina, we stop and join spectators enjoying fun day activities at a small beach. As I watch, four individuals are blindfolded and helped into two small dinghies. Officials then place buckets over their heads and plastic dustpans in their hands to use as paddles. Guided by voices calling from a diving raft about 100 feet off the beach, the contestants set off, paddling madly. The two teams are soon going in circles and neither complete the course.

I now notice that most of the onlookers are men, and they aren't watching the boats. Unobtrusively, all have their eyes peeled on nearby sunbathers, where three young Eurasian beauties are displaying most of their assets. Wearing only colorful thongs that accent the curves of buttocks, their slim, brown bodies are otherwise bare. As I watch, one woman gets up and saunters around, seemingly oblivious to the stares.

With our time growing short, we sign up for a full-day guided tour of the island. Our guide picks us up at the marina at 0800, driving a comfortable eight-passenger van. He proves to be a forty-something Englishman, who loves the French mystique of sexy women, hot-blooded men, and sophisticated culture. Our companions include two Australian couples from Brisbane and Sidney, and two young women who are a perfect foil for one another. Penny is from Sydney and is slim and blond in the outdoor Aussie manner. Gail comes from Paris, France, and her clothes are fashionable, her dark hair smartly styled, and her face carefully made up.

Our guide keeps up an exuberant patter as he drives north out of the city. We then cross the central mountains to the east coast, following a narrow, one-lane road, where the direction of travel is controlled and changes every hour. Road networks run in all directions through the rugged countryside, and several nickel mines sit high on ridge lines. Open-pit mines have removed whole mountaintops, and land erosion is obviously a problem. According to our guide, mine waste has polluted many rivers.

After leaving the one-lane road, we drive on until midday. Our guide then stops at a small restaurant in the middle of nowhere, and we're provided with a delicious meal that includes delicately seasoned pork chops and wine. Our next stop is a mineral spring that was once the site of a popular health spa. All that remains is a derelict building and a bit of stonework around a pool. As we've brought bathing suits, we stop long enough for a brief but rejuvenating dip.

Once on the road again, I ask our guide why the spa was closed. Choosing his words carefully, he explains, "In the early 1980's, the Kanaks (local native people) drove most of the white people off the east coast of the island. There were several deaths and two policemen were beheaded in the uprising."

He continues, "French authorities reacted quickly, sending in a squad of commandos, and there were more deaths. An accord was eventually signed, agreeing that a referendum on independence would be held in ten years' time."

Shocked by his words, I stare out the window in confusion, unable to reconcile the peaceful countryside around us with such violence. When we later stop at an east coast beach and tour a Kanak village, I find myself wondering if anyone actually lives there, as we see no one. Then we drive through another community and are told to close the windows, as people occasionally throw rocks.

Intrigued by what we've learned, we spend the rest of our time in Noumea finding out about the independence movement. The struggle had been going on for years, but became increasingly violent in the early 1980s. Events came to a head in 1984, when a group of white settlers reportedly ambushed and killed ten Kanaks. That event triggered more violence and murders, bringing the country to the brink of civil war.

Other than declaring a State of Emergency in January of 1985, authorities left the pot to simmer for three more years. In April, 1988, members of the independence movement took thirty-five hostages, all but one being members of the gendarmes and the military. In response, the authorities sent in commandos, who successfully freed the hostages. In the process, nineteen Kanaks were killed, as were two members of the hostage-recovery team.

Amid charges that many Kanaks died while in custody, a protocol for an agreement was negotiated. When it was signed four months later, the government had agreed to transfer more power to three regional assemblies and to hold a referendum on independence in 1998. (That referendum was held and approved the Noumea Accord, which gave more autonomy to local government and provided for another referendum to be held before the end of 2018, when the people would vote on whether or not to become fully independent.)

A few days after the tour, we treat ourselves to lunch in a downtown restaurant overlooking a park. The afternoon is pleasant and the food and drink excellent, so we quite enjoy ourselves. I then notice that benches in the park are filled with white faces enjoying the sunshine, while dark faces sit on the grass in the shade of the trees. We'd previously noticed that the two cultures didn't mix, but now recognize a tension. In fact, there's a highly visible police presence in the downtown area on Friday and Saturday, or whenever many people gather together. (The population at the time is 44% Kanak and 35% European, with most of the rest being immigrants from other French colonies.)

CHAPTER 34

Passage to Australia

Digging out charts and pilots, we now start planning the last leg of our voyage. Brisbane lies 840 nm to the WSW, and the SE trade winds that made the route challenging earlier in the season have started to subside. In fact, in coming months, north winds will blow down the east coast of Australia, bringing hot, humid weather and the occasional cyclone.

I pay particular attention to routes crossing Moreton Bay, on the Australian coast, as it is littered with sandbars. The buoyage system there is also the opposite of the one used in North America, and we keep reminding each other that the rule of *red right returning* has become *red right reaving*. We buy little in the way of provisions, knowing that Australian Agriculture is notoriously strict about what they allow into the country.

Having obtained our departure clearance the previous day, we're up early on Sunday, October 19, ready to go. But we hesitate, as the forecast is calling for light winds. In fact, boats at sea have been complaining about light winds for a couple of days. We leave anyway, as we're tired of sitting around the marina. We pay our bill at the office, top up our diesel tanks at the fuel dock, then set off for the north channel of the Passes de Boulari. We expect to be at sea for nine days.

Relaxing and soaking up the sunshine, we motor through sheltered waters for three hours, but as we approach the pass, a squall brings strong winds and driving rain. With visibility reduced to zero, Dave steers a compass heading out into open water. When the storm moves on, we stop and raise the sails, and now a huge expanse of open sea and sky beckons us onward.

At change of watch at 1600, winds are from the SSW at 10 kt, and a low, two-foot swell ripples across the water. At sunset, the wind gives a couple of 20-kt gasps, then dies. The air becomes still and the water flat. When the faint sound of a jet engine breaks the silence, I find myself searching the sky for an airplane.

As *Windy Lady* drifts along, stars begin to dot the sky and then a quarter moon climbs up out of the sea. With its pale light shining across the water, a weak 5-kt breeze rises out of the south, and we're soon making 2 kt. Shortly after midnight, the winds pick up to 5–10 kt and we make 4 kt. At noon, after twenty-four hours at sea, we log 90 nm for Day 1.

Long, regular, six-foot-high swells now push up from the south, and the wind drops to 5 kt. As the waves sweep beneath the keel, they turn the bow and knock the wind from the sails. Otto can't cope, so Dave struggles to keep *Windy Lady* moving forward during his afternoon watch. I do the same for half of the following watch, then the wind strengthens by just 2 kt and everything changes. The sails hold the wind, boat speed increases by a knot, and Otto goes back to work.

The wind dies during Dave's 2000-watch, then rises in the NNE and settles at 10 kt (a shift of 150 degrees). He tacks and resets the sails, but with winds on the stern, *Windy Lady* wallows in a four-foot swell and it's hard to keep her moving forward. Conditions worsen during my midnight watch, when winds veer to the north and increase to 15 kt. A squall with 30-kt gusts and driving rain then swoops down on Dave during the next watch, backwinding the sails. Other squalls follow, and in between, winds are light and variable. At the end of his watch, he writes in the journey log, "A night from hell!"

At 0800, the squalls are behind us, and winds are steady at 10–12 kt from the west, with seas about three feet. But at noon, south winds are gusting up to 20 kt and seas are back up to eight feet. We log only 85 nm for Day 2. The day then turns cloudy and cold, and although we're not far from the Tropic of Capricorn, it feels like we've left the tropics far behind.

Just after sunset, the winds back to the SSE and settle at 15 kt, and Dave makes 20 nm during his 2000 watch. They then gust from 10–30 kt during my midnight watch, and I fight the helm and make only 13. Now veering to the south, they settle at 20–25 kt, and we each make 24 nm during the next two watches.

Dave then rides ten-foot seas during his afternoon watch and makes 27 nm. I'm more cautious going into the night and put a reef in the headsail, so make only 24. Winds ease a bit overnight, and the squalls return come morning. We log 114 nm and 136 nm on Days 3 and 4.

During the next twelve hours, winds move back and forth between south and SE, while gusting from 15–25 kt. With incredibly rough seven-foot seas, we have to babysit Otto while on watch and don't get much sleep when off. Winds then drop to 10–20 kt during my midnight watch and seas become noticeably quieter. Suddenly feeling incredibly tired, I start dreaming of my berth. When Dave relieves me, I think I'm asleep before my head hits the pillow.

Two hours later, I'm jerked out of a deep sleep when *Windy Lady* starts heaving and twisting once more. I try to cushion myself against the movements while pretending that I don't hear the sails flogging or the hammering coming from the lockers. After forty-five minutes, I fly into a rage and storm out to the cockpit screaming, "Furl the g-- d--- sails! Do something! Anything!"

Dave stares at me wordlessly because the wind has died, leaving the boat rolling in four-foot swells, and there's nothing to be done. Still, after I've gone below, he does what I ask and drops the sails. *Windy Lady* then turns broadside to the swells and rolls over so far that I'm practically rolled from my berth. Admitting defeat, I wearily get up and start tracking down the knocking sounds coming from the lockers, securing items that have worked loose.

With winds light and variable, I don't even try to steer a heading during my morning watch. I just turn the bow as needed to keep wind in the sails. When the wind dies, leaving *Windy Lady* rolling in the swells with her headsail flogging, I furl in the sail and wait. When the wind eventually picks up from the SE, I pull the sail out again and slowly the boat moves forward. We start the engine at 1045, and at noon, log 117 nm for Day 5.

We run the engine for six hours, and as soon as the water is hot, we luxuriate in badly needed baths, after which I mop up the cockpit. We then relax in the sunshine, while admitting how much of a trial the passage has become. At that moment, a troupe of dolphins appears and four of them tail walk towards us. In the clear water, I see the shadowy outlines of others, some 100 feet away. The pod stays maybe ten minutes, racing back and forth alongside the boat, turning 180 degrees in the blink of an eye. As always, they cheer us up and I'm still smiling long after they disappear.

We start sailing again at 1730, with winds from the SSE at 7–12 kt and three-foot seas. As light fades from the sky, two pairs of small black and white birds appear, flying low over the waves. They appear to dip one foot into the dark waters before soaring up and away, and their white markings make them easy to spot. I've noticed them for the past few days and think they're a type of storm petrol.

Winds move back and forth between ESE and SSE at 8–15 kt for the next twelve hours, with squalls occasionally bringing 30-kt gusts and rain showers. As Otto can't cope, we hand steer. The wind then dies and we're left rocking in low swells off the coast of Queensland, Australia. At noon, we log 111 nm for Day 7. With 150 nm still to go, we now motor for twelve hours, then struggle to sail for twelve hours and log 103 nm for Day 8. Tired and frustrated, we finish the voyage under motor.

There is no sign of land as we approach the coast, but after dark, a cluster of lights starts to appear and disappear as *Windy Lady* rides up and down on a three-foot swell. At midnight, the lights still seem a long way off, and as we're both on watch, Dave sends me below to rest. He first asks me to find a waypoint that he can enter into the GPS to guide us in. Wearily, I look in the Queensland Coast pilot, write a position down, and hand it to him.

When he calls me up to the cockpit two hours later, I can't believe my eyes. Lights blaze across the water in front of us and *Windy Lady* is practically within spitting distance of shore. The water depth is only seventeen feet, and in fact, waves break on rocks to seaward. I'm suddenly wide awake, with an icy pit growing in my stomach as I realize that the position I gave him was actually on shore.

A quick glance at a chart reveals that we're inside Bray Rocks, and I then stand at the rail, my eyes probing the dark waters for signs of danger while Dave monitors the depth gauge and steers *Windy Lady* back to safety. After making our way to the correct GPS waypoint near the shipping channel, we see the red and green lights marking the entrance. Until then, they'd been hidden by lights on shore.

The shipping channel is the safest route across Moreton Bay, but is not without challenges, as the bow wave off a freighter recently damaged a yacht. I'm at the helm when we start in and steer a compass heading to the first waypoint, making sure to stay well over on the starboard edge of the channel. Before long, I see a couple of small lights moving towards us, but they don't look right for a ship. Then suddenly, the dark bulk of a freighter looms out of the darkness and races past, leaving *Windy Lady* rocking in a bow wave.

Thoroughly intimidated, I check frequently in both directions for traffic and see only the vessel moving away. But five minutes later, a huge, dark mass is steaming up behind. I barely have time to tighten my grip on the wheel before *Windy Lady* is again rocking in a bow wave. There's not much time to think as we're making 6 kt on a flood tide and the other vessels are moving much faster.

When daylight comes at 0530, we see the Queensland coast for the first time. We're now three-quarters of the way through the channel, and several more ships have gone by. Leaving the shipping lane, we cross to Deception

Bay, then enter the leads into Scarborough Marina and tie up at the customs dock at 1030 on October 27.

While thumbing through a pile of forms, the Customs and Immigration Officer explains that he's expecting sixteen boats to clear in that day (eleven show up). He quickly completes his work, then we wait several hours for the Agriculture Inspector. Within five minutes of his arrival, I am staring in dumbfounded disbelief, having no idea what hit us or why.

The officer doesn't say a word, just pulls out every container in every locker in the galley, opens it up, looks inside, shakes the contents, then piles the container on the galley table. He doesn't put the lids back on properly and spills rice all over the place, including in the tracks for the sliding doors. I watch in dismay as the pile grows higher, and the galley is a shambles when he's finished. He takes only the dried beans, butter, and eggs that I'd set out for him.

After moving *Windy Lady* to a berth on a nearby finger, Dave cleans up deck and cockpit while I restore order to the galley. It's late in the afternoon before we're free to relax in the cockpit and discuss the passage. We logged 863 nm during our nine days at sea, not much more than our rhumb line course of 840 nm, but high swells and light winds had made the crossing frustrating and difficult.

We never really appreciate the fact that we achieved our dream because the dream had become our reality. In a period of 507 days, we spent 102 days at sea and sailed 10,300 nautical miles (19,075 km). That experience changed us forever. It wasn't just the adventure, or the fact that we enjoyed living on the boat; most of all, we'd found a form of freedom that we never knew existed.

Windy Lady is our home for another thirteen years, and we have many more adventures—and still, so many stories to tell…

EPILOGUE

We spend the next five years in an around Australia, making our base in the beautiful, friendly Moreton Bay communities of Scarborough and Redcliffe. Buying a ten-year-old Ford Falcon station wagon, we fill it with camping gear, then drive 28,000 km as we explore the country, making a summer trip along the coastline, and a winter trip through the outback.

We learn much about the ancient landscape as well as the people who make the country their home. We spend exceptional evenings with people we've just met and never see again, while enjoying semi-permanent relationships with others. In Mount Isa, where Dave worked in 1962, we descend 3,000 feet into a mine, then visit a sheep station near the small town of Coonamble, where I worked as a jillaroo in 1968.

We log 8,500 km in another challenging cruising season, sailing back to Tonga, then returning via Fiji and New Caledonia. We're sailing up the Great Barrier Reef on our way to Thailand when *9-11* happens. With boats returning from SE Asia, we take refuge in Townsville and talk of war keeps us in country for another year. (*Beneath the Southern Cross, Dreamers and Doers, Part II*)

After making the passage to SE Asia, which is a very different sailing experience, we find a marina that we like in Malaysia. As the world changes, so do our plans, and we stay for eight years. We again buy a car and make several trips through Malaysia and Thailand, and spend a month hiking in Nepal, where we climb up to 18,000 feet in the Himalaya Mountains.

We go farther afield by air and spend weeks exploring cities as diverse as Hong Kong, Istanbul, Athens, and Lisbon. We spend three months in South America, first visiting Rio di Janeiro, then traveling overland through Bolivia,

Peru, and Chile. In Asia, we travel the Silk Route through China, peer down into Cuchi Tunnels in Viet Nam, and stare with disbelief at the site of mass graves in the killing fields of Cambodia. Some of the places we explore are far away in time, as well as miles, like the Delphi in Greece, Machu Picchu in Peru, and Angkor Wat in Cambodia. (*Exploring Far Away Places, Dreamers and Doers, Part III*)

GLOSSARY

Dave - somewhere in the North Pacific

Arlene in 40-kt winds off New Zealand

Windy Lady with the new dodger

Dave - at the helm

Arlene - up the mast

Outrigger canoe near Havannah Bay

US and Tongan ships in Neiafu

Hunga Village in Tonga

Visitors at Craig Cove

Mary and friends at Port Sandwich

Copra dryer in Vanuatu

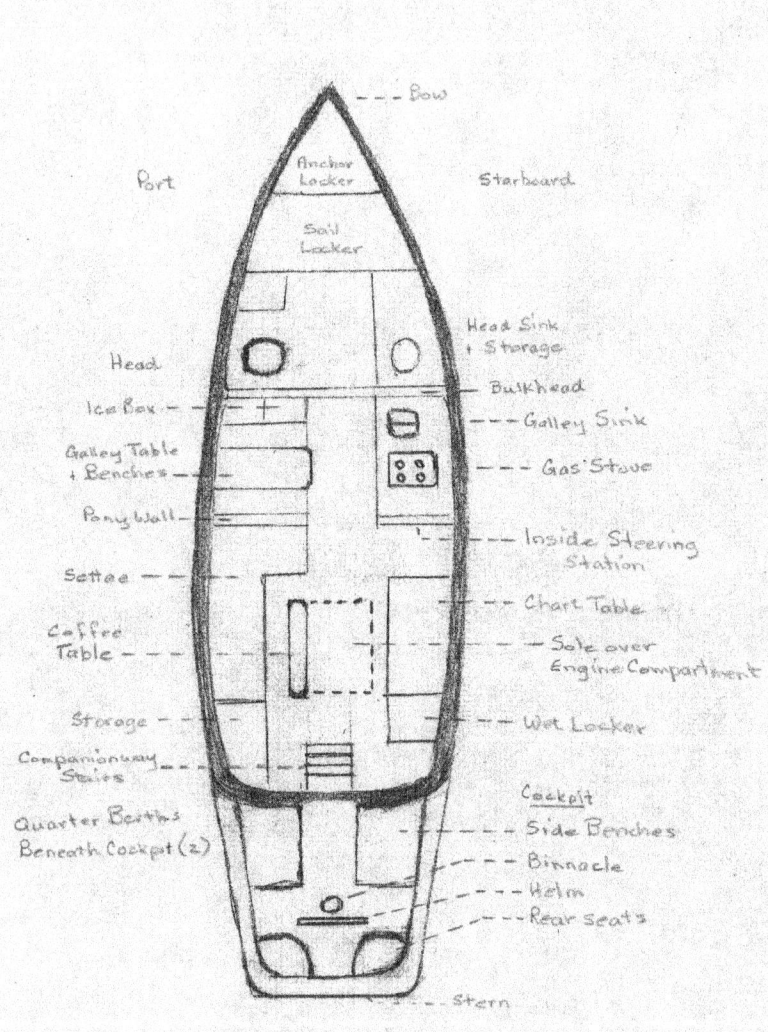

Windy Lady Interior and Cockpit

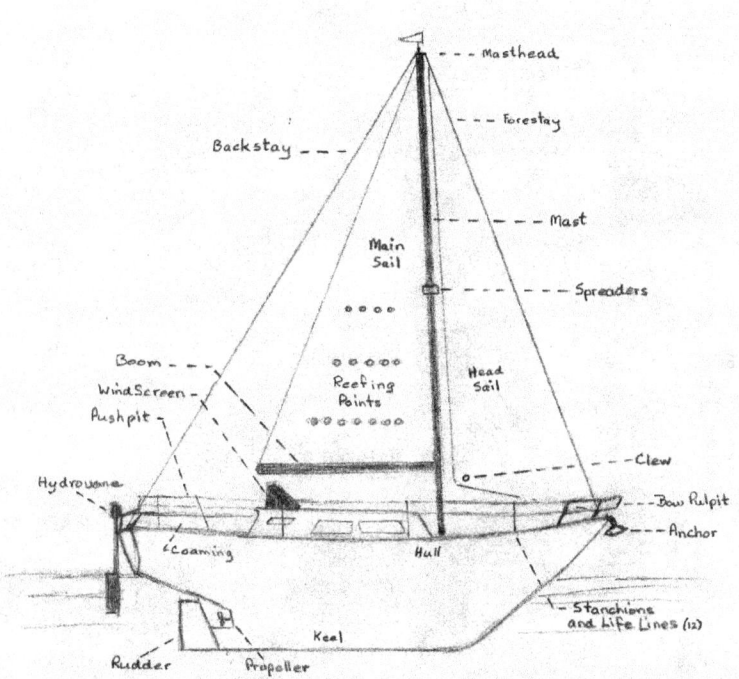

Windy Lady Exterior and Sails

PASSAGE PLAN

FOR SAILING VESSEL, WINDY LADY III
Description:
   40-foot cutter-rigged sloop monohull
   flush deck, aft cockpit with pilot house
   white with blue trim.
Port of Registry: Vancouver, Canada
Registration #804823.
Registered tonnage: 13.97

TRAVELLING TO HILO, HAWAII
   Departing Victoria Harbour on June 8, 1996 proceeding
through Strait of Juan de Fuca to Cape Flattery. Will stop
at Neah Bay only if weather dictates.
   Expecting to continue directly to Hilo, Hawaii.
   Intended route is 100 miles off the west coast down to San
Francisco, then west to Hawaii. Depending on winds, the
track will be approximately:
      SW to 130 degrees W, 45 degrees N
      S to 130   "   W, 35   "   N
      SW to 150   "   W, 25   "   N
      SW to 155   "   W, 20   "   N (Hilo)

FUEL ON BOARD: 750 liters of diesel
RANGE: 1200 NM

WATER: 900 liters
FOOD: Provisions for 24 weeks

RADIOS AND ELECTRONIC EQUIPMENT: Call sign CFL 4350
   VHF, ICOM IC-M58
   SSB, ICOM IC-700
      HAM VE0-DLB
   Radar, Furuno model 1721 (24 mile)
   GPS, Furuno GP-50 Mark 2

SAFETY EQUIPMENT
   RFD 4-man life raft
   8.5 foot white rigid dinghy on foredeck
   EPIRB, Lo-kata 406 (A78D00800500401)

S.O.B. David L. Ball, Captain
       Arlene L. Galisky, Navigator
       Brian O. Ball, Crew

EXPECTED TIME ON ROUTE: 24 days

Passage Plan

aft, abaft: near or toward the stern

autopilot: self-steering mechanism used under power

backwind: to deflect air onto the back of a sail

beam: the width, or widest part of the deck

beam reach: fastest point of sail, with wind coming over the beam

beat: point of sail, with the bow held as close to the wind as possible

bilge: lowest point inside the hull

binnacle: the stand in which a ship's compass is kept

blanket: to prevent the wind from filling a sail

boom: the horizontal spar that supports the foot the mainsail

broach: sudden, sharp turn caused by wind or sea that can cause a boat to capsize

broad reach: point of sail, with wind coming over the quarter

broadside: beam on to either wind or sea

bulkhead: a support below deck that strengthens a boat

buoy: a floating aid to navigation

chain plate: a metal plate used to fasten a stay to the hull

chandlery: a store selling boat supplies

coaming: the raised edge around the cockpit that keeps water out

cockpit: an opening in the deck from which a boat is steered

companionway: stairs between cockpit and cabin

course: direction in which a boat is steered

dodger: a spray shield that protects the cockpit

easting: distance traveled toward the east

fender: a cushioning object placed between boat and dock

flog: for a sail to flap or flutter when no longer supported by the wind

foredeck: deck area between mast and bow

forestay: supporting cable that runs from the bow to the upper mast

freeboard: distance from waterline to deck or gunnel

galley: kitchen area of a boat

gimbal: swing support that allows a stove to stay level in rough seas

grab rail: hand-hold fitting mounted inside the cabin

gunnel: the top edge of the side of the hull

HAM: restricted frequencies on an HF radio

HF radio: high-frequency radio used for long distances

hatch: an opening in the deck that can be sealed off

head: a marine toilet, or the room in which it is located

heading: the direction in which the bow points at any given time

headsail: sail attached to the forestay

heel: the angle of the boat to the water

helm: the wheel controlling the rudder

hove-to: to have sails/helm positioned so that a boat remains almost stationary

hull: actual body of the boat

jack line: a safety line running down the length of the deck

keel: an extension of the hull that goes deeper into the water

km: kilometer - equals .54 nautical mile

kt: knot - equals one nautical mile/hour, or 1.852 km/hour

lee, leeward: the side sheltered from the wind

lifeline: a cable running along the edge of the deck supported by stanchions

mainsail: principal sail on the main mast

mast: a pole on a boat that supports the sails

mb: millibar (a unit of atmospheric pressure)

moorage: a place to secure a boat to shore or sea bottom

nm: nautical mile - equals one minute of latitude, or 1.852 kilometers

pad eye: metal eye permanently secured to the boom

painter: a line attached to the bow of a dinghy

pooped: to have a wave break over the stern, can cause a boat to capsize

port: the left side of a boat when facing the bow

pulpit: guardrail around the bow

push pit: guardrail around the stern

quarter: the part of a vessel's side near the stern

reef, to: reduce the area of the mainsail using pre-established reefing points

rhumb line: shortest distance between two points at sea

rudder: an underwater vertical surface that steers the boat

scupper: a drain hole in deck or cockpit

sloop: a sailboat with one mast and one headsail

sole: floor of cabin or cockpit

spreader: horizontal support about halfway up the mast

stanchion: metal post supporting the lifelines

starboard: the right side of a boat when facing the bow

stays: strong cables supporting the mast that run fore and aft

staysail: a small jib sail attached to an inner forestay

steerage: the effect of the helm on a boat, or the act of steering it

tack: to turn a boat so that the bow passes through the eye of the wind

thru-hull: a fitting providing a secure hole through the hull below the waterline *toe-rail, rail*: the outer edge of the deck, usually raised

transducer: electronic device needed to measure water depth, boat speed, etc.

transom: the aft wall of the stern

turnbuckle: devise for adjusting tension on the stays

VHF radio: very high frequency radio, used for local communication

westing: distance traveled toward the west

whisker pole: a pole used to hold a sail out in light winds

windage: wind resistance of a boat

About the Author

    Arlene Galisky and David Ball lived on their sailboat in the South Pacific and Southeast Asia for sixteen years. Their personal journals and boat log provide the material for her writing. She presently lives in Kelowna, BC.